Wildlife
in Your
Garden

lumina
MEDIA

Wildlife in Your Garden

Project Team
Editor: Amy Deputato
Copy Editor: Joann Woy
Design: Mary Ann Kahn
Index: Elizabeth Walker

LUMINA MEDIA™
Chairman: David Fry
Chief Financial Officer: David Katzoff
Chief Digital Officer: Jennifer Black-Glover
Vice President Marketing & PR: Cameron Triebwasser
Managing Director, Books: Christopher Reggio
Art Director, Books: Mary Ann Kahn
Senior Editor, Books: Amy Deputato
Production Director: Laurie Panaggio
Production Manager: Jessica Jaensch

ISBN 978-1-62008-138-9

Library of Congress Cataloging-in-Publication Data has been applied for.

This book has been published with the intent to provide accurate and authoritative information in regard to the subject matter within. While every precaution has been taken in the preparation of this book, the author and publisher expressly disclaim any responsibility for any errors, omissions, or adverse effects arising from the use or application of the information contained herein.

lumina MEDIA

2030 Main Street, Suite 1400
Irvine, CA 92614

Printed and bound in China
19 18 17 16   2 4 6 8 10 9 7 5 3 1

Contents

Introduction

The purpose of this book is to help you reconnect with your wild side and the green space just outside your door by discovering the importance of the patch of earth that you tend and the creatures who find sustenance there. We have taken the wilderness out of most places where humans live, and now we are wondering why we feel unhealthy; why our air, food, and water is polluted; and why stress permeates modern lifestyles. *Biophilia*, the general tendency that humans have toward connecting with other forms of life, must be nurtured for our common good, and finding our place in relation to wild creatures is one way to restore ourselves.

How do we return our landscapes to being working systems that filter water and air? How do we grow food without pesticides? How do we encourage native wildlife to reestablish healthy populations? How do we prevent other wildlife from becoming a problem?

Although all of these questions may not be answered completely in this book, I hope that you find within its pages a starting point to coexisting with wildlife in your garden. I hope your approach becomes one of curiosity, respect, appreciation, awe, and understanding. If you have a garden, a yard, a community space, or an office with landscaping, a range of wildlife can become part of your daily routine, and this book will help you recognize those animals that you'd like to get to know better.

This book provides opportunities for understanding by exploring histories of selected animals, what they do, and why; animals' role in the ecosystem and their impact on your garden, home, neighborhood, community, and watershed; and the impact we have on animals and how we can encourage or discourage their presence. Each section will familiarize you with wildlife, ranging from abundant soil organisms all the way up to the largest and rarest mammals that may share your space. I encourage you, at any of these encounters, to first simply observe. What exactly is that moth, bird, squirrel, wasp, mouse, raccoon, or opossum doing? Try not to react to its presence—just watch. Does it visit flowers or gather seeds? How many different types of plants does it visit? Do you see it at night or in the morning? Does it show up reliably all year or just in certain seasons? Where does it take the food it gathers?

This act of slowing down and just looking at a subject is a technique employed by artists, hunters, biologists, and philosophers. The less threatening your presence is to wildlife, the more familiar you can become with the animals' normal routines, and the more details you will notice. It is very important that we don't disturb wildlife unnecessarily, especially during times of low resources, such as a long, hot summers or when they are storing up energy for the winter. This is a lesson for us to share with our children as well as teach to ourselves. Respecting space and similar ethical principles are important in your yard. Know why you are taking action before you do something, and consider the other living creatures that you will affect.

Permaculture (shortened from "permanent agriculture") is a holistic landscape design philosophy that holds a basic tenet of working *with* nature, not against it. Rather than seeing your yard as a perfect utopia—or as a battleground, where it's man versus nature—I like to think of gardening as a partnership with wildlife. We provide them habitat, and they do the work: pollinating flowers, planting seeds, turning soil, keeping populations in check, and breaking down and recycling nutrients. Rather than seeing ourselves as overlords of the land, we can be cooperative participants with the native residents.

I prefer not to label any wildlife as "good guys" or "bad guys" in this book; instead, I strive to provide basic information on what animals need and how they live. You can decide which ones to invite to dinner. I ask you not to think of your property as a space where you have the right to kill what you think does not belong. Do think of your garden as a wildlife refuge, where learning and understanding are your most powerful tools.

The information provided in this book may work well for the home gardener who can tolerate plant losses for a few seasons while his or her efforts to bring a natural balance to the garden play out. I also hope that gardeners and landowners consider the ideas and alternative solutions on a wider scale. Many resources exist for targeting those wild animals regarded as nuisances or invasive, and although I address some of these in their respective sections, you will also be able to access experts in your area. Alternatives exist for every problem, and looking at the reasons behind the issue often reveals the solution. With this approach, we can enjoy our sanctuary with wildlife rather than a creating a barrier that separates the two.

As Douglas Tallamy, author of the essential native plant landscaping book *Bringing Nature Home* points out, if we all work together to increase the biodiversity in our own yards, North American suburbia could improve on the protected public lands, such as national parks. At this time, 92 percent of suburban landscape is lawn. This holds great potential for renewing our connection with nature and giving wild things what they need to survive. Our yards could become the largest corridor of connected natural habitats in the developed world. It only requires some small modifications in our attitudes and our landscaping. You don't have to be big to make a difference in the world—if you need proof, just watch the insects.

1
Your
Garden

The basic steps in creating a garden that provides a safe habitat for wildlife and functions to improve the environment are:

1. Stop using pesticides.
2. Replace nonnative lawn turf with native plants.
3. Watch and enjoy.

Sound too easy? OK—I'm oversimplifying matters. You can delve as deep as you want to with Step 2, which can be a process that extends over more than your lifetime. Consider who will be tending the land after you are gone and what kind of legacy you will leave. Have a vision in mind, choose a starting point, and adjust as you go. Use the following concepts to check in with yourself and your garden periodically.

Make Observations

Before you set out to create a backyard wildlife sanctuary, make sure that you understand your local ecology. Find out what the native ecosystem was like before the area was developed. Go to your closest natural areas and spend time simply observing, preferably in all types of weather and all seasons. Take a notebook along and record your observations about the height of the tallest plants, the wildlife you see in each layer, the amount of water and whether it is flowing or still, which plants and animals seem to be thriving, and what might be missing from the landscape.

Talk with naturalists about native wildlife and what they have done to restore the habitats at their sites. Once you start these types of conversations, you'll notice that your observation skills will be sharper every time you see landscapes. As Marlene Condon observes in her *Nature-Friendly Garden* book, "The natural world does nothing that is nonsensical." You can take home some of the best ideas and try them out for yourself.

What do the natural areas in your locale look like?

Work with Natives

In nature, nothing exists in a vacuum. Communities, or guilds, of plants grow together because of mutually beneficial relationships, coevolution, and the right growing conditions. In *Gaia's Garden*, Toby Hemenway summarizes what wild nature does best, and we can try to emulate this in our gardens. "A healthy plant community recycles its own waste back into nutrients, resists disease, controls pests, harvests and conserves water, attracts insects and other animals to do its bidding, and hums along happily as it performs these and a hundred other tasks." So that's our goal. Native plants offer many advantages toward achieving this state.

In Rick Darke and Douglas Tallamy's book *The Living Landscape*, a native species is defined as "a plant or animal that has evolved in a given place over a period of time sufficient to develop complex and essential relationships with the physical environment and other organisms in a given ecological community." Some gardeners like to simplify matters by defining native plants as those that have been in the region since before Europeans arrived on this continent. Native plants generally, but not always, require less maintenance and care than exotic or ornamental species. They don't necessarily stay where you plant them, and they can become even more vigorous than you expected. Natives call for you to be adaptable because you can try to assert your will over them, but they may surprise you. As Darke and Tallamy put it, "Managed wildness and an invitational approach to chance happenings can sometimes accomplish things that would be impossible through more deliberate methods."

Intimate relationships between native plants, insects, birds, and other wildlife have evolved cooperatively over millennia. We need to keep an open mind and appreciate that the partnerships that this type of history cultivates are far more complex than the ones that we gardeners might develop with our plants. A few good reasons to select native plants are that they generally have deeper roots and prevent excessive runoff during heavy rains. They help filter and slow down stormwater. They provide essential sustenance to migratory species, such as the monarch butterfly. Also, compared to lawns, they absorb a great deal more carbon from the atmosphere, helping to reduce greenhouse gases.

Wild Ones

Wild Ones: Native Plants, Natural Landscapes is a national organization with a wealth of resources on working with native plants. You may find already-established local chapters in your area. For more information, visit www.wildones.org.

Echinacea, or purple coneflower, is a top pick for Midwestern gardens.

Landscape in Layers

Forest gardening, one aspect of permaculture, promotes establishing several vertical layers of plant communities that form naturally in a healthy forest ecosystem. Your home ecosystem may be prairie or desert, so take that into consideration and adapt the layers to match your area's climate. The following basic outline can be applied to most regions.

The tallest forest garden layer is the canopy. These are the dominant trees, the "roof" of the garden. The trees' crowns are the first to catch and store sunlight, filter air, and recycle oxygen and carbon dioxide. The size and conditions of these big beauties affects all the life underneath; likewise, they reflect the state of affairs going on far below the ground surface.

The layer below the canopy is the understory. This includes younger canopy trees and shorter growing tree species. They compete for light and adapt to maximize the efficiency of their leaves in capturing the sun's rays. Some leaf out before the canopy trees in the spring, and some have modified the anatomy of their leaves to function on lower light levels. This is where a graceful transition in design can be made from the towering canopy down to human-scale features.

1. Like a healthy forest, your garden should include multiple layers.

2. Trillium is a spring-blooming plant native to the northeastern United States.

The middle layer of life is the shrub layer. Shrubs and bushes are usually woody, multistemmed plants up to a height of around 15–20 feet. This layer can be a prime shelter for wildlife: a hiding spot midway between the safety of a high nest and the open foraging space on the ground. Berries, nuts, flowers, and foliage all provide something attractive, and a healthy shrub layer will encourage a diverse assortment of wildlife.

The herbaceous layer varies in plant height, with grasses and forbs (flowers and herbs) stretching up to several feet high or creeping low. The diversity of species increases as we move lower down in the forest garden layers, and although the individual plants consist of less mass, they are relatively more productive in their role of supplying food and returning nutrients into the soil. The herbaceous layer is where most of the interesting and colorful blooming plants take turns sharing their colors, fragrances, and textures throughout the seasons.

A layer that can touch all forest garden layers is the vine layer. Vines take up very little space and provide little surprises of color, seeds, and fruit throughout the shrub, understory, and canopy layers. Vines make productive fence decorations and can create screens for privacy.

Be cautious when selecting vines because there are some very invasive types (such as certain commonly planted nonnative varieties of honeysuckle and wisteria) that will take over. Opt for the native varieties so that wildlife will find what they need.

Perhaps the most critical layer for overall garden health lies below our feet: the ground layer. It includes several zones on the surface and below. Ground litter includes all kinds of plant and animal droppings, seeds, twigs, leaves, and dead wood, and it serves many purposes. It provides insect cover and food, retains moisture, and holds microhabitats for fungi, bacteria, and other microbes that break down the litter into soil.

The ground layer contains more life forms than any other layer. On the surface of the soil, you'll find mosses, algae, salamanders, and beetles, to name a few. Underground, most insects spend at least part of their life cycles in the soil, as do many reptiles and amphibians.

1. Vines add a decorative touch while benefiting other layers of the garden.

2. Swamp milkweed is popular with monarch butterflies.

3. A monarch caterpillar feeds on a leaf of swamp milkweed.

As for the impressive "roof" or canopy, it wouldn't be there without a foundation. The root systems of trees extend out from the trunks at least as far as the canopy branches and reside mainly in the 2- to 3-foot depth, where oxygen is available in the soil. Native grasses and wildflowers may grow deep taproots that plunge 6 feet or more into the earth. A community of mycorrhizal fungi and microbes release organic compounds into the soil that feed the plant roots.

In contrast, mowed turf grass adds very little support to the ecosystem, and the soil compacted by riding mowers makes is almost impermeable to water. Herbicides that kill forbs prevent a biodiverse system from establishing itself, and they set off a cycle of spot treatments for symptoms without addressing the underlying systemic malfunctions.

Likewise, removing nature's nutrient-rich gift—fallen leaves—takes away the soil-enriching and biodiverse benefits that leaf litter provides. Then we have to go out and buy topsoil, fertilizer, and compost; haul it home; and blend it back in to amend the soil. Douglas Tallamy sums up the wasted effort: "Plants make leaves, and we all freak out and get our leaf blowers and our rakes, we rake up all the leaves and put 'em in bags and treat 'em like trash. Then we run to Home Depot and buy

Zinnias add a splash of color and plentiful nectar to your garden.

mulch, fertilizer, hoses, trying to replace the ecosystem services we just threw out, but we can't replace the arthropods we got rid of." If we can let leaves stay where they fall or chop them up with a lawn mower and rake them to cover our garden beds, we'll be on our way to sharing the gardening work with Mother Nature instead of doing all of the work ourselves.

Understand the Food Web

You'll read about birdscaping and gardening for beneficial insects later in this book, but keep in mind that you cannot really garden for a particular type of wildlife exclusively. As Marlene Condon explains in *Nature-Friendly Garden*, "When you grow nectar plants for butterflies and hummingbirds, you will also attract moths, wasps, bees, and many other kinds of insects." Spiders and caterpillars will feed on them, and they will attract birds. Maybe even deer will join the party. Condon goes on to assert, "You need to accept that all of these creatures are part of your world and include them in your garden planning." This is our garden's food web.

We all know the concept of "the big fish eat the little fish." What do the little fish eat? Algae, plankton, insects. What do insects eat? Start with any food or animal, follow this thread to its source, and eventually you wind up at plants and, ultimately, the sun. Practically all life on Earth depends on the sun's energy, which is captured by leaves and photosynthesized. An animal eats the plant and absorbs energy, which is transferred to the next animal and so on. This is a food chain.

Switchgrass is a native grass that can grow several feet high.

Every food chain consists of producers, consumers, and decomposers. Plants are the main producers. Consumers are generally categorized as herbivores (plant eaters), carnivores (meat eaters), and omnivores (both plant and animal eaters). Decomposers help break down the nutrients and minerals and recycle them back into the system, which makes the system not such a straight line. There could be many food chains that interrupt or interconnect with each other. The term *food web* describes the various interweaving parts of food chains.

As with a spider's web, if one strand is broken, many others remain in place and do the same job. In permaculture, this is referred to as *redundancy*—the concept that multiple elements provide the same function. Redundancy puts less stress on any single member of the system, which is why more biodiversity, or a variety of life forms, helps increase a system's stability and resiliency. Lose one? No big deal. Another will fill in until balance is restored. A monoculture, on the other hand, which features a single predominant species, is more vulnerable to disease or predation. For example, many housing subdivisions are planted with one type of street tree. If you lose one, you might lose them all.

The ground layer nurtures both plant and animal life.

In Peter Bane's *Permaculture Handbook*, he compares our knowledge of our plant ecosystem with that of our ancestors. "The average Cherokee woman at the time of European contact knew and used approximately 800 species of plants for food, fiber, and medicine." Most vegetable gardeners today would be doing well to have thirty to fifty species growing, and, in a permaculture garden, that number could be multiplied by ten. Commercial, governmental, and industrial growers are not necessarily concerned about the heritage that they lose by decreasing plant diversity. It is up to the small-scale growers to preserve the native plants and heirloom fruits and vegetables and keep trying new ways to diversify the garden.

Know that Your Garden Matters

Douglas Tallamy, in *Bringing Nature Home*, explains why every plant decision you make is important. "Because food for all animals starts with the energy harnessed by plants, the plants we grow in our gardens have the critical role of sustaining, directly or indirectly, all of the animals with which we share our living spaces. The degree to which the plants in our gardens succeed in this regard will determine the diversity and numbers of wildlife that can survive in managed landscapes. And because it is we who decide what plants will grow in our gardens, the responsibility for our nation's biodiversity lies largely with us."

Bee balm (*Monarda* spp.) attracts bees, butterflies, and birds with its nectar.

Your property, with the ecosystem services it provides, is your place to make a difference in the world. The United Nations Food and Agriculture Organization

A honeybee on an apple blossom. Honeybees are important to apple pollination.

(FAO) defines ecosystem services as "the multitude of benefits that nature provides to society." The ecosystem comprises all living and nonliving parts of the environment and their interactions that benefit the world. Those essential services and benefits include cleaning the air, purifying water, providing spiritual connections, pollinating, stabilizing and forming soil, and providing recreation. The FAO estimates that all of this collectively adds up, worldwide, to a value of $125 trillion; however, "these assets are not adequately accounted for in political and economic policy, which means there is insufficient investment in their protection and management."

Tallamy and Darke delve further into the role of the garden in the larger environment in their book *The Living Landscape*. Ecosystem services that your very own garden can contribute to include:

- supporting human populations
- protecting watersheds
- cooling and cleaning air
- building and stabilizing topsoil
- moderating extreme weather
- sequestering carbon
- protecting biodiversity
- supporting pollinator communities
- connecting viable habitats

May you find inspiration in the good you are doing in your own little corner of the world.

Worms help gardeners in many ways, among them aerating the soil and producing nutrient-rich castings (waste).

Soil Matters

Originally printed in the April 2015 newsletter for the Lexington, Kentucky, chapter of Wild Ones: Native Plants, Natural Landscapes

Why care about the soil? Because soil is alive! Soil is the most biodiverse part of your garden ecosystem. Millions of organisms can inhabit a spoonful of rich, healthy soil. Every arthropod, bacteria, fungus, or worm plays a role that affects the other members of the soil community. They shred, graze, parasitize, and predate on each other, but they mainly take care of organic matter. Underground organisms process everything from leafy tendrils to tough tree trunks; they also build the infrastructure for plants' roots. They make nutrients available, disperse water, and open air pathways for good circulation, creating a healthy community or habitat.

The benefits of biodiversity in your soil don't stop with the plants. Recent scientific studies support the hygiene hypothesis, which theorizes that people who grow up in developed countries are too clean for their own good. Researchers are finding that early exposure to healthy amounts of bacteria, fungus, and even some parasites could build children's immune systems, leading

The soil in a healthy forest supports a thriving, biodiverse community.

to fewer inflammatory conditions as adults. Scientists are trying to identify which members of a healthy gut microbiome affect specific problems, ranging from Crohn's disease to autism.

Similarly, soil scientists are often interested in isolating the bacteria and fungi that create certain changes in soil chemistry and fertility. However, the USDA Natural Resources Conservation Service (NRCS) states, "Many effects of soil organisms are a result of the interactions among organisms, rather than the actions of individual species. This implies that managing for a healthy food web is not primarily a matter of inoculating with key species, but of creating the right environmental conditions to support a diverse community of species."

Where do you find the richest, most diverse, and most resilient soil systems? In forests. Forests can have up to 40 miles of fungus in just one teaspoon of soil, compared to several yards of fungus in a teaspoon of typical agricultural soil. Gardening with native plants and natural systems encourages a rich, biodiverse community above and below ground and mimics the conditions found in the wild forest. So go ahead and get some of that good dirt—er, soil—under your nails.

2
Insects:
A Respectful
Approach

The majority of gardening approaches portray bugs as the bad guys and easy-application pesticides as the answer to wiping out your woes. Sure, you can have a picture-perfect garden if you kill everything that might ever disrupt it. But that's no way to live and let live. The same synthetic methods used to control "pests" also bring a whole host of side effects: everything from collapsed colonies of honeybees to weak-shelled eggs in eagles' nests to many types of cancer in humans. Another alternative is to allow a little be-wilder-ment into your heart, and let it find a place in your yard as well. Do you have to love bugs and spiders to have a wildlife-friendly yard? Love is not required, but tolerance is.

Consider this insight from Nelson Mandela: "If you want to make peace with your enemy, you have to work with your enemy. Then he becomes your partner." Many bugs, creepy-crawlies, and slimy slitherers can be your garden partners, if you allow them to be.

Instead of listing every type of garden pest and the havoc they wreak, this section introduces some beneficial bugs. In nature, there is no such thing as "good guys" and "bad guys." Every creature—yes, even spiders, slugs, and ticks—exists for a reason, whether we understand their role or not. You may be surprised at how many commonly squished, swatted, or shunned insects are hard at work to keep your garden ecosystem in balance.

I like Jessica Walliser's definition of an ecosystem in her book *Attracting Beneficial Bugs to Your Garden*. "An ecosystem, in essence, is a community of organisms functioning hand in hand with their environment and each other to exchange energy and create a nutritional cycle. Insects are innately connected to each and every activity occurring in the ecosystem of your garden."

Aphids can suck the life out of plants, but they are a major food source for beneficial garden bugs.

It would be an oversimplification to call every creature covered in this section an insect or a bug, but since the average gardener does not describe a spider as an arachnid or a slug as a mollusk, I'll use the easiest terminology and lump them into the same category. Even including soil life is stretching the taxonomic boundaries if we want to acknowledge the fungus and mycorrhiza that make plant life possible below ground.

I'll admit that this does a disservice to the immense diversity within this group. Insects and arachnids comprise a whopping 80 percent of the world's animal species. They are everywhere, whether shockingly visible, mysteriously camouflaged, or microscopically minute.

Layers of Insect Life

Insects may be the least understood or appreciated type of wildlife, but they are by far the most abundant. Deserts, mountains, prairies, and forests alike harbor more six- and eight-legged creatures than reptiles, amphibians, birds, and mammals combined. It's not easy to estimate, but entomologists write in the textbook *Entomology and Pest Management* that there are 400 million insects per acre.

The forest floor allows mosses, fungi, and, of course, insects, to thrive.

Why not try and count them for yourself? When you step into your garden or yard, try surveying all of the habitats that are supporting insect life on all levels and during all life cycle phases. Try to lie, squat, kneel, and stand in just one spot as you take an inventory of the signs of wildlife at each of these levels.

Start as low as you can go. Important work is going on at ground level and below. According to the United States Department of Agriculture (USDA), there are more microorganisms in just one teaspoon of healthy soil than there are people on Earth! They are busily working through the leaf litter and animal remains, transporting and transforming nutrients. Springtails, beetles, mites, earthworms, and ants devour each other, deposit rich castings, lay eggs, and tunnel throughout the soil. Their normal life processes turn, aerate, and circulate humus without even the slightest hint of a spade or garden fork. Too small to see without a microscope, microbes such as bacteria, fungi, algae, yeast, nematodes, and protozoa process organic matter into forms that plants' roots can absorb.

Work up to the herbaceous layer, where flowers bloom and grasses sway, and look for some of the same soil creatures above ground. Beetles, roly-polies, leaf hoppers, lightning bug larvae, aphids, ladybugs, and slugs are a few of the crawling varieties. Many of these devour the others, while some simply scavenge the leftovers and make a fine life in the protective ground-cover plants. The winged creatures—bees and butterflies in the daytime and moths by night—are busy about the flowers, sipping nectar and gathering strength while they relocate pollen from one plant to the next.

Continue up into the shrubs that harbor our beloved songbirds. Caterpillars find the leaves delectable, and baby birds think the same about the soft, squishy caterpillars, which nature places within easy reach of nests. As if that weren't enough, more predators come along to feast: parasitoid wasps lay their eggs, predatory stink bugs attack with hidden weapons, and spiders trail their deadly decorations across flight pathways.

Head on up into the understory trees, where you'll find more flowers, fruits, and nuts. Winged insects pollinate, and cicadas reach their height of song season. Mantids await their prey patiently or catch a swift breeze to try another hunting stakeout.

Stretch up into the big shade trees that create our cooling canopy. Katydids resonate with the twilight, bark beetles burrow and evade drilling woodpeckers, and webworms cast their community hammocks across the crotches of branches.

To highlight the importance of insects in our gardens and in our lives as a whole, they are grouped according to the service they perform in the ecosystem. Sally Jean Cunningham's book, *Great Garden Companions*, points out some important, even critical, services that we humans really aren't too good at providing, such as pollinating, recycling resources, and maintaining a balanced food web. Think about it! How well can you pollinate every flower in your garden by hand? Are you able to chop up or chemically digest every dead animal and plant on your property so that the nutrients are released back in the right proportions to form rich, fertile soil? How about manipulating the intricate balance of nature's food web by providing the right amounts of the right nutrition at the right time for the wildlife that you want to attract? What if you overdo it? Can you then consume or destroy the right amounts of the overgrown populations so that everything is balanced again?

It sounds like a full-time job for an army, and that's what you are blessed with—an army of ecosystem service providers, especially when you plant native plants and landscape with natural processes in mind. Major players (and a few unsung heroes) are described in this chapter according to the main job descriptions that bugs are born to fill:

- **Pollination:** Flying and crawling insects that specialize in spreading genetic material among blossoms to fertilize and increase biodiversity. These include bees, butterflies, moths, wasps, flies, and beetles.
- **Population control:** Predators and parasitoids that help normalize numbers of prey species over time (and predators can become someone else's prey, too!). These include spiders, assassin bugs, dragonflies, and lacewings.
- **Recycling:** Scavengers and decomposers that break down dead and decaying plant matter and carrion and turn it into useful components in the soil. These include worms, centipedes, daddy longlegs, and sow bugs.

1. A juicy caterpillar on a leaf will be a lucky bird's next meal.

2. Cicadas are more often heard than seen from up high in tree branches.

3. Did you know that the daddy longlegs is not a spider? It is, however, a major player in your garden ecosystem.

Please note that some insects perform all three of these jobs; many are multitaskers! And all insects provide a food source to other creatures. Birds, lizards, frogs, fish, coyote, bears, and even people either eat insects or eat something that has eaten insects.

Pollinators

Who loves flowers more than you do? Pollinators! Gardeners have a lot in common with pollinators: we are attracted to the scent, color, and shape of flowers, and we survive by eating the food that flowers provide. For pollinators, it's the nectar, and for us, it's the fruit that develops after the plant is fertilized.

Types of Pollinators

Animal pollinators discussed in this section on insects and arachnids include bees, butterflies, moths, flies, wasps, and beetles. We'll discuss birds and bats later, in separate chapters of the book. Regardless, the general job description is the same for all pollinators: they visit flowers, looking for food, nectar, and pollen, and they inadvertently spread pollen to the reproductive organs of other plants, thereby fertilizing them and allowing them to reproduce through the development of seeds and fruit. Plant sex really is all about the birds and the bees!

Animal pollinators often are winged creatures designed to travel distances quickly and efficiently, helping nature spread plants' genetic material beyond the small area of your garden bed. But not all pollinators are live animals. Wind and water also spread pollen from one plant to another, ensuring that genes have the opportunity to make more varieties with different traits—in other words, increasing biodiversity.

Pollination Syndromes

Pollinators are fascinating to watch and, as you pay closer attention to their habits, you may discover their preferences. How does a flower attract a pollinator, and how does a pollinator pick a flower to visit? Like a key that fits a lock, the flowering plant has coevolved with its *vector*, or type of pollinator. These traits that attract a certain type of pollinator are called *pollination syndromes*; some are obvious, while others are a bit more mysterious.

Colors are probably the most obvious attractive quality of flowers, and hummingbirds certainly fixate on anything red. Colors also attract butterflies, and it is the sight of a milkweed in bloom that draws in a migrating monarch to dine on its juice. Butterflies prefer flower shapes that facilitate their landing, so upturned blossoms with sturdy petals, such as coneflowers, are a win.

Wasps are often underappreciated for their pollinating ability.

As much as bright colors mean food to butterflies and birds, the opposite is true for night-flying insects and bats. The flowers they visit are pale, usually white or dull shades of pink and green. Moths are drawn in by their keen sense of smell, and they find their

1. The coneflower's shape and ample head allow for safe landings.

2. Rosemary is among the plants whose flowers guide pollinators to the source of nectar.

dinner in the depths of strongly sweet tobacco flowers and Easter lilies. The fruit bats of tropical climates sniff out the musty odors of banana and agave in bloom.

What are flies attracted to? The smells that we are not attracted to, such as rotting meat. Not all flowers smell sweet and look pretty. Flowers that lure in flies, such as skunk cabbage or philodendron, have a putrid odor. Beetle-pollinated plants might not have an odor at all, or they may be strongly fruity or fetid smelling.

Birds generally have a weak sense of smell, although all pollinators have varying abilities to detect wavelengths of light beyond the color spectrum visible to humans. Patterns, colors, and designs convey secret messages to their intended audiences. For example, the human eye has three color receptors—red, green, and blue—whereas birds have four color receptors and can see a greater degree of complexity. Some birds are equipped to see violet, and others can even see ultraviolet (UV) light.

Bees' visible spectrum ranges from yellow through UV, but not the orange and red wavelengths. Certain flowers, such as penstemon and rosemary, display nectar guides, which could be compared to runway lights to guide pollinators straight into their sweet destination. Sometimes the nectar guides are visible to us, and sometimes they are masked in the UV wavelength.

Flower shape plays an important role in matching up with the right pollinator. Beetle-pollinated flowers, such as magnolias and dogwoods, are open and dish-like. Butterflies and hummingbirds can reach into tubular, trumpet-shaped blossoms in which nectar is concealed but accessible by using a long proboscis or tongue, and they dust the reproductive organs along the way. Wind-pollinated flowers have done away with showy flowers or even petals. Plants such as grasses and walnut trees must have their anthers (male reproductive structures) and stigmas (female reproductive structures) exposed to the air, letting go of pollen at the slightest breeze.

Bees: Buzzing with Life—By Amy Grisak

A healthy garden is alive with sounds—one of the most important being the gentle buzz of the myriad bees pollinating our fruits, vegetables, and ornamentals. A garden without these hard-working characters offers decreased pollination and becomes a source of frustration.

It's evident when bees are not in the garden. Squash and other cucurbits—pumpkins, cucumbers, melons, and the like—often start to produce, only to have the immature fruit shrivel and die. Other plants produce less.

Pollination by the Numbers

- 250,000 species of flowering plants on Earth
- 200,000 species of animals that pollinate
- 1,500 species of birds and mammals that pollinate
- 100–200 types of domesticated food crops in the United States
    - 15 percent of these are pollinated by domestic bees
    - 80 percent of these are pollinated by wild bees and wildlife
- $10 billion worth of crops pollinated by honeybees in the United States
- $13.3 billion annual losses due to honeybee poisoning with pesticides
- 42 species of pollinators are listed as endangered in the United States
    - 3 bats
    - 13 birds
    - 24 butterflies/skippers/moths
    - 1 beetle
    - 1 fly
- 185 species of pollinators are listed as endangered worldwide by the International Union for the Conservation of Nature (IUCN)
- 30–75 percent of food and fiber crops depend on pollinators
- 15–30 percent of food and beverages that humans consume are fruits, nuts, and seeds produced through pollination
- 80,000 hives kept by commercial honeybee producers
- 1.3 million colonies of honeybees to pollinate 615,000 acres of almonds in California
- 4,000 bee species native to the United States
- 700 butterfly species native to the United States
- 45 bat species native to the United States
- Hundreds of thousands beetle and fly species native to the United States

Sources: Native Pollinators in Agriculture Project and the Xerces Society's *Attracting Native Pollinators*

"Eighty-five percent of flowering plants need a pollinator in order to produce," says Ashley Minnerath, pollinator program administrator for The Xerces Society, a Portland, Oregon-based organization dedicated to the preservation of invertebrate species, including bees and other pollinators. Bees definitely make everything better.

Faced with colony collapse disorder, a devastating phenomenon known to wipe out entire hives with barely a trace, along with threats from pests and pesticides, European honeybees (*Apis mellifera*) grab most of the headlines. Many other species, however, are capable of ensuring adequate pollination.

The nonnative European honeybee arrived from England to Virginia in the early 1600s with the colonists. Along with honeybees, there are twenty to twenty-five nonnative species in the United States, Minnerath says. The wool carder bee and the horn-face mason bee are two of the more prevalent nonnative species seen in home gardens.

An accidental introduction in the 1960s, the wool carder bee (*Anthidium manicatum*) from Europe is so named because of the female's habit of gathering plant hairs ("carding" them, as one does with wool) to create her nest. They're solitary bees that resemble wasps, with deep-yellow and black markings. Minnerath says that they're mostly seen on the East and West Coasts.

In contrast, the horn-face mason bee (*Osmia cornifrons*) was introduced for pollination and then spread, Minnerath says. The species originated in Japan yet resembles our native mason bees and is often used for home pollination, so these bees are dispersed throughout the country.

Although there is a lot of press about the plight of honeybees, many people don't realize the astounding numbers of resident bees in our yards. Minnerath says that there are nearly 4,000 species of native bees in North America.

"Some of the native bees are more efficient crop pollinators than the nonnative honeybee," she says. A 2013 study backs up these claims, looking at forty-one crops worldwide. It found that the native bees were able to set the fruit at twice the rate of the honeybees.

This does not surprise Dave Hunter of Crown Bees in Woodinville, Washington. He's studied the behavior of pollinators for years and is convinced that encouraging native bee populations can mitigate the severity of honeybee losses throughout the country.

Honeybees are very efficient at what they do, Hunter says. "The honeybee is an industrious workhorse. One bee is a nectar gatherer. One bee is a pollen gatherer," he adds. Bees that gather the pollen remain very neat and tidy about the whole process, as the pollen goes into the pollen pockets on their back legs. Because of this meticulous nature, pollination is more of an accident than a certainty.

On the other hand, many solitary bees, such as the blue orchard bee (*O. lignaria*), will practically belly-flop into flowers because they're there for nectar and pollen. With pollen sticking to the tiny fur on her body, the orchard bee is off to the next flower, which will receive a generous dusting. "Virtually every flower she touches is pollinated," Hunter notes.

Bumblebees (*Bombus sp.*), carpenter bees (*Xylocopa sp.*), and sweat bees (*Halectidae sp.*) all offer another powerful pollination method.

1. A hardworking bee pollinates a cucumber flower.

2. *Halictus rubicundus*, a type of sweat bee, is a pollinator found throughout the United States and Canada.

3. The leafcutter bee was introduced into the United States in the 1920s to revive alfalfa crops.

4. Eastern carpenter bees pollinate through sonication (buzz pollination).

They exhibit what's called "buzz pollination," also known as sonication. The bee grasps a flower, and, after disengaging its wings from its flight muscles, it shakes its whole body at a frequency close to a middle C note, causing the release of pollen from the flower.

The most noted plants targeted for buzz pollination are those of the *Solanum* genus, such as tomatoes, peppers, and eggplants, but it's also very important for cranberries and blueberries. It's a fascinating process and one that's easily observed in the garden, particularly if you can pull up a chair alongside your tomatoes.

It's also important to understand when during the day various bee species go out to visit the flowers. Mason bees typically fly once the temperatures reach around 50 degrees Fahrenheit, and Minnerath points out that bumblebees will brave cool, rainy weather when honeybees are tucked in their hives.

Knowing that different bees aid in the pollination of the fruits and vegetables—with some species being generalists and others targeting specific plants—it's wise to encourage all of the pollinators in your area. "A diversity of bees, both the native and European honeybee, can help gardens be more productive," Minnerath says.

Planting for Bees

Choosing plants with bees in mind remains the first step toward creating a veritable pollinator oasis in your garden. Hunter recommends planting flowers in clumps. "Clumpy stuff will attract more bees," he says.

Break up the lawn by creating groups of gardens. An ideal situation will have some grass along with groupings of native bushes and plenty of flowering plants.

When choosing varieties specifically for pollinators, try to steer clear of the high-tech hybrids. "Hybrids and double-blossomed flowers are hard for bees to pollinate," Hunter says. Some varieties are developed for other characteristics, including no pollen in some instances, which also doesn't benefit bees.

Minnerath recommends native wildflowers, stating that they usually are the best sources of nectar and pollen for native pollinators. "Compared to nonnative plants, native plants are more likely to attract native bees and support a high diversity of butterflies and moths," she says.

When you look for locally native plants, check first at local nurseries because these plants will be well-acclimated to your region as well as the specific bee populations. For example, when the native golden currants bloom in April and early May in some parts of the country, they provide a valuable resource for newly emerging bumblebees. Willows offer another example of an important early-blooming plant. The native plants for your location are in sync with the native pollinator species.

Minnerath also stresses the importance of providing nectar and pollen sources throughout the seasons. "It is useful to include flowers that bloom early in the spring to provide food for newly emerging bumblebee queens," she says. "Similarly, it is important to provide flowers that bloom in late summer and fall to support new bumblebee queens for overwintering."

She recommends having at least three different plants blooming during each season to provide enough diversity to support local pollinators. Of course, more is better. For a visually appealing

Plants for a Seasonal Buzz

Spring
apples
apricots
cherries
chokecherries
dandelions
grape hyacinth
pears
Pulmonaria
Rhododendron
rockcress
violets

Summer
bee balm
blackberries
Echinacea
Echinops
fireweed
heather
hyssop
Joe Pye weed
lilies
phacelia
    (called "bees' friend"
    because it's such a strong
    nectar source)
raspberries
thyme

Fall
barberry
Echium
Sedum
witch hazel
Zinnia

balance in the garden, it's absolutely fine if some of these varieties are domesticated flowers. Natives are the best for providing pollinators with what they need, but the winged workers will definitely use other plants, too.

Depending on the severity of your regional weather, late winter and early spring are when the hardy bumblebees emerge from hibernation; other native bees continue to show up as the weather warms. In addition to the willows and currants, Nanking cherries offer early blooms. In the garden, lupine makes a spring appearance in most parts of the country, as do primroses and hellebores.

Later in spring, the garden bursts with variety, and it's easy to have more than the minimum of three species to accommodate pollinators. Foxglove, columbine, borage, allium, and cranesbill are all spring and early-summer blooming flowers that bring in the bees. During this time of the year, bumblebees and honeybees are out in full force, and more solitary bees emerge. "Mason bees come out when the temperatures are in the 50s [degrees F]," Hunter says.

Penstemons are a stunningly diverse and beautiful collection of well over 200 native and hybrid specimens that typically bloom in spring and early summer—and sometimes in fall if they are cut back during the hottest part of the season. Typically around 2 feet high, the tiny snapdragon-like flowers form dazzling spikes of brilliant blooms. Colors range from the most subtle pinks to hot reds and very close to a true blue. Whatever color you like, it's probable that you will find it in a Penstemon cultivar. Penstemons are an attractive nectar and pollen source for bees, particularly because the bloom time stretches so long throughout the season.

By the summer, poppies are usually brimming with bees during the cool of the morning, and hollyhocks are similarly crowded. Minnerath recommends milkweed, which is an important forage plant for Monarch butterflies that also makes a beautiful and fragrant addition to the garden with pinkish-purple, ½-inch-wide flowers that cluster into a ball shape.

Sunflowers of all shapes and sizes, including native species found throughout the country, are beacons to bees. The salvias, another sizable group of perennials found throughout the country, offer an important food source. Like the penstemons, they bloom throughout the season and come in an astounding range of colors. Agastache varieties appeal to both bees and gardeners; they are disease- and deer-resistant, providing a good option for planting along the perimeter of the property or in areas where deer browse.

During the summer and often well into the fall, herbs are a boon to bees, too. Minnerath suggests lavender, culinary sage, and basil varieties. When oregano is in bloom, the plant literally buzzes with activity—the only drawback is that when you cut the plant, you'll need to be extra cautious not to squeeze a bee between your fingers.

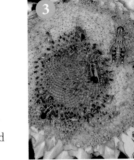

Whereas spring and summer are fairly easy times to provide ample nectar and pollen options, fall is a critical time of the year for the remainder of the native bees to gather enough food to overwinter. New England asters, sneezeweed, and goldenrod are several plants that offer good food sources for late-season bees, Minnerath says. Even though the time for the honeybee to put up large stores of honey for winter has passed, every bit of nectar and pollen helps pull the hive through the winter.

1. Yellow columbine is native to the southwestern United States.

2. The Payette penstemon boasts clusters of vibrant bright-blue flowers.

3. A sunflower head is very valuable in an insect-friendly garden.

Creating Bee Habitats in the Garden

In addition to planting with a food source in mind, it's important to consider how your garden fits the habitat needs of the bees in your region. Not all bees live in tidy hives. Bumblebees—a type of social bee like honeybees—live in a colony with a queen and female workers. Unlike honeybees, they live in the ground. Minnerath points out that bumblebee colonies last only one season, whereas honeybees persist throughout the year. At the end of the season, the old bumblebee queen, workers, and males perish, while the newly mated queens hibernate through the winter until the next season.

Because bumblebees need a place in the ground, consider keeping bare soil—particularly in out-of-the-way areas—available to encourage nesting. "Observe the pollinators you're attracting and what they're doing," Minnerath says. "If they're using specific areas to nest, protect those areas from disturbance."

Some of the other native species, such as mason and leafcutter bees (*Megachile sp.*), use holes in wood or plant debris or even premade homes with tubes provided by gardeners. These solitary bees make ideal garden allies because they are champions of pollination and extremely docile due to their nesting and life cycles. There might be only a little pollen and an egg to defend, and it's easier for the bee to look for more food and produce another egg instead of dying to protect it.

With social bees, Hunter says, "Everything is 'save the queen!' By contrast, solitary bees are gentle guys. They don't have a need to sting because there's nothing to protect. With a blue orchard bee, you can put your hand in front of it [on its way to its hole], and it'll land on you."

Solitary bees do require a little consideration, though, when you are providing what they need for their homes. Hunter says that mason bees require mud in the spring to create their nests, so it's important to offer wet areas where they can gather the necessary materials. As their name implies, leafcutter bees cut tiny circular sections out of plants; the greatest hurdle here is realizing that this is a valuable pollinator that needs just a few things for her home. The bee isn't a pest, so don't spray your plants.

Minnerath suggests leaving plants with pithy stems, such as elderberry and box elder, to give bees a natural place to raise their young. Plantings of bunchgrass are good places for bumblebees and other native bees to overwinter because they can crawl into the protected areas within the plants.

Out of the thousands of bee species, there are other solitary bees that nest in the ground. Cellophane bees (*Colletids sp.*) and sweat bees are a couple of examples. "Ground-nesting bees will need naturally occurring bare ground," Minnerath says. "Keep a watchful eye. Enhance and protect those areas."

1. The yellow-banded bumblebee is one of several species whose numbers have declined in North America.

2. Golden currant blooms in April and May and is very popular with bumblebees.

3. A European honeybee is attracted to the brightly colored "butterfly weed" (a type of milkweed).

Overall, a little chaos in the garden is a good thing, Minnerath advises. This gives bees places to hide, nest, and overwinter. Leave some of the sunflower or *Echinacea* stalks, along with clumps of perennials. When you're gardening with pollinators in mind, perfection isn't necessary.

One of the most important considerations concerning bees in the garden is minimizing, if not completely eliminating, pesticides. Pesticides are partly to blame for the demise of the honeybee, and the chemicals have devastating effects on native bee populations. "Yards need pests," Hunter says, "because if you don't have pests, you lose your beneficial insects." For example, if you have aphids on plants and spray them with poison, you will lose any ladybugs that come to feed on them. Many times, where there is a food source, the beneficial insects will follow.

In addition to curtailing your own spraying habits, you might also talk with neighbors about less severe methods. For example, rather than bringing out heavy-duty chemicals, consider using a blast

A Harvest by Bees

Even if you cannot grow these plants and crops in your yard or on your larger property, you might enjoy knowing the myriad foods that bees pollinate. Go ahead and feast your eyes on the bounty!

Fruits and Nuts		Vegetables	Field Crops
almonds	kiwifruit	asparagus	alfalfa hay
apples	loganberries	broccoli	alfalfa seed
apricots	macadamia nuts	carrots	cotton lint
avocados	nectarines	cauliflower	cotton seed
blueberries	olives	celery	legume seed
boysenberries	peaches	cucumbers	peanuts
cantaloupe	pears	onions	rapeseed
cherries	plums/prunes	pumpkins	soybeans
citrus	raspberries	squash	sugar beets
cranberries	strawberries		sunflowers
grapes	watermelons		
honeydew			

Source: The Natural Resources Defense Council

of water to clear off pests or adding row covers to prevent them from infesting crops. Both options are much safer for bees and other pollinators.

Having bees in your garden is a pleasure. Not only does it improve pollination and, ultimately, production, it creates a relaxing environment where you can see how these fascinating characters spend their busy days.

Butterfly Gardening—By Cherie Langlois

> *Happiness is a butterfly, which, when pursued, is always just beyond your grasp, but which, if you will sit down quietly, may alight upon you.*
>
> —Nathaniel Hawthorne, American author (1804–1864)

I don't know about you, but for me, there couldn't be a truer metaphor: happiness really is a butterfly. Taking a break from weeding to watch a sunny yellow tiger swallowtail flutter by and float down to a bee balm bloom. Reaching past little amber-colored skippers as they frolic among fragrant oregano blossoms. Holding my breath when an azure butterfly dances down to sit on my forearm for a few seconds before flying off again, my heart in tow. Each encounter and butterfly visitor

A Western tiger swallowtail.

brightens my world, brings me joy, and boosts my somewhat wild (OK, weedy) garden's beauty a thousandfold. How could I not want more?

Butterflies are so much more than happiness-making, living adornments for our gardens. Though not the efficient Type-A pollinators that some insects are (yeah, that's you, bees), butterflies still provide essential pollination services as they flit from flower to flower, sipping nectar.

Why is this essential? Well, most flowering plants—including many food plants—depend on pollinators like the butterfly to ferry pollen from the flower's male anthers to another flower's female stigma. In the butterfly's case, scales on its body and wings capture the pollen grains at one flower, and then the pollen rides along to be brushed off onto the stigma of the next blossom. Et voilà, a seed is born. Without pollen transfer, there is no plant reproduction.

Also, although it's not too pleasant to think about, butterflies and their larvae remain extremely important parts of nature's food chain. Spiders, dragonflies, parasitic wasps, frogs, and snakes all dine on butterflies and/or caterpillars, and so do many of the birds that bring beauty and song to our gardens. A garden a-flutter with butterflies signals a healthier environment for all.

Unfortunately, the butterfly's own situation isn't all sunshine and roses because many populations have experienced a sad, steady decline. The culprits? Primarily habitat loss—shopping centers, housing developments, and vast parking lots continue to obliterate native host and nectar plants—and the widespread use of toxic pesticides and herbicides. The famous monarch butterfly, for example, has declined alarmingly in step with the degradation of its wintering grounds in Mexico and California and the eradication of milkweeds—the main host plant for monarch caterpillars.

So here's my mission: Make my garden a better, healthier, lovelier haven for butterflies. Then sit on my porch on a warm spring or summer day and wait for happiness—and hopefully a butterfly or two. Care to join me? Here are some butterfly gardening basics to get us started.

Possibly the most well-known butterfly, the monarch.

A Life in Stages

In their winged adult form, butterflies dazzle us to such an extent that it's easy to forget they have other, not-so-flamboyant life stages with special needs. As insects in the order Lepidoptera, which includes moths, butterflies undergo a process called *complete metamorphosis* during which they pass through four distinct stages. If you want your garden to do more than attract a few passing butterflies, aim to meet the varying needs of each life stage in terms of food and/or habitat.

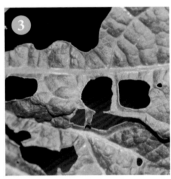

First comes the egg, which the female butterfly usually lays on a specific host plant's leaf or flower. Within a few days, a tiny caterpillar hatches and, like the colorful caterpillar in the popular children's book *The Very Hungry Caterpillar*, starts feasting on its host plant.

Growing rapidly, the caterpillar molts its skin several times until it reaches maturity and seeks a protected place to hang out (literally) and transform into a pupa, or chrysalis. After a span of time, depending on when it entered the chrysalis phase, a crumply winged adult butterfly emerges as if by magic from the dried shell. Within the first hour or so, the butterfly's wing veins fill with a fluid called *hemolymph*, and its wings slowly unfurl and dry. Then it's time to fly, feed on a strictly liquid diet, and find a mate—fast, because many butterflies live only a few weeks.

1. The butterfly lays its eggs directly on a leaf or flower.

2. This green caterpillar is a swallowtail larva.

3. If you host butterfly eggs and caterpillars, be prepared for holes in your leaves.

Gardening for Eggs and Caterpillars

While adult butterflies are usually happy to sip nectar from a variety of flowers, their caterpillars (larvae) tend to be picky eaters, feeding on only one or several specific host plant species. For example, monarch caterpillars feed exclusively on milkweeds, zebra swallowtail larvae munch on pawpaws, red admiral caterpillars favor nettles, and painted lady larvae prefer thistles (though they'll also dine on hollyhocks and pearly everlasting).

Yes, many plants that larvae like to eat are what most people consider weeds: think clover, plantain, and nettles. You don't have to let your entire garden run rampant with weeds to provide food for caterpillars (but why not let a little weedy patch persist, if possible, for their feeding pleasure?). Plants that both feed caterpillars and beautify gardens include coneflowers, asters, snapdragons, violets, lupines, and certain milkweeds. Some, such as butterfly milkweed and hollyhocks, also serve as butterfly nectar plants.

Don't expect your host plants to have pristine, hole-free leaves! If seeing caterpillar-gnawed plants bothers you, consider hiding them in the less visible areas of your garden or camouflaging them among nonhost flora. Caterpillars eat a lot, however, so you'll want to provide them with groupings of food plants rather than just one plant here and there.

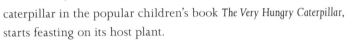

Just Say No to Pesticides

You wouldn't invite human guests to dinner and serve them up a delectable dish tainted with arsenic, would you? Then neither should you invite butterflies and their young into your garden to dine on poisoned plants.

Incorporating hardy, bug-resistant herbs and natives into your butterfly garden will make it easier for you to garden organically, shunning toxic pesticides made to kill insects—bad and beneficial alike. Your happy butterflies (not to mention the birds and the bees) will thank you.

To research which butterfly species inhabit your area and for species-specific host plant recommendations, consult *Butterflies of North America* by Jeffrey Glassberg or another good butterfly guide. Also check out the regional butterfly gardening guides from the North American Butterfly Association (www.nababutterfly.com).

Gardening for Butterflies

Butterflies will sip from a wide variety of blooms, but they tend to favor nectar-rich flowers that present nice, stable landing surfaces, such as coneflowers and heliotrope, and spiked flowers that allow them to easily meander from blossom to blossom, such as bee balm, lavender, and salvia. Butterflies gravitate toward purple, blue, and pink flowers as well as red, yellow, orange, and white. By the way, to obtain salts, protein, and other needed nutrients, many butterflies also imbibe liquid from some not-so-pretty sources: rotting fruit, mud, sticky sap, animal excrement, and even dead animals.

Although you'll often see exotics like butterfly bushes and hollyhocks on butterfly-garden plant lists, it makes sense to incorporate native plants and wildflowers into your butterfly garden as much as possible. As authors Bill Thompson III and Connie Toops explain in *Hummingbirds and Butterflies*, natives are plants that would have grown within 50 miles of your yard at the time when Europeans arrived in North America. The authors point out that not only do native plants have important evolutionary ties with native butterflies, which makes them ideal food sources, but they are "adjusted to local soils and climates, are more drought-tolerant, and are usually more disease-resistant than exotics."

In other words, native butterfly plants are often easier to grow and maintain than exotics, which is good news for time-strapped gardeners. Depending on where you live, native plants both beautiful to gardeners and attractive to butterflies include showy milkweed, butterfly weed, aster, yarrow, goldenrod, lupine, bee balm, violet, phlox, purple coneflower, pearly everlasting, and redbud. For more suggestions, check the aforementioned books.

When planning and planting your butterfly garden, try to incorporate a mix of perennial and annual flowers of varying heights and with different bloom times, enabling you to offer a nectar buffet from spring to fall. Since cold-blooded butterflies need warmth to get moving, plant butterfly flowers where they'll receive full sun for most of the day, preferably in multiple-plant blocks that will be easy for butterflies to spot and visit. Don't have room for a big in-ground garden? No worries. Window boxes, sunny patio pots, and other containers filled with bright nectar plants lure butterflies, too.

Remember that these delicate insects weigh practically nothing. Planting native shrubs and trees (or employing fences and walls) as butterfly-garden windbreaks, if needed, will help keep wind from battering butterflies' fragile wings and can also help shelter them from rain. Ground covers, brush piles, leaf litter, old logs, and snags also offer protection as well as places for all life stages to hibernate. After you add some flat stones to your garden as butterfly basking spots and a shallow container filled with damp sand for puddling (sipping moisture from puddles or wet sand/soil), you're well on your way to creating a butterfly haven.

Cocoon, What's that Secret You're Keepin'?

Unabridged version of this article was originally printed in the November 2013 newsletter for the Lexington, Kentucky, chapter of Wild Ones: Native Plants, Natural Landscapes

The romantic idea of a lowly caterpillar munching along and then one day becoming the beautiful, graceful creature it has waited so long to become captures our imagination and is the stuff of fairy tales. But do we really know what happens during that miraculous transformation inside the cocoon?

First, a few definitions: a *caterpillar* is the larval form of a butterfly, moth, or skipper. A *cocoon* is the silk covering that encloses the pupa. In general, moth caterpillars spin various types of cocoons from their silk, and a *chrysalis* is a protective shell of a pupating butterfly. A distinct difference is that the chrysalis is a structure formed within the caterpillar itself, and this structure is revealed when the caterpillar sheds its skin one final time.

The diversity of cocoon designs varies from a silk hammock to a rock climber's sling to a leaf-litter-woven sleeping bag. Depending on the species, the complete reorganization that happens within can last from a couple of weeks to several months. Unable to react to predators with anything more than a twitch, the cocoon camouflages and protects the vulnerable creature inside it.

Slicing into a cocoon may reveal the state of the pupa, but it destroys the life. If you do it at just the right stage, you find it filled with wet goo, the disintegrated caterpillar. This slop is made of imaginal cells, which are undifferentiated, similar to stem cells. These terms describe the blank slate of possibility, the basic building blocks that will construct the new winged form. The protein-rich soup will multiply and organize cells into

1. Common buckeyes are known for their large "eye" spots.

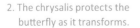
2. The chrysalis protects the butterfly as it transforms.

A Butterfly Mini-Mini-Guide

Clouded Sulphur
(*Colias philodice*)

A common butterfly of fields and roadsides, the cheery clouded sulphur tends to sit on flowers with its black-bordered, bright-yellow wings closed. While males are always yellow above, the females can be either yellow or greenish-white. The caterpillars enjoy munching on alfalfa and clover.

Common Checkered Skipper
(*Pyrgus communis*)

Named for their brisk and skipping flight, skippers might not appear as dazzling as some butterflies, but they are adorably little. Adaptable to just about any habitat, including cities, the common checkered skipper has dark, white-checkered wings and prefers to sun with its wings open. Its larvae prefer noshing on mallows and hollyhocks.

Common Buckeye
(*Junonia coenia*)

The aptly named buckeye transforms itself from cryptic leaf mimic to big-eyed, bird-startling bug monster by simply spreading its wings. Look for distinctive multicolored eyespots on the fore- and hindwings and reddish-orange bars on the forewings. These migratory butterflies enjoy puddling, and the caterpillars adore plantains, snapdragons, and monkeyflowers.

Monarch
(*Danaus plexippus*)

Arguably the best-known butterfly in North America, the monarch flaunts rich orange wings boldly veined with black and adorned with double rows of white dots on the black margins. Each year, these dazzling butterflies stage an amazing multigenerational migration, journeying back and forth from wintering grounds in either central Mexico (for central and eastern populations) or along the California coast (western populations). Monarch larvae munch on milkweeds, incorporating these plants' nasty-tasting toxins into their bodies.

Mourning Cloak
(*Nymphalis antiopa*)

This unmistakable butterfly has dark maroon-brown wings with blue-spotted and yellow margins. Mourning cloaks hibernate during the winter and can live for ten months, making them one of the longest-lived butterflies. The larvae prefer to dine on cottonwoods, willows, and birches.

Painted Lady
(*Vanessa cardui*)

Another impressive winter traveler to warmer climes, the painted lady flashes wings of orange, black, and white on top and an intricate pattern of gray, white, brown, and rose below. These medium-sized butterflies have a quick, erratic flight, and the males often hang out on hilltops while scoping out their surroundings for mates. The caterpillars favor thistles but also nibble hollyhocks and pearly everlasting.

Spring Azure
(*Celastrina ladon*)

True to its name, this little silver-blue beauty is often one of the first butterflies to emerge in spring. Thought to include several variable species, spring azures flock to flowering herbs, and the males are keen puddlers. The caterpillars relish various flowers, including blueberries, dogwoods, and wild lilacs.

Tiger Swallowtail
Western (*Papilio rutulus*)
Eastern (*Papilio glaucus*)

It's easy to see where this common garden visitor gets its name: viewed from above or below, its yellow wings bear striking black tiger stripes. "Tailed" hindwings sport a blue iridescence, more so in females; in the eastern species, the dimorphic females can be either yellow or black. Look for male swallowtails congregating to puddle in muddy areas. While adults enjoy sipping from honeysuckle and bee balm, among other blooms, the caterpillars chew on the leaves of trees such as cottonwood, tuliptree, and alder.

legs, wings, sexual organs, and other parts designed for a completely different purpose in life. The caterpillar's body was designed to eat and store fat; the winged butterfly or moth is all about mating: two different bodies for two different life stages.

With advancements in technology, a glimpse inside the mummy-like pod is possible. X-rays have been used to display internal structures. Computed tomography (CT) scans create multiple views and can show more dimensions within an object. With a technique known as Micro-CT, researchers have scanned and recorded the entire metamorphosis of a single caterpillar. Magnetic resonance imaging (MRI) shows more contrast between different soft tissues, and the multiple images lend themselves well to animation sequences.

Dr. Richard Stringer peered inside monarch chrysalids with an MRI at Duke University Medical Center, recording images over ten days. Hundreds of images create a composite 3D portrayal of the changes taking place. Animators took Dr. Stringer's research and illustrated the butterfly life cycle in the film *Metamorphosis*.

The MRI showed brain tissue forming as early as day one of the chrysalis and that the breathing apparatus remains functional throughout the process. Researchers have found that some butterflies and moths will remember lessons learned as caterpillars, such as particular smells to avoid. Even with the high-tech magnifying glass peering inside the womb of a chrysalis or cocoon, it remains baffling that these creatures dissolve and something orchestrates their resurrection.

Moths

In nature, there are many examples of wildlife that take shifts performing similar ecosystem services or filling a niche. Butterflies pollinate during the day, and moths do the same at night. Moths and their flowers tend to be duller in color because moths navigate in darkness and communicate through scent.

Contrary to popular belief, moths are not actually attracted to light; instead, they are disoriented by it. Their eyes are designed to see by the light of the moon and stars, and, like many flying insects, they navigate in relation to the brightest light, which would normally be the moon. Bright outdoor lighting, candles, and fires draw them in because moths have to constantly shift their position to keep the light at the right angle for their navigation system to work. The closer the light, the more disoriented they become. When they reach the light, it could trigger their internal "switch" that tells them it's daytime, causing them to go to sleep. These are a few of the fascinating theories that scientists are researching about moth behavior, and it's a good reason to use outdoor lighting minimally and appropriately. Many night creatures are suffering due to light pollution,

The royal walnut moth is found in North America, most commonly in the southern United States.

Monarch Waystations—by Susan Jonas

A version of this article first appeared in the ~~Danville Advocate-Messenger~~ newspaper in August 2013

Garden clubs across North America want you to plant weeds in your garden. That's right. These folks are on a mission to add milkweed plants to gardens all over the continent. Without them, the beautiful gold-and-black monarch butterflies will be in serious trouble.

Gardeners, and others who keep a close eye on the natural world, have noticed a sharp decline in the number of butterflies, particularly monarchs. Like the scarcity of honeybees and amphibians, this is one more sign that all is not right with our world.

In 2012, monarch numbers declined by 59 percent compared to 2011. These figures have caused the World Wildlife Fund to declare the eastern monarch migration to be endangered. What can we do?

Monarch Watch, a national organization sponsored by the University of Kansas, has designed a plan to create "Monarch Waystations" all across America at schools, businesses, homes, and municipalities to sustain the butterflies during their life cycles and migrations. The Garden Club of Danville, Kentucky, and the Lexington, Kentucky, chapter of Wild Ones are both committed to this mission. Once you understand how important and how easy it is, these folks hope that you'll join them.

Two Kentucky gardeners are especially committed. Joanna Kirby of Lancaster is president of the Garden Club of Kentucky, and one of her goals is to establish Monarch Waystations all across the state with the help of local garden clubs. Linda Porter of Danville is known as "The Butterfly Lady" and gives presentations to schools and other organizations throughout the state. Both have certified their own gardens as Monarch Waystations.

You've probably seen adult monarchs sipping nectar from many varieties of flowers, but you may not know that milkweeds are the only plants that monarch caterpillars can eat. Without milkweeds, the monarchs cannot survive. The adults lay their eggs on milkweed plants, and the little caterpillars begin munching as soon as they hatch.

And that is the problem. While milkweeds used to be common in fields and fencerows, they are fast losing habitat to development and due to the use of herbicides. With a name like milkweed, it is no surprise that generations of farmers and gardeners have considered the plant just that: a weed. Now we know better.

Monarchs are one of nature's truly remarkable stories. Populations of the tiny but tough creatures migrate each year from Mexico to Canada and back. It takes four generations of monarchs to make their way from overwintering in Mexico all the way to Canada during the summer and then back to Mexico for the winter.

The monarchs you may see in gardens in the summer and fall will only live two to six weeks before they lay eggs and die. Providing there are enough milkweeds, those eggs will hatch into butterflies that complete another segment of the migration. It is becoming harder and harder for the butterflies to find enough milkweeds as they cross the country.

If you have a flower garden, you probably already have many of the plants that provide nectar for adult monarchs. With the addition of at least ten milkweed plants and some management practices, you could certify your garden as an official Monarch Waystation. Of course, the butterflies don't care if your garden is certified or not, but registering it lets Monarch Watch keep track of the locations and numbers of Waystations across the country.

First, you need at least 100 square feet of space in full sun. The total may be split into several locations, which makes it easy to convert an existing flower garden or landscape.

Second, plant ten or more milkweed plants, preferably of two or more species (caution: milkweed sap can severely irritate your eyes; if you cut the stems, wear gloves or wash your hands and keep your hands away from your face). They are not always easy to find, but if enough people ask for them, local sources will begin carrying milkweeds. In the Bluegrass area of Kentucky, they are readily available at three local nurseries.

Third, plant at least four nectar plants to keep something blooming throughout the growing season. They may be native trees, shrubs, and wildflowers or the common annuals already in many gardens, such as petunias, lantana, salvia, and zinnias.

The fourth step concerns the way you garden. Plants should be relatively close together, to provide shelter, but not crowded. Eliminate the use of herbicides and insecticides. Leave some dead plants over the winter to provide shelter for eggs or chrysalises; cleaning up in the fall may destroy next year's butterflies. If you prefer to tidy your garden, at least loosely pile the dead plants in an out-of-the-way spot until spring.

Last, find complete information and register your garden as a Certified Monarch Waystation at www.monarchwatch.org. You can fill out the application online or by mail. There is a processing fee, and you can add an attractive metal sign for an additional cost so that others will know that you have a special garden and can learn from you.

Thanks to the campaigns of garden clubs all across North America, hundreds of Monarch Waystations have been installed in home and commercial landscapes ... preliminary counts showed an increase in monarch sightings during the fall 2015 migration.

and some cities have established ordinances that help preserve the night sky and nocturnal wildlife.

Moths are gaining in popularity, and mothing (the act of finding, identifying, and recording moths) is catching on like birding has. Since mothing is relatively new, it's fun to make exciting discoveries that can further the body of scientific knowledge of moths. Approximately 12,000 species of moth live in North America—enough to keep moth-ers occupied for quite a while.

The giant cecropia moth is larger than a grown man's hand.

Foster Moth-ers: The Cecropia Story

Unabridged version of this article was originally printed in the November 2013 newsletter for the Lexington, Kentucky, chapter of Wild Ones: Native Plants, Natural Landscapes

Eat, sleep, have sex, and die. The life cycle of the huge, beautiful cecropia moth can be simplified to those few acts. Nonetheless, it is providing entertainment and fascination for some Wild Ones members in Kentucky. Like many dramas, this story starts with death.

Amanda Cawby was on her way to a drive-in movie when wings flapping on the ground got her attention. "It looked like a hurt bird, and I was afraid someone would run over the poor thing," she said. She recognized it as a giant silkworm moth, and it died shortly after she placed it in a container. It left behind ten little nuggets that resembled Grape Nuts cereal, which turned out to be the eggs of North America's largest moth: *Hyalophora cecropia*.

She took the eggs to her butterfly-loving friend Betty Hall, who thought they might survive. She put them on maple leaves and left them alone. Around ten days later, little black fuzzy larva hatched out. Six lived and grew into their barbs, filling out as plump, pale-green caterpillars, 4 to 5 inches long, armed with colorful, medieval-looking spiked knobs. When they formed their cocoons around seven weeks later, Betty put them in a protected cage outdoors and let them spend the winter just hanging out. "I held my breath that all would go well," she said, and let nature take its course.

The following summer, when all six adult moths emerged and stretched out their 6-inch wingspans, Betty was thrilled. One of them appeared to be a female, with a larger abdomen and less bushy antennae (the males need those extra sensory appendages to sniff out the females' "come-hither" pheromones from, literally, a mile away). Betty placed this special lady in a large mesh cage with hopes that the moth would attract a mate and that she could witness the act.

It didn't take long before a male found her and mated with her all day long. The next morning, he was gone, and that same day, the female began laying her eggs, at least seventy. After that, Betty said, "She deserved to be free," and she released the female moth. The moth would die within days

What Are Caterpillars?

Graceful, elegant butterflies all spend a very important portion of their life cycles as caterpillars, with segmented, wormlike bodies and three pairs of legs. They can be hairy, spiny, smooth, spotted, outlandish, or dull-colored. They can camouflage themselves or mimic unsavory items like bird droppings or spun glass. Who would want to eat that?

The important role of caterpillars in the food web cannot be overstated. They keep birds alive. To keep caterpillars alive, we need to supply their food source: native plants. Technically, caterpillars have a parasitic relationship with the plants they eat; parasites depend on their hosts for sustenance but don't usually kill them.

According to Douglas Tallamy, specialization is the rule, not the exception, in the natural world. Most caterpillars need a very specific host plant for early stages of growth, which may be a different type of plant than what their adult versions visit for nectar. The sphinx moth drinks from and pollinates phlox, but it needs red coral honeysuckle to host its larvae, which are a type of hornworm. The threatening "horn" appendage could scare off mama birds looking for juicy, tender food for her babies. But another predator awaits: the caterpillar might become the host for a parasitic wasp that will lay its egg on, or in, the caterpillar, ensuring a long, slow death. But first there must be some phlox and red coral honeysuckle to set the stage for this inevitable drama.

Caterpillars are high in lipids and proteins and rich in carotenoids, all important for reproduction. Caterpillars also make great baby food. They are soft, easy to digest (no pesky exoskeletons to get caught up in a young bird's throat), full of nutrition, and plentiful. How plentiful? The parents can deliver food every three minutes all day long, and they will use a variety of species.

So, if you are concerned about some eastern tent caterpillars, gypsy moths, bagworms, or any number of other perceived pests in the form of caterpillars, don't spray pesticides, even if they are organic or all-natural. Instead, look to the birds to take care of them, and you can sing a sweet little song along with the baby chickadees.

of giving birth. In fact, the adults are made only for breeding, with no functional mouthparts or digestive systems.

Maple and black cherry trees in Betty's yard hosted this third generation, the grandchildren of the original deceased moth. Again, around ten days later, they began to hatch. This time, Betty wanted to share the experience with other moth foster parents if they could provide the right food—mainly maple, cherry, apple, or birch leaves.

Many larvae found homes with friends in central Kentucky. Ann Bowe took three under her wing, and Floracliff Nature Preserve took in five. On a quiet day inside the nature center, they could be heard munching on maple and cherry leaves. Around mid-August, all of the local caterpillars were at various stages of forming cocoons, and Laura Baird's was the last. She said, "At this point, I'm eager for the little guy to wrap it up. Literally." It appears that cherry leaves may have plumped them up faster than maple.

A mating pair of cecropia, the largest species of moth.

What really happens while the pupa hides inside the cocoon is a bit of a mystery. Ann Bowe's curiosity was sparked by watching the caterpillars she keeps in her kitchen. She wondered how they wove their cocoons because they looked like they barely moved. Unlike a butterfly chrysalis, the cecropia caterpillar spins silk into a pod, incorporating leaves for stability and camouflage. Within, it undergoes changes on a cellular level, protected and safe, for up to nine months.

Checking back with our foster moth-ers as the saga continued, it seemed as if they'd bridged the insect–human divide. Laura stated, "Raising caterpillars has made the entire world of insects seem more approachable and fascinating to me." Ann has gotten friendly with hers, and they even allow her to pet their harmless spikes. The creatures were also the source of artistic inspiration: Floracliff Nature Preserve hosted a nature journaling workshop in July, and artist Pat Greer made a watercolor study of one while the entire class marveled at the size of its scat.

The survival rates of the rescued eggs' offspring were mixed. Ann raised two caterpillars that looked healthy and overwintered well in her enclosed, unheated back porch. The first to emerge was unable to fly and did not survive. The second one was in perfect condition and flew away as soon as it could. Beverly at Floracliff continues to foster caterpillars and keeps hers caged, outdoors, on a porch.

It is important for the cocoons to stay at a cold temperature for several months. Five out of six survived and flew away in June of the first year. The second year, they took six more caterpillars from Betty, and only one survived. In the wild, the survival rate of caterpillars is typically around 2 percent. Raising a caterpillar in captivity will actually help it live to reproduce.

If Amanda had never picked up that dying mother, this door to cecropia affinity may not have opened. Amanda explains, "I am not an animal rescue person necessarily, just big-hearted." Ann added, "I've raised lots of butterflies, but this was quite different, in part due to the overwintering and in part due to the size of these beautiful beasts." As for Betty, who raised many butterflies before the cecropia moth crossed her path, she confessed that she was "just winging it."

Flies and Wasps

The first astounding thing you may learn about these forgotten pollinators is that they actually do something besides annoy and scare us! Flies and wasps are so much more than uninvited pests at our picnics. They play critical roles in pollinating our food plants, and they perform other important ecosystem services, such as population control (of other insects, not of people!). If you have learned to embrace bees (metaphorically) and appreciate them for the labor that they give their lives to do,

<aside>
Moth and Butterfly Resources

See Betty Hall's homegrown blog and beautiful photographs from her suburban nature sanctuary. She has a simple guide to raising black swallowtail butterflies, which can be useful for any butterfly or moth: www.bettyhallphotography.com.

The Butterflies and Moths of North America (BAMONA) project collects and shares citizen science data and generates regional checklists that can get as specific as your home county: www.butterfliesandmoths.org.
</aside>

Flies are often seen as pests, but they do important work, too,

then you are well on the road to giving wasps a chance, too.

Bees, wasps, and flies can be difficult to tell apart. Some harmless flies mimic bees or grow larger than wasps or even dragonflies. Look at the wings if you can; bees and wasps have two pairs of wings (they belong to the order Diptera, meaning "two wings") whereas flies have only one set. The heads are also distinctive. Bees generally have obvious antennae whereas those on flies are stubbier and downturned. Flies' eyes are much larger than those of bees. The pollen-carrying ability of bees is also more noticeable. Female bees are equipped with hairs on their legs and underside to carry more pollen for their larval offspring.

Flies

Do you like to eat strawberries, onions, or carrots? Thank a fly. Flies are very efficient pollinators because they don't have to supply a nest with fuel for the winter. They can work on pollinating later into the season and in colder climates than bees can. They usually visit tubular flowers appropriate to the size of their sucking mouthparts; these are shorter tubular flowers than those that butterflies and moths visit.

Hover flies, also known as flower flies or by their family name—syrphid flies—are commonly mistaken for bees. Their striped bodies and coloration confuse predators, but they are capable of moving in ways that bees don't, hence the name "hover" fly. Hovering in place is not a typical bee behavior; a bee generally lands and rests its wings while the flower's outstretched petals support it. The larvae of hover flies are great predators on aphids as well.

Even more mimicry comes with aptly named bee flies, some of which are equipped with long proboscises to probe for deeper nectar, just as bees do. Their hairy bodies also allow more hitchhiking pollen to be transported.

That's Redundant

Even though specialization pairs up pollinators with flowers, you may see many types of beetles, flies, wasps, and butterflies on the same plant. This is nature's way of ensuring that the job gets done through *redundancy*, which is also a principle that permaculture gardeners integrate into their ecosystems. Think about how you can provide a multitude of options to feed these flies and wasps, and they will return the favor by spreading pollen around as they do what comes naturally.

Wasps

Wasps are not as well equipped to probe deeply into flowers, and their smooth bodies discourage much pollen from clinging to them, but they are still pollinators. They visit easily accessible flowers, such as goldenrods and Queen Anne's lace, accidentally dropping a few grains of pollen as they move about. With the exception of a few

social wasps in the family Vespidae that may be aggressive when defending their territories, wasps are generally mild-mannered and serve our gardens well as predators of other insects.

If you see a wasp feeding on a flower, it is probably in the nonsocial genus *Pseudomasaris*, known as "pollen wasps." The dozen or so species in North America look like small yellow jackets. Pollen wasps prefer pollen from only two plant families, the Hydrophyllaceae (waterleaf) and Scrophulariaceae (figwort) families. Less common wasps that may also visit flowers for nectar include the colorful, wingless velvet ants.

Beetles

If you were to guess what the most diverse group of pollinators is, you may guess bees or butterflies. Although they have impressive numbers of natives in North America, they can't top the 30,000 species of beetle in the United States and the 340,000 species worldwide. And that's only what scientists have identified so far! According to fossil records, beetles and flies were probably the earliest pollinators, going back 150 million years to the beginning phases of the co-evolution of flowers and insects, which led to the specialization of more pollinators and the wide variety of flower shapes we have today.

Magnolias and water lilies allow beetles access to their open, disc-like flowers and lure them in with their musky aroma. For many beetle species with a short life span, the timing of food availability is important if they are to eat, mate, and deposit eggs before they die. Soldier beetles, whose larvae are predators, eat and mate on sunflowers, coneflowers, and goldenrod. Other beetles that regularly visit flowers as adults include blister beetles (when threatened, they can release a chemical that can blister human skin), scarab beetles (important for pollinating native magnolias), and soft-winged flower beetles (who mainly eat other insects on flowers but spread some pollen while they're at it).

The Xerces Society guide, *Attracting Native Pollinators*, sums up the incremental contributions that beetles make to the flower world. "Despite the damage they cause with their chewing and

1. The scarlet lily beetle is named for its appetite for lilies and related plants.

2. It's easy to see why syrphid flies are often confused with bees.

3. Pollinator wasps in the United States resemble yellow jackets.

4. The soldier beetle is one of the main pollinating beetle species.

Neonics Endanger Pollinators

Adapted from an article by Linda Porter and Susan Jonas, Garden Club of Danville, Kentucky, and Wild Ones native landscaping organization, originally published in the Danville Advocate Messenger, March 8, 2015

Concern is growing over a class of pesticides widely used on farms and in home gardens. Even if you garden organically, it's hard to escape them. These are the neonicotinoids, developed in the mid-1990s. Neonics, for short. At first, they were welcomed as safer alternatives to the chemical pesticides then available.

Neonics are systemic chemicals. They are absorbed by the plant through the roots or leaves and carried through the vascular system, making the entire plant toxic to insects, from roots to flowers, even the nectar and pollen. Exposure endangers bees and other insects by disrupting their immune and nervous systems.

The active ingredients persist in plants and in the soil for months, if not years. For annuals, this could be the entire life of the plant. Untreated plants may absorb chemical residues in your garden soil from the previous year.

Neonics are widely used in agriculture and horticulture because they are less toxic to humans and animals than previously used pesticides. This sounds like a great idea if you want to kill an infestation of aphids in your garden, but it doesn't stop there. If it was treated with neonics as a seed or seedling, then that pretty coneflower providing lunch to a visiting butterfly or caterpillar just might be the insect's last meal, even if you don't use pesticides yourself.

Here's the alarming part: many, if not most, nurseries rely on neonics to control insects in greenhouses, where millions of bedding plants are grown. A major study by Friends of the Earth, BeeAction.org, and the Pesticide Research Institute found that 54 percent of annuals and perennials tested in large garden centers have been treated with neonics. Growers say they can't control harmful insects without them. You may unknowingly purchase these plants, intending to provide habitats and food for bees and other pollinators but ending up harming them.

Some sources feel the whole problem is overblown. Others predict another "silent spring." It's up to each gardener to decide what to do, if anything. Here are our suggestions:

- Do not buy neonicotinoids for home garden use. Be aware that some potting soils contain neonics. Some common neonics found in pesticides include imidacloprid, acetamiprid, dinotefuran, and clothianidin. Look for them on ingredient labels.

- Ask before you buy plants. If [sellers] can't or won't tell you whether their plants are neonic-free, don't buy from them and tell them why.

- Take care using any pesticide, even organics like insecticidal soap. Follow directions for safe application and use sparingly.

- Grow your own plants from organic seeds. They are safe and available at most garden centers or online.

Maybe it's time to see the beauty of a less-than-perfect garden. A garden that is healthy for beneficial insects, with a few bugs and chewed leaves, will likely have far fewer harmful insects. Mother Nature has a way of keeping things in balance. We would do well to work with her.

rummaging, a little pollen sticks to the beetles' bodies and gets transferred from anther to stigma. Because of the abundance of these insects, even that small amount of pollen adds up, making beetles significant pollinators." Let us learn from the beetles and find inspiration in the small solutions we can create in our home ecosystems.

The Buzz on Pollinators

Understanding that the flowers on the plants in your yard could provide pollen that will be transferred to another yard and another plant, and vice versa, you may begin to get the sense that your small wildlife habitat is a fragment of a much larger picture. Whether it's a 3,000-mile monarch migration or a beetle scooting under a neighbor's fence, pollinators, as with most wildlife, dwell where they need to, regardless of our boundaries. Recognizing the importance of how you choose to handle insects on your property will affect your neighborhood and beyond. Be brave and let your neighbors know that you've chosen not to spray any insecticides, that you are encouraging beneficial insects, and that you'd appreciate their help by doing the same.

Sharing your observations about important pollinators can greatly help worldwide efforts to educate people. Citizen scientists are volunteers who collect data for research, and they are contributing to the understanding of how these amazing little pieces of the wild world fit into bigger puzzles. Information from citizen scientists can lead to critical discoveries.

You Can Help!

Here are some ways to join the pollinator rescue movement from the comfort of your own backyard habitat:
- Citizen Science Central: birds.cornell.edu/citscitoolkit/projects/find
- Monarch Watch: monarchwatch.org
- Million Pollinator Garden Challenge: millionpollinatorgardens.org
- Pollinator Task Force: whitehouse.gov; enter "pollinator" in the search box

Population Controllers

There simply is not enough room on the planet for every seed to become a plant.

—Marlene Condon

Since the human population has boomed in the past century, we are putting more and more pressure on our resources, which often results in conflicts. In the natural world, populations wax and wane, and what seems like an influx of a prey species one year will lead to a rise in that species' predators. Soon, the predators reduce number of prey animals, leaving them with less to eat; thus the predator's population inevitably drops. This happens naturally over years, and we must have patience to really witness the cycles of life.

Whether you call it a firefly or a lightning bug, this insect is an efficient predator that helps keep balance in your garden's ecosystem.

Your garden is a microcosm of natural cycles, reflecting the patterns of the universe on a small scale that you can see for yourself. Insects offer an intimate view of the realities of the world, playing out dramas that would seem brutal and shocking if we were to reenact them for a civilized audience. Yet, while you may appreciate the way that bugs go about their business, you may be less empathetic when it comes to their eating your prize-winning rose bush, your shady cottonwood tree, or the crocus bulbs that you carefully arranged so they would bloom first thing in the spring. Varying forms of biological controls, integrated pest management, and beneficial insects are the safe alternatives to spraying, which usually results in a ripple effect of hurting more wildlife than we intended.

We have not thought of every way to kill bugs. Our chemically engineered concoctions have tragic side effects (DDT led to thin-shelled eggs in birds of prey), yet we seem to have overlooked the incredibly vicious yet efficient world of bug-eat-bug. While happy little pollinators are nectaring it up out there, and industrious little scavengers are cleaning up messes, creative killing machines are going about their business as well. Dive-bombers, weapon-wielding hunters, seductive lures, infiltrators—nature has tried everything. Predators and parasitoids are the two main agents of insect population control.

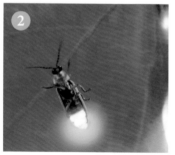

Predators

A variety of insects and arachnids serve the ecosystem by chowing down on other insects. The following predators are common garden inhabitants, often providing curiosity, amusement, and pleasure at their discovery. You may just be grateful that they are doing the dirty work for you.

Beetles

The big world of beetles holds a wide range of predators. They are classified in the order Coleoptera, with nearly 400,000 identified species.

Ladybugs

Let's start with the cutest beetles, ladybugs. More properly known as lady beetles or ladybird beetles, more than 450 species, both native and imported, live in North America. All are generalist predators, especially effective in their tiny alligator-like larval form. They are best known for controlling aphids, with adult ladybugs eating hundreds a day and the larvae eating much more. Spraying aphids, even with a mild soap, could cause these pretty little predators to disappear. Killing ladybugs would mean wiping out a great beetle that also eats the larvae, eggs, and adults of thrips, mites, mealybugs, and scale.

1. Ladybug larvae are best known for being effective eliminators of aphids.

2. Fireflies intrigue children and adults alike with their green glow, but their work in the garden is not as well known.

Fireflies

The fascinating firefly is another beautiful beneficial. Also known as lightning bugs (which is slightly more accurate because they are not technically flies but beetles), these jewels of the night are major predators of slugs, snails, worms, and other soft-bodied larvae. There are approximately 150 firefly species in North America, and they each have distinct flashing patterns to help them find mates of their kind. Like that of the lady beetle, firefly larvae look very different from the adults that we see flying and flirting. The larvae, sometimes called glowworms, resemble pill bugs with their plated, armorlike bodies. They emerge from eggs harbored in moist ground cover like moss or leaf litter. (As an aside, less moss in your landscaping means fewer lightning bugs, which means more slugs and snails.)

The larva uses the unique ambush technique of climbing onto a snail's back, waiting for it to pop its head out, and then attacking. It injects paralyzing enzymes into the snail before digesting it.

More Beetles

Ground beetles, a family of between 2,000 and 3,000 species in North America, also consume a wide variety of ground-level goodies by regurgitating digestive fluids to soften them up. They are nocturnal predators, discreetly hiding under stones or logs during the day. At night, they hunt mites, earthworms, caterpillars, slugs, and snails.

Another 3,000 species belong to the rove beetle family, also discussed in the section on recyclers. Their wing covers are shorter than those of ground beetles, leaving their abdomens exposed. However, when threatened, they use their flexibility to curl themselves into a scorpion pose, although they don't have stingers. Although the adult and larval rove beetles consume some of the same prey as ground beetles, they also go for wood-eating insects such as termites, bark beetles, root maggots, and many more. These hunters use their strong, sickle-shaped jaws to catch quick insects and crush them. Be careful because they could pinch you, too. Some have defensive (and offensive) odors or secrete chemicals that can blister human skin.

Soldier beetles, around 470 species, resemble adult fireflies with long antennae. Adults fly well and pollinate flowers by day, while the larvae live a darker life in the leaf litter, hunting at night. Like rove beetles, their jaws are instruments of death. They

1. *Amara aulica* is a ground beetle found most often in northern climates.

2. *Platydracus stercorarius* is a common small rove beetle.

The blue-eyed darner is a strikingly colored dragonfly.

capture insect eggs and larvae, such as grasshoppers, cucumber beetles, caterpillars, root maggots, rootworm larvae, aphids, and mealybugs. You can attract these masterful hunters by planting pretty flowers, such as catnip, milkweed, and goldenrod.

The colorful family of around 100 species of tiger beetle hunt in similar ways to the big cat after which they are named. The larvae use their energy wisely by waiting out their prey in ground burrows and then quickly flipping out and grabbing their victims. Hook-like projections anchor the larva in the ground while it drags the ant, fly, or grasshopper into its burrow and chows down. An adult has strong, sharp jaws that catch prey and whack it against the ground until it stops struggling. It then uses digestive enzymes to partially digest the prey before eating it.

Dragonflies

Beautiful but deadly describes the 450 North American species of long and strong fliers in the order Odonata, which includes dragonflies, darners, and damselflies. Stealth is their strength in taking other flying insects, such as mosquitoes, bees, moths, aphids, and anything else they can catch. Damselflies are not as well equipped for flying, and they generally hold their wings vertically, rather than out to the sides as dragonflies do, when they rest. They need water to survive, so a pond is ideal for a backyard dragonfly habitat, as are large, flat stones where they can sun themselves.

The female dragonfly dips her abdomen under the water's surface to lay eggs, sometimes with the male holding her steady. Aquatic plants are necessary for darners because they thrust their eggs into slits in the stems. Some other species glue their eggs to plants or under stones. When the nymphs, called *naiads*, hatch out, they are ready to eat tadpoles, mosquito larvae, and even small fish using a bristly lower "lip" that grasps prey quickly.

Naiads live a relatively long life for insects—from eleven months to several years. When they molt for the last time, they crawl ashore, split their exoskeletons open, and unfurl their translucent wings. Dragonflies live for only about another month as full-grown adults. An adult dragonfly will mate several times during that short life, forming a heart-shaped mating wheel with its partner. Some species, such as the common green darner, actually migrate from the United States to Mexico each year.

Flies and Wasps

Don't swat that fly! Most garden flies are valuable pollinators, predators, or parasitoids—or all of the above. Robber flies, for example, are one of the most aggressive flying predators. With around 1,000 species in North America, their appearance ranges from stout and hairy, like bumblebees, to sleek and trim, like damselflies. Their bearded faces and a hollow divot between their big eyes make them look like masked robbers. They find high perches to await unsuspecting victims and then drop down on them, taking their enemies by surprise. The robber fly grasps its prey with strong, bristled legs; injects paralyzing and digestive enzymes into it; and returns to the perch to finish its liquefied meal.

Robber flies are opportunistic predators, taking anything from butterflies to bees. Some species also sip flower nectar. Their larvae control underground populations, eating insect eggs, root maggots, and grubs.

A smaller but important predatory fly is the aphid midge or gallfly. It resembles a mosquito, but the adult doesn't thrive on blood, preferring the nectar and pollen of Queen Anne's lace, dill, thyme, and wild mustard instead. Like mosquitoes, aphid midges thrive in high humidity and fly at night, sometimes doing their mating dance in large masses. Smart adults lay their eggs near the larvae's food source, which is any leaves with aphids. The larvae can eat between ten and eighty small insects, including mites, mealybugs, and cabbage aphids, during this stage of life. If you see tiny, bright-orange larvae all over the flowers that aphids like, especially roses, think twice before trying to get rid of them. They could be your roses' best friends!

Lacewings

Have you ever seen a sandy trail or barren area where little cone-shaped holes create a pock-marked effect? Did you ever see what made the small depressions? I've seen these all my life but didn't know what they were until a few years ago, when I was told that they were the work of ant lions. Ant what? The larvae actually do resemble little lions, with big heads, bristly bodies, and short legs. They are also called doodlebugs, as if that's any help in describing an insect. They walk backward, using their long,

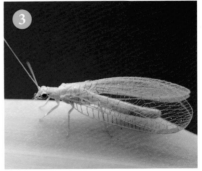

1. The robber fly's appearance lives up to its name.

2. Lacewing larvae are sometimes called "ant lions."

3. A green lacewing adult.

spiny jaws to munch on the ants or ticks that happen to fall into their traps. The adults are a type of lacewing that resembles the dragonfly, with semi-transparent wings that fold up like tents rather than into the "T" shape of dragonfly wings at rest.

Other types of lacewings—and there are thousands in North America—are also predators, many of them specializing in one particular species of aphid or mealybug. Dustywings, brown lacewings, and green lacewings are three main families. The adults are nocturnal, and you may find them clinging to screens at night. Take a look at their delicately veined wings, but don't let their beauty fool you—they are voracious predators that will even eat each other! Lacewing adults and larvae consume a variety of garden insects, including Colorado potato beetles, leafhoppers, whiteflies, mites, thrips, scale, and mealybugs. One single larva can eat up to 600 aphids before maturing.

Centipedes

Millipedes and centipedes may look similar, but their habits and family trees are very different. Millipedes are scavengers; centipedes are hunters that eat a variety of insects, spiders, and snails. You should never handle a centipede because they use their poisonous claws to subdue their prey and can pack a nasty sting. They prefer moist, dark areas and are commonly found under logs or boards in moist soil.

Mantids

Although they look harmless and aren't a threat to humans, mantids are some of the best carnivores in the garden. Twenty species live in North America, and three are nonnatives from Europe and Asia. All reproduce prolifically; up to 200 nymphs hatch out of egg masses that resemble papier-mâché, and they eat anything they can catch, which winds up being any type of insect, including moths, grasshoppers, crickets, caterpillars, bees, beetles, and other mantids. Their lightning-fast strikes and strong jaws can crush insect exoskeletons easily.

Mantids are very patient ambush predators. Camouflaged and observant, they spend 95 percent of their time just waiting for the right moment to strike. They are very territorial, so if you see one in your garden, that's probably all there is. Some species will catch a breeze and float to a new hunting ground. Others are strong fliers and spend time hunting in the higher branches of trees.

Other Insects

True bugs are characterized by their mouthparts, which have a piercing-sucking ability—all the better to drain the life out of plants or animals. Assassin bugs and damsel bugs are impressive predators with sharp, switchblade-type mouthparts, called *rostrums*. The bug keeps its weapon hidden under raptor-like front legs until it has hold of its prey, which could be a cucumber beetle, an aphid, a hornworm, or one of a variety of other insects. It then releases the curved knife and injects a toxin that kills and melts the prey's insides. The bug then sucks up the innards of its victim, leaving nothing but an empty shell for the recycling crew to dispose of.

Big-eyed bugs look small and cute but are voracious insect-eaters. They consume sixty-seven different species of insect. Cover crops can increase their populations, as can a diverse array of flowering plants because they will drink the nectar.

Arachnids

More than 3,000 species of spider live in North America. All spiders have silk glands, but not all of them make webs. Patience and camouflage also lend them the upper hand (or eight) as predators. About 40 percent of all spider species are webless hunting spiders, lying in wait for their victims. Their natural habitat tends to be meadows, so a thick layer of mulched grass creates great shelter in the garden, where hunting spiders can pounce on root maggots and cutworms. Crab spiders wait inside a single flower until a pollinator visits and meets its end.

1. The praying mantis, or *Mantis religiosa*, is found across the United States.

2. Unfortunately, the crab spider often preys on beneficial pollinators.

Web-spinners find their prey by feeling the vibrations of and seeing struggling insects in their webs. They are highly mobile and can travel quickly to dispatch their victims.

One particular spider, the fishing, or bolas, spider, practically goes fishing. Barely noticeable unless you know what to look for, this highly specialized predator lures in moths very cryptically. The adult female spider dangles a single strand of silk off the end of a leaf. A dab of a sticky ball, or *bolas*, will snag the moth, but the secret weapon is the chemical lure. The bolas spider arms its nearly invisible fishing line with a specifically developed sex pheromone designed to attract male moths of a certain species. It can bring them in from hundreds of yards away, and every species of bolas has a unique spider–moth relationship.

Parasitoids

Parasites don't usually kill their hosts, and they live their entire lives on or in their hosts, fully dependent on them for life. Parasitoids, on the other hand, spend a portion of their lives off their hosts and ultimately kill their hosts.

Wasps

You may not be a fan of wasps, perhaps because you've had an unfortunate encounter with the nonnnative German yellowjacket, a type of wasp. Although they are great predators of insects, wasps also defend their underground nests and can sting. Most wasps do not sting, however, and many are excellent population controllers through more complex means than a simple catch-and-eat method. Jessica Walliser, horticultural and beneficial insect specialist, says, "Parasitic wasps are highly sophisticated and intriguing insects—and they are my favorites of all the natural enemies." There are more than forty families of parasitic wasps that range in size and behaviors. The most common garden wasps are the braconid, chalcid, and ichneumon wasps.

1. A tomato hornworm covered with parasitic braconid wasp eggs, which will kill it slowly.

2. Tachinid flies are both pollinators and parasites.

The parasitic, or, more accurately, parasitoidal, wasps' usual mode of operation is that the female will lay eggs inside a host. The host could be any type of insect; they often choose caterpillars, but they also pick true bugs, beetles, and flies. It is in the larvae's best interest that the host keeps living for a while, so when the eggs hatch, the larvae start by eating their host's less vital organs. When they are ready to pupate into adults, they work their way out to the surface of the host, spin cocoons, and spend a few days developing into adults.

Some wasps insert a single egg into a smaller host, such as an aphid. You may find the shells of aphid mummies on your plants. Others colonize a caterpillar, such as a tomato hornworm, with hundreds of eggs. They use what appears to be a large stinger but is actually an ovipositor, an elongated egg-laying tube. The scariest-looking ones puncture wood to reach larval insects, such as bark beetles. These wasps aren't aggressive at all, but don't mess with them because they could hurt you in defending themselves.

Flies

Tachinid flies, all 1,300 species in North America, play the same role as the parasitoid wasps. They lay eggs in caterpillars, and the larvae eventually suck the life from their hosts. The adults are great to have in the garden as pollinators, even though they look like pesky houseflies. Another subtle way that they fly under the radar is through the technique that certain species use to put their larvae inside the host. They maneuver to lay their eggs on a leaf, in the line of consumption, so that an unsuspecting caterpillar, such as an armyworm, will swallow them up.

Some tachinids follow the songs of crickets and katydids to find hosts. Others find their hosts by detecting chemical clues emitted from the plants being eaten, a sort of call for help. Imagine your blackberries sending out word that Japanese beetles are devouring them, and along come some pregnant flies to the rescue! It will take one or two weeks for them to do their dirty work, but if you allow these natural processes to play out without interfering by using synthetic controls, you may find your problems solved by doing practically nothing. The only real work you need to do is plant flowers to attract a great diversity of pollinators, many of which also serve as population police.

The Balance of Predators and Prey

As you can see, the insect world can take care of itself when given the right habitats to support a wide variety of life. Try a hands-off approach for a few seasons; your garden may suffer short-term losses, but you may be rewarded in the long run with a community of predators and prey. At a minimum, these creatures will stay and eat if there is food, keeping populations in check, and they will move on or die if there is no food. At best, they will provide essential ecosystem services that benefit life beyond your property line by keeping your plants healthy, which in turn stabilizes soil, filters water, and cleans the air we breathe. In any case, try to watch the insect life in your garden. Notice the cause-and-effect chains of events, and you will discover another world of entertainment.

Recyclers

When I was a kid, I used to hate to take out the trash. It was messy, stinky, heavy, and always too full. As a teenager, I became more educated about recycling, and I began volunteering to take out the trash because I knew it was up to me to make sure that the plastics, paper, and glass were separated. I would drive to a recycling center when I got a good load, and this became a routine that I looked forward to. I didn't know many ways that I could personally make a change in the world, but the

physical evidence that my family's waste was not going into a landfill was a small, simple reward. If I had to do the same job every day for the rest of my life, I probably would not enjoy it as much. This is one reason why I appreciate nature's recyclers.

Nature's recyclers create the nutrient-rich soil that plants need to thrive.

Of course, in your garden or in any natural setting, the presence of plastics, paper, and glass is at a minimum. The recycling that happens here is the decomposition of organic matter and the breakdown of minerals, resulting in the beautiful, nutritional matrix that your plants and all life in the ecosystem depend on: the soil. Insects, bacteria, fungi, and the other soil microbes do the majority of recycling that maintains the soil. Toby Hemenway, in *Gaia's Garden*, explains that nature makes soil from the top down and from the bottom up. Plant roots pull nutrients up and use them as needed. "By 'top down,' I mean the constant rain of leaf litter from above that decomposes into fluffy earth." In a natural forest ecosystem, a prairie, or even a desert for that matter, soil builds itself over time. Fertilizers are already in there. Hemenway says, "Nature doesn't rotary till, and we don't need to, either."

Insects are responsible for turning everything—yes, everything—that falls to the ground into the ground: maple leaves and dogwood tree trunks, mockingbird feathers and shrew bones, raccoon droppings and snail shells. Everything returns to the earth with the help of what ecologists classify as decomposers, scavengers, carrion feeders, or detritivores. You'll recognize many of these also as predators and pollinators. Some may send shivers up your spine at the first mention, but as we get to know them better, we can understand that, in the right amounts, these creatures are gardening for us. And if they show up in numbers that seem out of proportion to the workload, we need to sit up and pay attention to what that says about the ecological balance in our backyard habitat. Following are some of my favorite recyclers—insects that work as tree trimmers, earth movers, and garbage collectors.

Flies

The saying "like flies on #*@%" (well, you know) is based on fact. Larvae of flies in the family Muscidae, which includes our common houseflies, live in dung, carrion, or other decomposing organic debris, eating bacteria or preying on other dung inhabitants. Everyone poops. That's a fact of life (and the title of a funny children's book by Taro Gomi). For wildlife, we give it names like "scat," "castings," or "dung," and I especially like the word for what the caterpillar makes: "frass." Call it what you will, but we don't find it socially acceptable to deal with it. That's another reason to value nature's recyclers—they clean up scat, so we don't have to.

Dung beetles are found all over the world.

Beetles

Dung beetles are an obvious answer to the problem of poop and, perhaps less obvious, to the problem of too many flies. Some species lay their eggs in dung, and the larvae feast on fly larvae and nematodes, keeping their population in check while breaking down the excrement. Other kinds of dung beetles will actually eat the dung, gleaning all of the moisture and nutrients they need. Certain species known as tumblebugs match up with a mate, roll balls of scat into a straight line by navigating by the moon, find a soft spot, and bury the scat. They do everything in their scat habitat: mate in it, lay eggs in it, and

Slugs

Slugs are definitely low on the list of lovable garden critters, but that could be due to the imbalanced predator–prey state in most gardens. If you see too many slugs eating your favorite plants, it means that there's either too much moisture and an excessive amount of rotting leaves or mulch, or a lack of reptiles and amphibians. Improve the habitat for frogs, toads, turtles, garter snakes, and salamanders, and you'll see fewer holes on your strawberries and lettuce. Small rodents, such as moles and shrews, should also be welcomed if you have unwanted slugs; they will gobble the slugs up! Additionally, you can make your garden less appealing to slugs' sensitive, slime-activated touch receptors by using fuzzy-leaved foliage, such as lamb's ears, or strongly fragranced herbs and flowers, such as lavender and salvia.

Have you provided some good trees and shrubs for songbird habitat, and have you seen some foraging in the ground? Great! They're here to help as well. To make bird-friendly slug traps, simply lay planks of wood for garden pathways, and slugs will gravitate to the planks' undersides during the day. Flip the boards over, step aside, and let the birds have their way with them. Slugs make great baby-bird food, and no other beneficial bugs are harmed in the process.

otherwise cherish the prize they've fought off other tumblebug couples to win. A bonus is that they are fertilizing your garden in the process as nitrogen from the manure is slowly released into the soil. Bill Clymer, PhD (parasitology), from Amarillo, Texas, was quoted in an article in *The Horse* online magazine about the benefits of dung beetles. "The tunnelers (beetles that bury brood balls) are actually the most beneficial," says Clymer. "They bury the manure under the pat, aerating the soil and fertilizing it. Their activity helps water percolate into the soil, enhances root penetration by pasture plants, and reduces contamination of water sources. If manure is buried instead of sitting on the surface, water runoff won't wash it away into the streams."

Fungi and Slugs

Another fact of life is that everyone dies, plants and animals alike (you got an idea of the death and carnage going on in your garden in the section on population controllers). Someone has to clean up the bodies. Our friends, the fungi, do the primary work for plants. This work goes on subtly, out of sight, until their fruiting bodies—mushrooms—make an appearance. The list of other beneficial decomposers might sound like a list of pests to kill: bacteria, flies, beetles, slugs, and snails. But hold your fire. As for these last two, Marlene Condon's book *Nature-Friendly Garden* argues that slugs and snails "are actually critical to the proper functioning of the home landscape." They consume tons of organic matter, and, in turn, earthworms eat slug scat, processing it even further.

Worms

The digestion continues with what Aristotle called the "intestines of the Earth"—worms. Most fishermen and gardeners are familiar with night crawlers and red wigglers. While neither of these are native to North America, and there is some concern about nonnative worms becoming invasive in already-fragile forests, we know that they are very effective at speeding up the decomposition process. If you have a compost bin with worms, you can witness that easily for yourself. Worm castings are rich fertilizers with bioavailable minerals such as calcium, magnesium, potassium, and phosphorous. Worm burrows aerate the soil and increase water access throughout as well.

More Flies and More Beetles

Believe it or not, nature even keeps the dirt clean. Trash cleanup happens underground, in burrows where bumblebees lay their eggs. Flies in the genus *Volucella* mimic bumblebees so they can enter these burrows without alarm. The flies lay their own eggs, and, when the fly larvae hatch, they clean up the nest, eating egg casings, dead bees, and other debris, all without harming the bumblebees. A group of beetles called rove beetles, with around 2,900 species in North America, also do a great service of cleaning up maggot bodies as they scavenge through the soil.

Roly-Polies or Pill Bugs

I have always had a fondness for the tiny little critters I call "roly-polies." I was surprised to learn, though, that they aren't actually insects. They are crustaceans, in the same class as lobsters and shrimp, but they have evolved to live terrestrial lives. Also known as "pill bugs" because they roll up into little balls when threatened, they are close kin to sow bugs, which are also known as wood lice. Interestingly, some of these isopods (as they are further classified in the order Isopoda) may not have forgotten all of their water-loving DNA; certain species will care for their young nymphs in water-filled pouches on the undersides of their bodies. Their segmented, many-legged bodies resemble those of centipedes, but they don't sting. They are great little debris feeders, so they are happy to munch on your leaf litter and decompose it for you.

Even More Beetles

Another surprise guest that you might find chewing on woody, coarse debris is the click beetle. A description from the book *The Living Landscape* explains this fascinating creature's evasive tactic: "A spine on the ventral surface of the first thoracic segment hooks into a notch on the second segment. Applied muscular pressure causes the spine to snap loose with a loud click, flinging the beetle several times its body length out of harm's way."

The click beetle's apparatus reminds me of the springtail, a much smaller, moisture-loving, soil-dwelling organism. Springtails are those tiny whitish bugs in your soil (up to 10,000 per square meter) that seem to disappear as soon as you try to catch one. They are mainly scavengers, fragmenting bits of decaying plant matter so it can be further decomposed. A powerful appendage called a *furcula* is pinned up under the abdomen until the creature needs a quick escape. When released, the furcula can fire the tiny springtail head

over tail for a distance that would equal a human jumping over the Eiffel Tower. Just try and find where it lands!

Daddy Longlegs

The daddy longlegs—now there's a misunderstood garden helper. I bet you've heard the myth about them being the most venomous spider—except that their fangs are too small to bite a human. First, they aren't even spiders (although they are arachnids, sporting eight fantastic legs), and, second, they aren't even equipped to produce venom, much less kill another insect. Not much is really known about the 10,000 or so species of daddy longlegs in the world, but it seems that they are fairly gentle scavengers that spend the nighttime close to the moist crevices where they hide during most of the day. At night, they venture out to eat nearby carcasses, dead wood, and small debris.

Millipedes

Millipedes also evoke undue fear because of their similarity to their potentially stinging cousin, the centipede. Millipedes don't bite or sting humans, but they can be deadly predators. A toxic gas that they emit through their pores is meant to kill ants and irritate the eyes of other predators. As with any wild creature, you should not handle them or stir them up needlessly; this chemical irritant could blister your skin.

As for millipedes' role as recyclers, they are great plant shredders, working on anything that falls to the ground and making it small enough for bacteria and fungi to break down further. They are considered one of nature's best composters, and they can live for up to ten years!

1. Roly-polies (or whatever you call them) are prolific decomposers of garden debris.

2. The springtail is ready to jump at a moment's notice.

3. Millipedes don't sting, but they do emit a toxic substance.

4. Cicadas can help trees by "pruning" a few branches.

Cicadas

Up in the higher layers of the trees, singing insects could be providing some specialized gardening services. They keep the system healthy by pruning branches and clearing out dead wood so that new life can reach the light. Cicadas spend only a few weeks of their astoundingly long lives (up to seventeen years for some species) above ground, where they find their way to treetops and vibrate as loudly as possible, with the sole purpose of attracting mates. If successful, the female will lay her eggs in small slits in the bark of branches. This may result in a few branches being cut off, but it doesn't destroy the tree; in fact, most trees will thrive better with a little pruning. To dispel further misconceptions, cicadas can't bite or sting, and they are not locusts, which are a type of grasshopper.

Still More Beetles!

The Xerces guide *Attracting Native Pollinators* explains that some beetles "lay eggs on or within dying or weakened trees, where their grublike larvae burrow beneath the bark or through the wood. The presence of tunneling beetle larvae is important for wood-nesting bees, such as leafcutter and mason bees, because the female bees construct their nests within abandoned beetle tunnels. A lack of sufficient tunneling beetle larvae may limit local bee populations." The relationship is even more complex. "Because decaying wood is not a good source of nutrition, these larvae may take several years to develop fully, often relying on symbiotic microbes in their guts to digest cellulose in the wood."

In addition, some species of beetle disperse a trail of fungi as they burrow through the bark. The fungi effectively digests the trees' tissue, making it edible for the beetle larvae. Beetles bring attention to diseased or dying trees. They display interdependence with other organisms by creating an important habitat. At least three species of beetle use infrared-sensing organs to detect forest fires—not to escape, but to occupy the charred wood with their eggs. An influx of bark beetles indicates a shift in a normally healthy tree community, which would be able to defend their tissues with a sticky resin. Heat and drought will weaken the tree's water reserves, and, just as a dehydrated person is susceptible to disease, the trees cannot fight off too many beetles.

Recycling in Nature

Where would we be without nature's recyclers? As Peter Bane explains in *The Permaculture Handbook*, nothing is wasted in nature. "Structures invariably break down, whether they are the ephemeral walls of cells, the delicate tissues of leaves, the bones of animals, or the very rocks of the Earth's crust, but none of the parts are lost . . . The leftovers are remade in a miraculous dance that has endured for four billion years." How nice that your garden hosts more of these miracles than you'll ever witness.

Insect Habitat

Like all animals, insects need the basics for adequate habitat: food, shelter, water, and space. They are well equipped with sensory organs and mysterious instincts that scientists have yet to explain, all of which guide them to the places where they can thrive.

Food

There are two types of food: prey insects and plants. Prey insects can include leafhoppers, aphids, slugs, caterpillars, and a variety of others. Plants are just as diverse, but most insects are specialists, which means that they can eat only certain plants. Generalists, on the other hand, are more adaptable and can survive with a wider palate.

Douglas Tallamy explains that the leaves of no two species of plant have the same chemical makeup, which gives each species a particular and unique taste, digestibility, and toxicity. For us, spinach tastes different from kale, which tastes different from romaine lettuce, but they are all green leaves. The variations in taste, bitterness, and texture are usually minor to us, but, to insects, they can mean a difference between survival or starvation. Even when hungry, they will pass up leaves of hundreds or even thousands of plant species because they literally just don't have the right chemistry.

Selecting native plants for your garden is critical to nurturing beneficial bugs. Nonnative plants are not palatable to native insects, and that's the point. Many exotic ornamental plants have been selected because they are "pest-free," and the horticultural trade banks on this promise. Meanwhile, beautiful butterflies, such as the spicebush swallowtail, struggle to find spicebush or a sassafras tree, where the female needs to lay her eggs so that her larvae will survive.

Tallamy explains that nonnative plants not only have escaped planted gardens but also have invaded large spaces where native plants once grew, thus changing significant areas of natural ecosystems. The coevolution of native plants and the insects they host is a much slower process than the quick relocation that man has put them through.

A grasshopper feeds on a flower.

The National Wildlife Federation's report on landscaping at colleges, "The Campus Wild," agrees. "And while an argument can be made that anything green is better for wildlife than bricks, walls, and pavement, not all greenery is created equal from a wildlife point of view. Wildlife-useful plants typically end up with holes in their leaves—a reminder of the link between caterpillars and birds. Nearly all

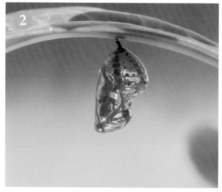

1. A green dragonfly finds shelter in mulch.

2. A chrysalis uses a leafy plant for camouflage and shelter.

songbirds are fledged on a diet of insects, and those insects have to eat something, too. Regrettably, the majority of exotic (nonnative) flowers, shrubs, and other horticultural offerings are the equivalent of a 'food desert' for native insects and wildlife."

Shelter

The same plants that feed bugs also shelter them. Remember that insects need shelter in all phases of their life cycles: egg, nymph, larva, pupa, and adult. The appropriate type of shelter for each life stage may be distinctly different. Insects usually lay their eggs on the leaves of plants that will feed the nymphs or larvae.

Some butterflies and moths wrap themselves in leaves as camouflage when forming chrysalides; therefore, don't trim your perennials in the fall. The dead parts of plants can provide just as much shelter as the living parts. Standing stems are much-needed winter habitat for certain insects, such as mantids. The mulch between and beneath plants is just as important for other insects, such as aphid midges. Create a permanent mulch boundary with straw or dried leaves that never gets tilled, dug, or planted in. Hiding spots are important to enable bugs to escape predators, stay warm, and wait out the winter.

Water

Place rocks and pebbles in ground-level shallow pans. Waist-high birdbaths with sloping sides are also inviting. Any shallow water source with sloping sides will invite insects to land for a refreshing sip, and it also attracts bug eaters such as salamanders, birds, and frogs. To prevent mosquitoes, rinse out the basins with a strong spray from the water hose every few days.

Beneficial insects are sold commercially, but there's no need to buy them if you plant the right attractant plants and provide adequate water and shelter. They know how to find what they need and have been doing so for thousands of generations.

Space

Nobody likes to be crowded, and every habitat has its limits. Pay attention to the edges of your garden and notice how air flows and circulates through it. Is there room to fly, burrow, tunnel, run, and climb without major interference? We usually think of ourselves and larger mammals as having territory issues, but many insects will also claim boundaries and fight off intruders.

Consider colorful space when planning your garden and try to provide large swaths of color to attract pollinators. Plant flowers in groups of seven or more to amplify the sight and smell for those insects seeking landing and feeding places. Also consider the space you'll want to occupy while you are in the garden and make sure that you account for your proximity to bees, wasps, ants, and other insects that may mistake you for a threat.

Which Plants to Plant?

Know how to plant for your specific ecoregion's pollinators by using the zip code search function at the Pollinator Partnership's website: www.pollinator.org/guides.htm.

Watch and Learn

Now that you've gotten acquainted with some of the helpers working in your garden, your forays outdoors could take a turn toward the scientific. To identify and learn more about the multitude of insects you may encounter, equip yourself with a hand lens, a binocular, and some field guides. You may want to start with the *National Audubon Society Field Guide to North American Insects and Spiders*. This will help you narrow down your options, and then you can use more locally specific identification tools to find genus and species classifications.

Inspecting leaves closely will reveal eggs, larvae, and signs of insects worth investigation. These signs could point more to health than to distress, and identification of the insects helps us interpret the signs. As Marlene Condon points out, insects don't want to completely destroy plants any more than you and I want to burn through all of our food crops. Her book *Nature-Friendly Garden* reminds us, "If you have a plant that has attracted an abundance of insects that seem to be weakening it, the plant probably has an environmental problem that needs to be addressed, or your yard is not home to the predators necessary to keep those particular insects in check." Wildlife of all sizes and shapes fit niches in the ecosystem and keep the parts working in harmony.

In conclusion, entomologists estimate that between 95 and 99 percent of all insects are beneficial or harmless to human endeavors. Only by sterilizing all of the outdoors, paving over nature, and installing plastic turf would you be able to control the amazing dance of life going on in the garden. This might be a difficult vulnerability to admit—that we are not really doing the gardening! The tiniest of animals is much better at it, and they work together better than we do. Once we can let go of our conqueror attitude and recognize our relationship with our planet's other inhabitants, we will find it much easier to coexist with the creatures in our gardens, yards, and community spaces.

Close observation will reveal the diverse life in your garden.

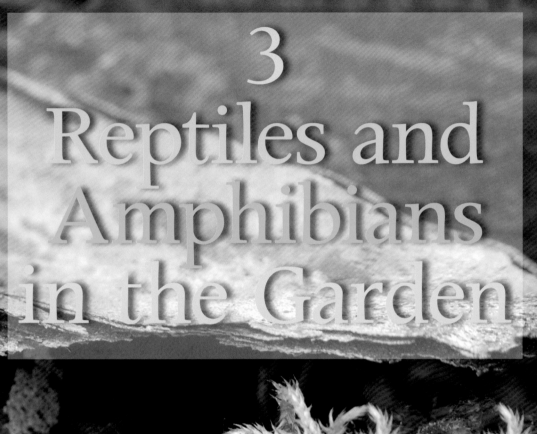

3
Reptiles and Amphibians in the Garden

hy is it so easy to overlook the cold-blooded members of the food web? Although they are a diverse group of animals, with a wide assortment of adaptations and specializations, they are small, shy, and relatively quiet, and they are becoming quite rare.

Reptiles and amphibians are less adaptable and more specialized than some other types of animal. Each area of North America holds special reptile and amphibian populations that occur nowhere else. Relocating them to places for which they are not suited is not a good idea for their sake or for your area and could upset the ecosystem's balance of both their home and your garden, not to mention result in the death of the animal.

Reptiles and amphibians are collectively known as *herpetofauna*, or, informally, as "herps." People who like to identify and learn about herps are herpers, just as birders go birding and moth-ers go mothing as hobbies. Reptiles include crocodiles, alligators, snakes, lizards, and turtles. Amphibians include toads, frogs, salamanders, and newts.

Many similarities bring reptiles and amphibians together. One thing they have in common is that they are ectothermic, or cold-blooded, meaning that their body temperature depends on their surroundings. To get warm, they find sunny spots; to cool off, they head for the shade. In extreme temperatures, they may estivate, which is similar to hibernation, in which their body processes slow down to a minimal level of functioning.

Their differences outweigh their similarities, however. Reptiles, whose name derives from the Latin *repere*, meaning "to creep," live mainly on land. *Amphibian* means "two lives," referring to the animals' ability to live on land and in water. The structure of their skin reflects their habitats and life cycles. Reptiles have dry, tough, waterproof, scaly skin, which can aid them in climbing. The skin of amphibians is smooth and permeable, allowing water and air to pass through.

With a few exceptions, most reptiles and amphibians lay eggs, but there are differences. Reptilian eggs have leathery, flexible shells, whereas amphibian eggs are encased in a jelly-like substance and must stay in water for their survival.

Taking the Ecosystem's Pulse

Reptiles and amphibians let us know where the ecosystem stands in terms of its health. Their permeable skin cannot tolerate pollution, and other environmental factors affect their health dramatically. An overgrown fungus can effectively suffocate them by coating their skin. Malformations, extra appendages, and missing parts could be the results of increased radiation due to ozone depletion or an increase in parasitic worms due to an imbalance of snail populations, likely caused by fertilizer runoff.

The presence of herps in a garden means that there are a variety of plants, insects, and habitats to support great biodiversity. The absence of herps in an area where they are expected to live indicates that something in the environment is lacking or unhealthy. The website eNature.com brings the importance of gardens to the surface: "Frog conservation measures start at home. Reducing or eliminating pesticide use is one effective step, since homeowners apply ten times more pesticide

and herbicide per acre than farmers. Composting to reduce or eliminate fertilizer applications is also advised, and every effort to protect wetlands, even the smallest seeps, pools, and marshes, provides necessary frog habitat."

The scarcity of herps in the wild is largely due to loss of habitat through development, habitat fragmentation, water pollution, and increased stormwater runoff. Mortality from trying to cross busy streets is another big reason that snakes, turtles, and frogs don't survive long. If a healthy population of herps graces your garden with their presence, you'll be glad they did. Beyond the important role of indicating the system's health, reptiles and amphibians provide essential services as both prey and predators in the food web.

1. Turtles often congregate in the same sunny spot.

2. Herps bask in the sun to stay warm.

3. Fewer pesticides mean a healthier habitat for water-dwelling creatures.

4. Frog eggs are an easy target for fish, birds, and other predators.

Predators and Population Control

The snake in the Garden of Eden was very interested in sharing fruit, but have you ever wondered why it wasn't offering Eve a bite of a mouse? That is a much more plausible scenario, but maybe it wanted to keep all the mice for itself. The snakes' reptilian and amphibian friends are also carnivores, making them wonderful population police in your garden. It is much easier to think of a snake as a predator than it is to imagine a happy little frog or subdued salamander stalking its prey and swallowing it whole. But that is exactly what they do. Like the bug-eat-bug world, reptiles and amphibians duke it out in the herp-eat-herp world. For example, salamanders eat substantial amounts of insects, snails, slugs, and other invertebrates on land. Not only do they control populations, they also play the role of recycler, converting those nutrients back into the soil as scat.

Remember that although other garden residents may be rodent hunters and insect eaters, the most stable and resilient ecosystems contain overlapping elements that do the same jobs. Redundancy in the system provides a backup plan.

Herps as Prey

In permaculture, a partner principle is that each element in a system serves more than one purpose; reptiles and amphibians are not just consumers: they also certainly provide a food source to many other members of the wildlife community. If all of the eggs laid by frogs every summer were to hatch and survive, we'd surely be overrun by frogs in no time. Fish, herons, other amphibians, and the larvae of many water insects all devour the eggs and tadpoles. This is an important foundation of any wetland food web.

Amphibians are an especially important link because the abundant nutrients found in the pond algae, which the young amphibians eat, create a protein source for larger mammals and birds. This doesn't mean that they go down without a fight. Reptiles and amphibians use surprising means of defense, and colors are one of their main warning signs; brightly colored frogs, snakes, and salamanders use their colors to warn predators of the toxins they carry, but not all fly conspicuous warning flags. Some amphibians, such as the pickerel frog, are stealthily camouflaged but will secrete irritating poisons that repel most predators. Some reptiles, such as horned lizards, look tough and unpalatable, and if the enemy makes it past their appearance, the lizard might resort to squirting blood from its eyes.

Where and What Types of Herps Are in the Garden?

Reptiles and amphibians don't stand out in your garden, and that's the way nature intended. Camouflage is the herp's best friend. The patterns on snakes, turtles, and frogs mimic the dappled shadows of woodland floor or the buff-and-tan variations of prairie plants' stems. Slow movement and stealth keep herps in sync with their prey while out of the notice of predators. The warm days that draw us outdoors may draw herps under logs or deep in mud to keep their body temperatures comfortable; they don't burn energy to regulate their internal temperatures. They eat less often than mammals or birds and therefore are spotted out hunting less frequently.

Whether or not you see them regularly, reptiles and amphibians can live throughout the several

layers of a forest garden. The ground layer is the most critical space for water-dependent amphibians. Life begins either in the water or underground, such as tadpoles swimming in the pond and turtles burying their eggs in soft earth to incubate. Snakes, lizards, and salamanders depend on the small mammals, insects, and birds they find in burrows and dens.

The herbaceous layer of grasses, flowers, vegetables, and fruit provides much-needed shade for their sensitive skins and also hosts many

A pair of garter snakes rests among the dry leaves.

insects and small mammals that nourish the herp community. Under the right conditions, salamanders and toads will keep slug and snail populations under control. Although amphibians won't stray far from water, some lizards and turtles will forage throughout the garden's beds and paths.

If your garden habitat includes shrubs, understory, and canopy, you could also be providing good places for tree frogs and climbing salamanders to find shelter. Like vines that traverse all layers of the forest, a few types of snake climb up to higher limbs. For example, the black rat snake can ascend tree bark by digging its scales in like tiny cats' claws and contracting its muscular body to defy gravity's pull. Don't fear, though—these climbing snakes are not venomous.

The American toad is common in the Northeastern states and Canada.

The thrill of discovering more astounding adaptations awaits you when you give herps a space to thrive in your garden. In this chapter, we'll explore the various types of reptiles and amphibians and learn how to encourage and attract them with the proper habitat.

Frogs and Toads

What's the difference between frogs and toads? Toads are actually a type of frog. Generally, toads' legs are shorter, they don't have webbed feet, and their skin is drier and bumpier, which are all good adaptations for living a life that is more connected to earth than water. Of the ninety-five species of frog in North America, twenty-one of those are toads.

Frogs and toads are amphibians and rely on water, even if they don't spend their entire lives in it. They need to be near water with aquatic plants to reproduce, hatch their young, and keep their skin moist. The springtime is when most frogs and toads are noticed in gardens because their mating activity also relies on wet weather.

Just because you don't see or hear them in the colder months, don't assume that frogs aren't around all year. Frogs generally don't migrate to warmer climates, but they will move from their breeding pools to deeper lakes for the winter. Frogs have amazing adaptations to get through the cold weather. Aquatic species, such as the northern leopard frog, hibernate under water, settling down on the muddy bottoms of ponds. Terrestrial frogs, such as the spring peeper, will burrow into leaf litter or a crack in the earth and spend months in a state of torpor, with its life systems running at a bare minimum.

Some species of frog, such as the wood frog, have a type of antifreeze protein in their circulatory systems that allows them to go into a suspended state until they thaw out. This is a fine way to spend the season when no food is available.

Frog Adaptations

When you think of frogs and toads, you may think of bulging eyes, loud calls, smooth skin, camouflage patterns, big jumps, lightning-fast tongues, and maybe even poison. All of these characteristics serve them well within their habitats.

As low-lying prey, frogs have unique eyes that can keep a lookout in all directions at the same time (ever notice how hard it is to sneak up on a frog?). Unlike birds, whose eye sockets don't allow their eyeballs to move around inside their heads and who have necks that allow for a great range of movement, frogs can rotate their eyeballs independently and see almost 360 degrees around them, but they don't have very flexible necks.

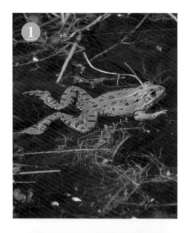

1. A frog's long legs are made for swimming and jumping.

2. The frog's large, round eyes give it an almost 360-degree range of vision to look out for predators.

As hunters, frogs have strong vision, especially the ability to see colors and depth in the dark. A membrane that frogs and other nocturnal animals have at the back of their eyes, the *tapetum lucidum*, reflects light and amplifies it, similar what the shiny cup of a flashlight does.

Underwater, tadpoles' eyes are more spherical, adapted to the water's refraction of light. As they metamorphose into adults, the lenses change shape and flatten. Frogs also have nictitating membranes to cover and protect their eyeballs as they swim. Hunting is more difficult underwater, so frogs rely more on their sense of smell while below the surface. Because frogs' eyes have adapted to focus on movement, hunting is next to impossible if their prey is still.

Another unusual way that frogs that use their eyes is to help them swallow. Wiggly water striders, mosquitoes, or other insects get shoved down into the frog's gullet with pressure from the eyes. In some species, such as the leopard frog, the eyeballs retract into the mouth as deeply as they bulge out from the head. This little extra shove from above is as purposeful and helpful as swallowing.

Even though frogs have teeth, the teeth mainly serve to hold the food inside the mouth rather than to chew. The frog's tongue is attached at the front of the mouth, so it's great for grabbing food and dragging it inside, but the tongue is pretty useless when it comes to swallowing. If you are lucky enough to watch frogs catch and eat their meals in your garden, take a close look and watch their eyes as the food goes down.

Frogs don't hang out at the watering hole to drink; they're there to soak it up. Their specialized skin absorbs moisture and electrolytes. The moisture enables them to take in oxygen through their skin as well. If they get too dry, they can suffocate. Toad skin is a bit tougher, so toads can spend more time away from water. To maintain this all-important organ—the skin—frogs shed frequently.

Unlike with snakes, you aren't likely to find a frog skin in your garden. Nature wastes nothing; frogs eat their own skin.

Frogs can also secrete mucus to keep their skin moist and help them evade predators (ever try to hold on to a squirming frog?). The mucus also protects their delicate skin with beneficial bacteria that can keep fungus from taking over. A very widespread fungal infection, Chytridiomycosis, has reduced the amphibian population worldwide. It causes an overgrowth of keratin on the skin surface and interferes with the breathing and absorption of electrolytes. Scientists continue to study this fungus and are trying to understand how it is being spread. Nurturing the life in your soil so that all parts of the ecosystem thrive is a good preventive measure.

What Are Sirens?

Sirens are a genus of salamander that resemble eels and never develop hind legs. Hellbenders and mudpuppies are examples of the largest types of sirens, which can grow up to 30 inches (76 cm) long. Some live in shallow, muddy ditches while others prefer fast, well-oxygenated water. They don't need to come to land, so they keep their aquatic bodies rather than sprouting the extra legs needed to navigate solid terrain.

Salamanders

What is a salamander? Salamanders are amphibians, but, unlike frogs, they have tails, which makes them look a little more like reptiles. Salamanders are their own scientific order, Anura, which also includes newts and sirens. A newt spends most of its time on land, and a siren spends most of its time in the water. Adaptations vary widely depending on the species, and they match the habitats in which they have evolved to live.

Salamanders' toes say a lot about their lifestyle. Of the 150 or so species in North America, scientists can tell them apart not only by their colors and sizes but also by how many toes they have. Their feet may be designed for digging or climbing, or they may be fully webbed for swimming. They don't have claws, but some have adapted toes that function like claws and enable them to scale trees, some as high as 60 feet (18 meters).

Many salamander larvae, called *efts*, start out breathing underwater with gills. Newts develop lungs and keep their gills, and some species lose their gills and develop lungs. Most salamanders, though, don't use lungs or gills but breathe through the skin and thin membranes in the mouth and throat.

All salamanders need to keep their skin moist, whether it's the toad-like skin of a land-dwelling newt or the smooth, moist skin of a siren; they could die if they dry out. Since you are not likely to see salamanders out in the open, their presence can be a clue to weather patterns. Marlene Condon reports:

A baby Northwestern salamander.

The red-bellied newt is mainly terrestrial, found in coastal woodlands of northern California and southern Oregon.

"A red eft (the immature terrestrial form of the eastern newt) is more likely to be seen wandering around following a rainstorm." Woodland salamanders spend all of their life cycles on land, but that land must provide ample humidity. The red-backed salamander mother will protect her two dozen eggs for up to two months, wrapping her body around them so they won't dry out.

Salamanders tend to be nocturnal and find their way in the dark, under leaf litter, and in water with incredible accuracy. Unlike frogs, salamanders have small eyes, but they can perceive wavelengths that extend into the ultraviolet range. Unlike lizards, they have no outer ears, but they can sense low-frequency vibrations that warn them of predators. The aquatic life stages of some salamanders also have lateral-line organs that sense changes in water pressure. Whether underwater or on land, salamanders' sense of smell and touch helps them find mates. They even have the ability to navigate their way home by the earth's magnetic field using a type of sensory organ that scientists are still trying to understand.

Most North American salamanders measure between 2 and 5 inches long, although a few species, such as the aquatic two-toed amphiumas, can reach 3 to 4 feet in length. Salamanders' bellies drag on the ground because of their long bodies and short legs. They match their prey's speed, slowly taking slugs, snails, and earthworms for food. Some species have quick tongues that grab ground-dwelling creatures and pull them up to their sharp little teeth.

Some salamanders are poisonous. Even cute little newts, so small and unassuming, can pack a deadly punch. The rough-skinned newt, one of only six native newts to North America, contains a type of toxin that can kill a healthy adult human, so don't eat it! It won't hurt anything that doesn't mess with it. Only the common garter snake may be able to tolerate it, but the snake then loses muscle control and can easily fall prey to hypothermia, a bigger snake, or a raptor. Other types of newts also have glands on the backs of their necks and at the bases of their tails that produce a potent venom. Even the gel that surrounds their egg clusters contains a toxin.

Self-protection also comes in the form of mates taking turns babysitting; for example, the spiny salamander curls around its eggs and turns them occasionally, preventing predators and disease. Some newts will wrap leaves around each individual egg, which can number in the hundreds.

Although we would typically associate salamanders with their watery birthplace or the moist earth, a few species of salamander climb up into the canopy layer—wherever they can find the necessary hydration and proper conditions. Mole salamanders, as their name implies, stay in burrows or rotting logs, eating earthworms or grubs.

Salamanders may be one of the most telling indicators of good ecosystem health. They are extremely susceptible to pesticides and fertilizers, so they will not stay where the environment has pollutants. Disturbance of wetlands, siltation of streams, and fragmentation of natural areas has also impacted salamander populations detrimentally. Many types of salamander are widespread throughout the East, yet there are isolated pockets of certain salamanders that have evolved with and belong to a particular place, such as the high elevations of northern New Mexico, where the Jemez Mountain salamander lives.

To enjoy salamanders in your own backyard, it is best to start with a field guide specific to your area. The best time to find them is after a rain in the warmer months, and the best places to look are under rocks and logs. Safety tip: always tip a large rock or log toward you, so that any creatures you disturb do not make a run for it, straight at you! (This is especially important in areas where venomous snakes live.) After you take a look and take a picture, gently let the rock or log settle back as you found it. Imagine leaving a friend's home just as you found it, and your hosts will not be stressed by your visit.

Lizards

Lizards are generally small, land-dwelling reptiles. They are predators of insects of all types, as well as prey for birds and mammals. A wide variety of evasive and defense mechanisms help them survive and make them interesting animals to observe in the garden. Their adaptations must serve them well; lizards make up the largest and most diverse group of living reptiles.

Lizards in North America are divided into eight families and 155 species. Their bodies, diets, and activities vary depending on their sex, age, and surrounding environment. Whatever type of lizard you see on your property is likely to be the only species around, although southern and warmer climates host more varieties.

Lizard Adaptations

Spotted, striped, or banded; colorful or plain, lizards stir up flashes of interest as they dart around or laze away the days sunning themselves on rocks. Unlike snakes, lizards have external ears, and they have legs, with the exception of legless lizards. Like those of all reptiles, their scales are made of keratin, the type of protein that also produces fur, feathers, and fingernails. Keratin also tips reptiles' toes with claws, another distinguishing characteristic that separates them from amphibians. These claws help them traverse ground-level terrain, such as sandy soil and leaf litter, as well as climb fences, walls, and trees to find habitat.

Green anoles are plentiful in some southern states, particularly North Carolina.

1. The coloration of the venomous gila monster is a warning to potential prey.

2. Geckos are more fragile than many other lizard species.

Quiet, stealthy hunters, lizards are skilled at stalking their prey with catlike moves. They wait until the perfect moment to strike with a quick tongue, swallowing their meals whole. One exception is the chuckwalla, a vegetarian that eats flowers, leaves, and fruit.

Many lizards hide in plain sight. Anoles, also known as chameleons, can shift colors from green to brown and back to green. The color is affected by hormones, temperature, environmental colors, and mood.

Lizards have good vision, especially color vision, which relates to colorful parts of their bodies and physical displays. The gila monster's color scheme—black, orange, yellow, and red—is similar to that of a hornet, a monarch butterfly, or a coral snake, and these are colors that mean beware! The hefty gila monster carries a potent venom that helps it digest its prey as it bites into it. Another example of lizard color use is the male green anole's bright red dewlap, which resembles a fan of skin on its throat below the chin. It waves its dewlap in a flashy display of attention-getting color reserved for attracting a mate or defending its territory.

Some types of spiny lizards look drab to our eyes, but they hide secret warning signals beneath their scales. When threatened, they can flex their scales to reveal iridescent colors, some that are visible only to other lizards and predators that can detect ultraviolet. Otherwise, blending in with the natural surroundings keeps most lizards hidden from their number-one predators, birds. Many species are camouflaged to match the leaf litter or dusty earth where they hunt.

Quickness and agility are additional evasive techniques. Whiptails and racerunners, with deceptively blue-colored tails that distract predators, can run up to 17 miles per hour. Geckos are native to Mexico and the southern United States and are best known for their ability to scale walls and ceilings as if they are immune to gravity. Each of their small toes has microscopic bristles that not only add traction but also include tiny suctions cup on their tips.

Horned lizards resemble ferocious little dinosaurs with spiked, flattened bodies. Their horns are specialized scales that make it difficult for a predator to swallow it whole.

Horned Lizards:
Texas Dinosaurs Are Not Quite Extinct

When I was growing up on the high plains of Texas, my friends and I would find the occasional horned lizard in a field or backyard. It was fairly normal to hear our parents and grandparents tell us how they used to find them all the time. There were so many of them, and they were so easy to catch, that many of the older generation had kept one as a pet. Everyone had a story about a horned lizard—about it squirting blood out of its eyes, about turning it over and rubbing its belly to help it fall asleep, or some other tall tale to which I just rolled my eyes in disbelief.

One of the classic stories took place in my granddad's home town of Eastland, Texas. "Old Rip" (short for Rip van Winkle) was a famous horned lizard that was encased in the cornerstone of the county courthouse. It survived in a state of hibernation for thirty-one years until the old courthouse was demolished and Old Rip was discovered—alive!

After I had grown up and returned to my hometown area to work as a park ranger, those childhood stories came back to me. As I led visitors on guided tours, occasionally they were amazed to see a horned lizard on the trail, referencing the same stories I'd heard from my parents' generation. Some people even told me that they had bought them as pets, ordered through the mail, but none seemed to survive very long in a shoebox, being fed crickets.

Why did older generations have so many fond memories while younger folks had never even seen one? Why had horned lizard numbers drastically declined? The old-timers' stories became a fascinating curiosity to me. I learned more about horned lizard behaviors and their importance as indicators in the ecosystem.

Captivity is hard on lizards because they are very sensitive to their environment and instinctively driven to live as their ancient ancestors had evolved to live. It turns out that the blood squirting from their eyes is true, but not necessarily as a defense mechanism. It is an uncontrollable reaction to being disturbed, basically as a way of releasing a sudden surge in their blood pressure. On the other hand, the idea that rubbing their bellies relaxes them didn't hold up. It's more like they freeze from fear, almost in a state of shock, rather than relax. If that's not stress, I don't know what is. If so many people hadn't tried to keep them as pets, maybe we'd have more today.

Many of the thirteen species of horned lizard in North America are now listed as species of special concern or otherwise protected in their various states. But the folks who harassed them as children and the wild reptile pet traders were not the only culprits. Another major reason for the toad's demise is the disappearance of their favorite food, ants. Not just any ants, but red harvester ants.

These were the ants I would watch trekking across the sidewalk to open holes in the ground, busily moving seeds, while I sat at a picnic table on my lunch break. Every once in awhile, I might get a bite from an ant that strayed up my pant leg, but otherwise they were harmless little harvesters. They eat a variety of seeds and grains, which helps out the grasses, forbs, and shrubs in the arid landscape by dispersing their genes farther and wider. While these ants were busily doing their ecosystem services of turning soil and spreading seeds, horned lizards would keep their population in check by eating up to seventy a day.

Unfortunately, most people don't know their ants, and as development has increased, so has the indiscriminate use of pesticides. Many people don't know their weeds, either. Increased use of herbicides killed off native herbaceous vegetation, the food source of the harvester ants. These harvester ants were doing the South a favor, keeping invasive fire ants at bay. As soon as fire ants made an appearance, even more pesticides were employed to fight all ants, thus packing another punch at the horned lizards' food source. The last remaining fragments of their natural habitat has also been subdivided into housing, businesses, parking lots, roads, and other barriers that keep far-ranging, slow-moving lizards from finding a meal.

The alligator lizard is not in the alligator family but sports hardened bone-like plates (which are otherwise reserved for crocodilians) on its body for protection. If it weren't for a small, flexible band of scales along its sides, the alligator lizard would not be able to take a breath and fill its lungs.

The gecko's skin, on the other hand, is very fragile and easily damaged. Like most lizards, they escape harm by shedding their tails when caught. Their tails will grow back, but without bones, and it requires a great amount of energy for a gecko to regenerate its tail.

Pheromones are another means of communication among lizards. These chemical signals mark territory or announce breeding availability in a language that is picked up by the reptile's sensitive odor receptors. We don't often think of lizards as "talkative animals," but geckos can be quite vocal, calling like birds or chirping like crickets, especially when defending their nesting sites. Some lizards, such as certain types of racerunners, are all female and don't even need to mate; they lay unfertilized eggs that hatch into more female lizards.

Lizards in the Garden

Where are you most likely to see a lizard? In the sun. Where are you most likely to hear a lizard? In the shade. Some species are attracted to rocky terrain and escarpments. The fence lizard, as its name implies, is likely to be seen on a fence because it is out of the shade but high enough that other ground-dwelling predators won't notice it. In any garden, warm spots are a requirement for lizard habitat because they have no way of producing their own heat and do not have the ability to shiver when cold.

Conversely, lizards cannot sweat when they are hot, so too much sunshine doesn't suit them, either. Little bits of shade make a big difference. Skinks, a type of shiny, dark-colored lizard, are more likely to be found in cooler, moist portions of the garden, such as under rotting logs or decomposing leaf litter. Reptiles would rather not be out in plain sight, so if you have diversity in your layers, your garden could harbor many more lizards than you'll ever see. Don't assume that the sound of rustling leaves is a foraging bird or a squirrel; it could be a lizard.

Unlike amphibians, lizards do not have to keep their skin moist to breathe; thus, they are found throughout the drier regions of North America. Like amphibians, however, they need to hibernate in the winter, so hidden spaces in rocks, crevices, and stumps are ideal. In return for providing a

pesticide-free, diverse habitat, lizards will perform their population-control services on a long list of garden creatures. Lizard food includes moths, grubs, flies, grasshoppers, caterpillars, spiders, cockroaches, beetles, snails, slugs, crickets, and even small mice.

Crocodilians, like the American alligator, should not be making appearances in your garden.

Gators and Crocs

At the other end of the reptile spectrum are crocodilians, the heaviest and largest cold-blooded creatures in North America. They take some of the lizard's characteristics to an extreme with their stealth, camouflage, and predatory instincts.

Crocodilia is an order that consists of only two families: alligators and crocodiles. There are only three species in North America, but they make a big splash. American alligators and spectacled caimans make up the alligator family and live in the coastal Southeast from Texas to North Carolina and as far inland as Arkansas. The American crocodile has a more limited range in southern Florida and Puerto Rico. Alligators are more abundant and are found in freshwater habitats. Crocodiles can tolerate salt water, so they are found in coastal and brackish waters. Crocodiles are much shier and more reclusive than alligators, and the American alligator is far less aggressive than those in other parts of the world.

Unfortunately, many of the reports of alligator or crocodile sightings in gardens are due to illegally releasing pet reptiles or illegally keeping wild gators in captivity. Crocodilians fill an important niche in the ecosystem as a top predator. Deer, wild hogs, small mammals, birds, snakes, insects, amphibians, and other reptiles round out the gator's diet. Anywhere there is water in a warm climate is a good place to find a gator in its natural habitat. They create their own space by digging or wallowing out a shallow pit that holds water during dry periods. This is so important for other species that the alligator is considered a keystone species, one that other life in an ecosystem rely on for habitat.

Crocodilians are similar to turtles in that their bodies are designed for swimming and for walking on land, but they are much quicker and more agile than turtles are on land. A female alligator will make a large nest, using her entire body to dig, move vegetation, and mound up earth. After laying between twenty and fifty eggs in the nest, she will cover it with more vegetation and defend it from predators for the next sixty-five days. The nest-guarding behavior is very different from that of other herps, who are not only solitary before and after mating but generally don't hang around after they deposit their eggs.

Alligator hatchlings preparing to emerge begin calling out, and the other egg-encased young get the message that it's about time to break out. The call also beckons the mother to uncover the nest, and she may help the hatchlings emerge if any are having difficulties cutting out of the leathery eggs with the temporary teeth on the tips of their snouts.

Crocodilians are more vocal than other reptiles, making barking, grunting, croaking, or other deep sounds. They slow down their body functions to survive temperature extremes, and they bury themselves in mud for insulation while they are in either estivation (in the heat) or hibernation (in the cold).

Alligators were hunted extensively until the 1960s, and they have since made an impressive comeback in areas with freshwater lakes, streams, and rivers. Unfortunately, their habitat has decreased and become more populated by humans. If your garden is wild enough to handle them, it is possible to live in harmony with these reptilian predators. Just make sure that they have their space. It is illegal to feed crocodilians, so they will have to depend on nature's supply of food. Even though they usually avoid humans, they may harm children, swimmers, and even pets. If you want to fence your garden and keep crocodilians out, make sure that your fence is at least 4½ tall to prevent them from climbing it.

Snakes

Snakes strike fear in the hearts of many gardeners, while others are delighted to see a serpent in the midst of their fruits, flowers, and vegetables. Why such extreme reactions? It depends on how much you know about snakes.

Snakes take us by surprise. Something about their stealthy appearance startles us, and we startle them equally. Fear is usually based on the unknown. Let's take a look at snakes from a safe distance and arm ourselves with knowledge so we can discern when and how to encourage snakes in the garden.

Venomous or Not?

All snakes are capable of biting if disturbed, so leave them in peace if there's no reason to move them. Although most snakes are not venomous, it would be very unpleasant to have a snake's powerful jaws snap down on your skin.

If you see a snake in your garden, the first step is to identify it. If you are leery of snakes and likely to run at the first glance, a great way to help build your snake identification skills is to make flash cards. Get a field guide to reptiles of your region, photocopy or draw the individual snakes,

and have a friend quiz you in rapid succession. The more familiar you become with the colors and patterns of venomous and nonvenomous snakes, the quicker you can make a correct identification in the garden.

Venomous snakes in North America include various types of rattlesnake, copperheads, cottonmouths, coral snakes, and sea snakes. These comprise around 5 percent of the approximately 115 species of snake in the United States and Canada. Here are some tricks to help with snake ID.

Sound

Rattlesnakes are ambush hunters—very well camouflaged but alert to any intruders approaching. Fortunately, they would rather retreat than waste their venom on something too big to swallow, and they will give you an audible warning before they strike. So if you hear their buzzing whirr sound, you have already gotten too close. Stop, back away slowly, and watch from a distance, paying attention to where the rattlesnake moves. Many snakes will also shake their tails in warning but do not carry poison that could hurt a human. They can trick you by rattling tall grasses or dry leaves rather than their tails.

Shape

Venomous snakes hold their poison in pouches in their jaws, so they have wider, more pronounced, triangular heads than nonvenomous snakes. If you don't see a venomous snake side-by-side with a similarly shaped nonvenomous snake, it can be hard to tell the difference. That's a benefit for the nonvenomous snake; mimicry of a deadly snake can fool other predators in addition

1. The harmless garter snake is sometimes called the "garden" snake.

2. If you can hear a rattlesnake shake its tail, you've gotten too close.

3. As its name implies, the black rat snake is a predator of mainly rodents.

4. The venomous cottonmouth is among the snakes classified as pit vipers.

to you. A combination of the head shape and markings is usually the best way to confirm your identification.

Markings

Rattlesnakes obviously have a different type of tail than the rest of their body; similarly, young cottonmouths and copperheads have bright yellowish-green tails. These three types of snakes are pit vipers, and if you get close enough to see their eyes, you'll see that they have slitted pupils rather than round ones. Another general rule is that solid colors or horizontally striped patterns indicate nonvenomous snakes, such as black rat snakes, smooth green snakes, and garter snakes. Cross-bands, splotches, spots, or any other pattern require further identification clues.

Population Control

All snakes are reptilian predators—specialized ectothermic carnivores. They are intimately connected to their environment, a trait that cold-blooded animals share. If the weather cools off or heats up quite a bit, the snake slows down, and so does its digestion, wasting no energy when food is not available. Depending on the species and its habitat, the size of prey can vary from small insects to large birds and even medium-sized mammals.

A snake's common name may provide a hint about their habitat and related food source. Black rat snakes are often seen in gardens and primarily eat rodents, such as mice and chipmunks, but will also eat birds' eggs and young birds. King snakes will eat other snakes, along with rodents and birds. Water snakes eat tadpoles and dead or dying fish. Hognose snakes prefer to eat toads. Green snakes mainly eat garden insects like hornworms, crickets, and grasshoppers. Mole snakes hunt moles, and gopher snakes eat gophers. With this diverse array of food, snakes impact many different populations in the garden and cannot be blindly labeled as good or bad. If they find enough to eat, they are probably necessary to keep something else in balance. If they don't find what they need, the snake population will decrease to match the food supply.

Some snakes can climb trees, putting birds' nests at risk.

Snake Life

Remembering that everything in nature has a reason, every feature that makes a snake a snake serves a purpose. As reptiles, their long bodies are covered in scales (not slime), which aids their ability to climb without any legs. For example, black rat snakes are often seen in gardens because they can traverse trees and rough walls. The scales also help prevent loss of moisture through the skin. Snakes shed their outermost layer of skin, including the eye covering, once or twice a month to enable continual growth.

Play It Safe

Take precautions when working in any garden or natural area with snake habitat, whether you have seen snakes or not.

- Be aware. Understand the seasonal and daily habits of animals in your garden and be conscious of snakes' preferences in relation to the temperature.
- Wear gloves. Although your hands should never go into a crevice or under debris where you can't see, even a thin layer of leather could make a difference if you surprise a snake.
- Wear boots and long pants for the same reason. Your feet are more likely to disturb a snake in tall grass. Step on top of logs, not over them. Position yourself so that you can see where you will place your foot when you step down.
- Carry a walking stick or long-handled garden tool to turn over debris from a distance. Run the long tool through any high grasses or herbaceous ground cover as a gentle notice to any snakes who may be hunting or resting in the shade; also do this before you mow your lawn. Most young garter snakes don't survive to adulthood due to lawnmowers.
- Know what to do in the case of a snake bite.

Snakes' internal organs are elongated, and their bones are light and flexible. Although they are relatively small, they can eat prey larger than their heads (have you ever tried that?) by releasing the ligament holding their jaws together. Those long, flexible bodies are also uniquely ideal for following burrowing rodents, such as voles and gophers, into their underground domains.

Snakes' senses are focused on taste, smell, and touch. They hear without ears by sensing vibrations through the ground, and they taste before eating by sniffing the air with their forked tongues and transferring the aroma to a pair of receptors in the roof of the mouth, called the Jacobson's organ.

Rather than relying on their sense of sight, pit vipers can detect infrared frequencies with a type of heat sensor that is attuned to finding warm-blooded mammals and birds. The "pit" on the front of the viper's head is actually a unique organ that translates infrared light waves into heat, so pit vipers such as rattlesnakes, cottonmouths, and copperheads can sense their prey in the dark.

Like turtles, snakes will lay eggs in ground-level nests from which babies will hatch around two months later. However, no venomous snakes in North America lay eggs, so if you find snake eggs in your garden, rest assured that they cannot harm people. A few species of snake, including rattlesnakes, copperheads, garter snakes, and water snakes, hatch their eggs inside their bodies and give birth to live young.

Approaching Snakes in the Garden

It depends on the habitat, but, generally speaking, snakes will be where the temperature is comfortable and food is available. Stacks of firewood, brush piles, sheds, basements, and thick vegetation all give snakes protection and shade and harbor their prey. Snakes sun themselves in open, flat areas, which unfortunately often means roads. If you can safely encourage snakes to move along to wilder terrain, you'll help their survival, and natural population control will be able to run its course.

Any wild animal will feel threatened by a larger creature, such as a human. Snakes are no different. Almost all snakes will retreat to safety when startled because they would rather not put up a fight and waste precious energy. One exception is the male black racer, which sometimes charges larger animals when defending its breeding territory. Otherwise, hissing, coiling, and tail-shaking are behaviors that any type of cornered snake will exhibit as a warning, whether they are venomous or not.

You should always treat snakes with respect and take snake bites seriously. Of the several thousand venomous snake bite cases in the United States each year, an average of five people die—a number that would be much higher if the victims did not get medical treatment. The US Centers for Disease Control and Prevention provide this first-aid refresher about dealing with a snake bite.

- Seek medical attention as soon as possible (dial 911).
- Try to remember the color and shape of the snake, which can help with treatment of the snake bite.
- Keep still and calm. This can slow down the spread of venom.
- Inform someone what has happened.
- Apply first aid if you cannot get to the hospital right away.
- Lie or sit down with the bite below the level of the heart.
- Wash the bite with soap and water.
- Cover the bite with a clean, dry dressing.
- Do not pick up the snake or try to trap it.
- Do not wait for symptoms to appear. If bitten, seek immediate medical attention.
- Do not apply a tourniquet.
- Do not slash the wound with a knife.
- Do not suck out the venom.
- Do not apply ice or immerse the wound in water.
- Do not drink alcohol as a painkiller.
- Do not drink caffeinated beverages.

Snake Feng Shui

As a final thought on snakes, consider that they can bring much awareness to the state of our gardens. We usually discover them while we are cleaning up the garden, moving brush, weeding mulched beds, or tidying up tools, which provides insight into creating snake habitat—they like to hunt, rest, and lay eggs where stuff accumulates. For a healthy serpentine environment, carefully consider accumulations in your garden and whether these spots are being recycled into their next phase at a natural rate or not. Stagnant pockets could be a problem, whereas areas that change with the seasons will encourage a normal predator–prey relationship that coincides with abundance and limitation of resources.

Turtles

Turtle is the all-inclusive name given to animals in the order Chelonia, a group of reptiles that form shells on their backs. Tortoises and terrapins are types of turtles; tortoise is to turtle as toad is to frog: the tortoise is the land-dwelling version of the turtle. The term *terrapin* generally refers to semi-aquatic turtles.

The lives of most turtles are tied to the water, either salt or fresh. Their feet are designed to help them swim gracefully, and their beaks help them eat fish and mollusks in the water. Tortoises, on the other hand, have clubbed feet for walking on land and don't need a body of water to survive. Terrapins spend most of their lives on land near brackish or swampy water.

Female turtles emerge from the water to lay eggs in the ground. They need warm, soft earth, so sunny, sandy beaches are ideal for some species. Other turtles lay their eggs in ground nests beneath vegetation. The eggs are soft and leathery, and, in some species, the sex of the young is a product of temperature: males result from lower temperatures and females from higher temperatures. When the young hatch, they instinctively scurry toward the water, unaided by any parental guidance. The vulnerable nests of sea turtles in particular have been impacted drastically by development along coasts, water pollution, light pollution, and predators.

Baby turtles are born carnivores and become omnivores as they grow up. Turtle diets vary depending on the species of turtle, native habitat, and available options. All turtles need protein, which often comes in the form of slugs, worms, aquatic insects, and marine life, for healthy development. Many species, such as land-loving box turtles, become more vegetarian as they mature and will eat flowers, leafy greens, vegetables, and fruits. Some will eat native poisonous plants that they have evolved to tolerate, which will also make the turtle taste bad to predators. Some turtles even eat stinging insects, jellyfish, and cacti.

All turtles, whether land or water-based, must breathe air. However, they have ways of staying underwater for extended periods of time. Some species, such as sea turtles, can take in dissolved oxygen from water through specialized tissues in their cloaca. Another adaptation is the ability to circulate water through the mouth and throat, where the lining of blood vessels extracts oxygen.

Since turtles are ectotherms (cold-blooded), they bask in the sun on logs, rocks, islands, or banks to warm up. When it gets

1. The gopher tortoise is the only tortoise native to North America.

2. A common aquatic species, the red-eared slider, basks in the sun.

3. The turtle's hard shell, made of cartilage plates, provides a safe retreat.

very cold, they will burrow into mud and spend the winter in torpor, a type of hibernation. Similarly, to escape extreme heat, tortoises find cool relief by digging down and burying themselves. The ground level of your garden may offer the perfectly balanced climate-control system for these reptiles.

Shell

The turtle's shell is made of stiff cartilage plates fused to the vertebrae and ribs. It includes the spinal cord as well. The top (or back) is the carapace, and the bottom (or belly) is the plastron. The tail is connected to the backbone, which is why you should never pick a turtle up by its tail or else you risk dislocating its spine. A turtle can feel pressure and pain through its shell. Land tortoises have shells with air pockets to lighten the load, and swimming turtles have more streamlined and flexible shells to enable efficient movement.

Shells protect turtles from a wide range of threats, from wildfires to raptor claws. Relying on this barrier as their main defense mechanism, quick reactions or evasive moves are not turtles' strengths. The quickest part of a turtle's body may be the head and neck. Carnivorous turtles, such as snapping turtles, can quickly turn and grab prey or fend off a threat with a powerful and painful chomp. Snappers' heads are heavier, too, hefting more weight into their bite. Another useful adaptation that makes up for their lack of agility is the wormlike lure inside a snapper's mouth; it attracts fish looking for a meal, and, before they know what hit them, they've become turtle food.

Even though the shell makes a great shield, there are still predators that can kill and eat turtles. On land, hawks, ravens, foxes, coyotes, raccoons, and smaller predators such as minks and cottonmouth snakes will easily eat turtle eggs or young hatchlings. At sea or in fresh water, predatory turtles, large fish, and crocodiles prey on smaller turtles. However, once the shell forms and hardens, it can protect the turtle for decades.

Do not mistake the shell for a reason to handle turtles excessively; they are easily stressed. Unless they are in harm's way, it's best to let them move about at their own relaxed pace.

The massive Galapagos tortoise is the world's largest living tortoise species.

Slow and Steady

Turtles and tortoises may be the underdogs in a race, but when it comes to longevity, they've got us all beat. Small turtles may live sixty to seventy years, and the largest have set records of close to 200 years! Their DNA changes very slowly, so they are less likely to suffer from age-related conditions. The heart, lungs, and kidneys of a 100-year-old tortoise could be as healthy as a young turtle's organs. On the other hand, turtles are not highly adaptable to changing climates. Even though they can move to cooler or warmer places and retreat within their shells, two-thirds of the world's turtles need fresh water, a resource that is diminishing at a fast pace.

Turtles have walked and swum this planet for more than 200 million years. They've survived dinosaurs and massive die-offs of other life forms and have steadily held their ground. Today, however, turtles are the most endangered type of vertebrate in the world, with 58 percent of turtle species on the brink of extinction. Whether swimming in the sea or trekking through the desert, turtles are having a harder time than ever surviving loss of habitat, hunting, the pet trade, and environmental degradation.

Turtle Gardens

You can keep turtles happy in your garden by providing a pesticide-free water source, a wide variety of native plants to attract insects, and some accessible sunny spots where they can warm their shells. Water turtles will need a pond, the more natural the better. They need nooks and crannies for hiding and hibernating, piles of rocks for perching, and shallow edges for climbing out onto the banks. Tall pond plants provide ample shade and create more humid micro-climates. Mini-habitats also attract turtles; by varying the pond's edges, you can create little coves for them to explore.

Box turtles are one of the most common backyard turtles, although their population is severely declining due to habitat loss and mortality from being kept as pets. There are four species and several more subspecies in North America, all of which have a special hinge on the plastron to completely shut themselves inside the shell. Box turtles are more like tortoises, completing their life cycle on land. They are especially attracted to thick leaf litter, which harbors insects and slugs while giving them a place to sleep at night and tunnel through during the day. Box turtles also enjoy muddy or boggy areas where they can cool off.

Turtles select their nests very carefully, scoping out warm spots by looking closely and rubbing their noses around in the dirt. Even after digging a nest, a turtle may

Help a Turtle Cross the Road

If you happen upon a turtle crossing the road, and it's safe for you to stop and help, take a few precautions to make sure you are giving it the help it needs. First, notice the direction it is headed and take a quick survey of the land on the other side to know where you will place it. If the ground is sloping toward the road, it could topple back into traffic, so find somewhere level or gently sloping away from the road to set it down. Keep in mind that turtles are designed to gracefully maneuver underwater, but on land, they are awkward, clumsy, and on the defensive. Most turtles can bite, and some will express urine when threatened, so be cautious about handling them. Hold smaller turtles by placing your fingers under the plastron and your thumbs on top of the carapace, belly side away from you.

For larger turtles or snapping turtles, grab at the very back of the carapace with one hand on each side, turn yourself around, and walk backward while gently sliding the turtle across the road. If you have a car mat, blanket, jacket, or shovel, you could use it to slide the turtle across so it doesn't get too scratched up.

When you reach the other side, simply rotate yourself again so the turtle is facing the right direction (away from the road). Turtles have a destination in mind, either for nesting or breeding, and they are following their instinctual cues when they cross roads. Take a bit of satisfaction in knowing that by helping a turtle cross the road, you've just lent Mother Nature a helping hand.

The box turtle is a common backyard visitor.

decide that it's not suitable and keep on looking. This nest site is critical to survival. Should you be fortunate enough to witness a turtle nesting in your garden, make sure to identify and protect the site with some type of flagging or barrier that does not obstruct the sun's rays from warming the earthen incubator. Every winter of their adult lives, which could last a century, they return to the ground to spend the cold season. Some, such as painted turtles, will actually return to their birth nests when it is time to hibernate.

If you see turtle activity in your garden, keep dogs away from their habitat. Let your neighbors know as well. If you can identify the species of wild turtle that has graced your garden with her offspring, report it to your local fish and wildlife office because many are endangered or threatened species. You can also contact the Turtle Rescue League (www.turtlerescueleague.com) for more information or to get a "Turtle Crossing" sign.

Herp Habitat

Reptiles and amphibians are delicately interconnected with their environments. As with all wildlife with which we share our gardens, we should simply prepare their habitat as an invitation, and they will settle in if the environment suits them. Never import reptiles or amphibians from wild areas or pet stores. This is how invasive species are spread and environmental damage results. Create an outdoor environment where native plants and animals can coexist as naturally as possible.

One of the most important ways to help herps in your garden is by refraining from tilling soil. Remember that much of a reptile or amphibian's life cycle happens underground, whether it is an egg incubating, a mother seeking a suitable site for nesting, or a herp hibernating or cooling down. Turning soil in garden beds may be necessary at certain times of year, but if you want wild herps, your garden must include wilder areas where the circulation of soil and humus is left to natural processes all year round. A healthy reptile and amphibian population indicates that you have a healthy insect population, which is supported by a healthy native plant population and healthy soil. So, in many ways, herps living in the garden can mean that the food web is in good shape.

Food

Most reptiles and amphibians eat lots of bugs, and a variety of native plants and flowers will attract pollinators. Vegetable, fruit, and flower gardens with wanted or unwanted moths, butterflies, aphids, grasshoppers, ants, wasps, flies, beetles, and various forms of insect larvae will provide nutritious meals for land-dwelling herps. Dragonflies, mosquitoes, water striders, and all kinds of aquatic insects and their larvae will feed young amphibians well. Algae is another must-have for tadpoles just starting out life.

Shelter

Shelter for the youngest reptiles and amphibians matters for their survival. The eggs of most reptiles are tough, but they need an insulated subterranean nest to keep them safe. Loose dirt or sandy areas that get sunshine are ideal. Amphibians need aquatic plants because they attach their vulnerable, soft eggs to the stems. These plants will also provide shelter for the adults.

Carol Buchanan's book *The Wildlife Sanctuary Garden* reminds us that what is underfoot is important herp habitat. She writes, "Everything you do to enrich the soil helps amphibians. For example, if you allow autumns' fallen leaves to remain on the ground and decompose naturally, frogs (and other small creatures) will hibernate under them. The winter's rains decompose the leaves and make a wet place for frogs to hibernate in … I sometimes leave a pile of leaves in the yard over winter. In the mid- or late spring, I spread the leaves out, gingerly, so as not to disturb creatures before they're ready to migrate back to the wetland habitat."

1. A log pile in the garden provides opportunities for shade and shelter.

2. Herps can help with insect control in your garden.

Other easily overlooked herp habitat is created by mammals. Amphibians will use abandoned or seasonal burrows near water, so think twice before plugging up your chipmunk or mole holes. Snakes cannot dig holes but will use those made by rodents. Stumps and exposed tree roots also make great habitats.

Sometimes our garden messes are the best habitat for our wildlife friends. Keep your frequently used materials in an area that makes sense to your workflow, and purposefully create rock or log piles where snakes and lizards can hunt and lounge without disturbance. Piles of things provide plenty of gaps for hiding in the shade while the surfaces can be perfect sunbathing spots with a quick escape below always a possibility.

Even land-dwelling amphibians have shelter needs that differ from those of reptiles. Toads are hunted by skunks, snakes, and birds. An easy way to create shelter for toads is to make a toad hole from a broken terra-cotta pot, a concrete drain pipe, or other circular form. Dig it partially down into the ground in a protected area, such as tall herbs, native grasses, or flowers, and fill the bottom with soft sand. Tall, uncut plants, especially near a pond, provide shelter where bullfrogs can wait to ambush their prey. If they get startled, they can easily jump into the water. The water itself is a shelter, too. Most amphibians will bury themselves in mud for the winter. Turtles can sink down into it, too, and stay until the spring thaw.

Large, flat, open areas where the sun hits during at least two or three seasons of the year are essential, too. Because reptiles and amphibians need to warm their bodies, if you can build a rock wall or leave out sheets of plywood or large, flat stones, you may be occasionally graced with the presence of sunbathing snakes, turtles, and lizards.

Water

Obviously, amphibians need water. If you are considering building a pond on your property, do plenty of planning before you dig. For example, fish will need a deeper pond that won't freeze completely during the winter. Likewise, amphibians need places to burrow in the mud, and a pond liner could interfere with their hibernation cycle.

For the most wildlife diversity, a natural pond could be the answer, if it suits your property. *A Popular Guide to Garden Ponds* by Dick Mills describes a natural pond this way: "A natural pond can be of any size … The cross-sectional profile should be shallow rather than steep-sided (although some deeper areas of water can be included for better stability of water conditions) to allow easy access for amphibious animals, insects, and birds."

Where to situate the pond on your property will be your biggest decision because it will be influenced by and also influence the tree cover, the slope, the drainage, the availability of rain or irrigation, the types of plants that will flourish, and the view. The best place for a natural pond might be where water naturally pools on your property, whereas ornamental ponds can sit in a contained area where the water level is constantly maintained with pump systems. Other important aspects to understand include algae growth, cleaning, and types of pond liners. For warm climates, a light-colored pond liner or light-colored rocks will help keep the temperature moderate. If your garden gets a good amount of rain, you can make it into a bog garden. Bog plants like to have their roots in water all the time. Some native plants to feature include irises, arrowhead, pickerelweed, rushes, and sedges. You may want to hire a pond installer or consultant to help you plan and construct your garden's water feature.

The edges are important because they create the transition zone between land and water and should allow for easy entry and exit. Taper the edges with some type of "beach" and provide plenty of hiding places in tall aquatic plants. Floating logs for basking and overhanging plants for shade are crucial for regulating cold-blooded creatures' body temperatures.

Although it is tempting to stock a pond with exotic fish, never put goldfish or other nonnative fish in a water garden close to a

A garden pond should provide easy entrance and exit and plenty of basking spots.

natural stream, pond, or river. Exotic species can become invasive and outcompete native wildlife. Also be very careful with any chemicals around water because amphibians' skin is especially sensitive to toxins.

Space

Most reptiles and amphibians are solitary and territorial. Bullfrogs, for example, live alone except for mating or fighting. On the other hand, some frog species benefit from crowding in large numbers; the unison songs of chorus frogs provide a blanket of sound that eludes predators. Giving herps the space that they need is the key to living in harmony with them.

If you handle any live reptiles or amphibians, do so with caution. Remember that some herps excrete irritating or harmful toxins; conversely, handling them with even a gentle touch can sometimes harm them. Bug spray, sunscreen, moisturizers, or other skin products could block pores on their sensitive skin and prevent them from breathing.

When encouraging herps in your garden, give some consideration to whether you want to have fish in the same habitat as amphibians. Fish are the primary predator of frog eggs, and larger fish may eat baby turtles, too.

Remembering that the space below our feet is another creature's habitat invites us to consider gentler ways of being at home in our garden. April Pulley Sayre's book *Touch a Butterfly: Wildlife Gardening with Kids* recommends making the habitat a special place where we slow down and be intentional with our footsteps, voices, and actions. Sayre says, "Having a 'toad abode' or 'toad corner,' a special place where kids walk slowly, carefully, respectfully, and watch for toads can add a new dimension to the garden and your family's routine. Creating loud and quiet areas, fast and slow areas, in a garden is not just about what plants we plant or paths we create but how we decide to act, as well."

Remember that because snakes can't hear you coming, you should give them a heads-up before you surprise them. Walk your lawn before you mow to gently encourage snakes to head for cover. Better yet, replace your lawn with native grasses and flowers and let it be the cover.

Help Herps Recover

Why does the herp cross the road? Instinct. Reproduction. Feeling the ingrained need to migrate to pools for breeding or land for laying eggs. Turtles are often found crossing roadways or as unfortunate victims of passing vehicles. In forested areas, salamanders crawl across the roads at night.

Some wildlife-conscious communities have coordinated volunteers who assist in stopping cars while salamanders cross the road. States such as Vermont and Michigan, as well as the province of Ontario, collect reports of local herp sightings. Their region-specific websites accept data from professional or amateur herpers who have information to contribute. In addition, a couple of large-scale amphibian and reptile citizen-science programs exist. You can participate by adding your own observations.

Do you enjoy frog song? Want to use your music appreciation for a greater good? The Association of Zoos and Aquariums runs FrogWatch USA (www.aza.org/frogwatch), an information-collection program to which volunteers report the calls of frogs and toads during the spring and summer.

Herpmapper (www.herpmapper.org) is a collaborative and user-friendly effort to map herp sightings worldwide. A mobile app makes it easy to snap a picture or record sounds and upload your findings to the website. It is an interesting storehouse of both current and historic records.

4
Birds:
Part 1

Birds bring us into nature. They call us outside with their morning songs. They capture our attention with a swooping, soaring, or splashing wing. They bring our eyes up and out, beyond our path or window, into unknown reaches of tree canopies or limitless blue sky. Birds provide a splendid gateway to our gardens, and many converts to wildlife gardening begin by creating habitat for birds. This can lead to a healthy addiction to the natural world, going deeper and learning more about all the pieces of the wildlife puzzle. Indeed, when you give birds the food, shelter, water, and space they need, you are by default giving so many other life forms a home as well.

Gardening for birds means using plants wisely. The ground, herbaceous, shrub, understory, and canopy layers of a forest garden all provide something for sustaining bird life. Likewise, as Thomas Barnes's book *Gardening for the Birds* illustrates, "Every species of bird has a special place for nesting and feeding in the habitat it uses."

Douglas Tallamy's book *Bringing Nature Home* and the website by the same name (www.bringingnaturehome.net) share research into which plants are best for attracting and hosting various specialist insects. Caterpillars in particular provide essential nutrition to birds, especially young hatchlings. When you select what to plant, choose to plant bird food by growing plants that feed insects as much as they feed us or benefit the environment. For example, various types of oak, cherry, willow, birch, poplar, crabapple, blueberry, maple, elm, and pine will support more than 200 species of insect. The greater the diversity that your garden supports, the better chances birds will have of finding food that suits their needs.

Although it's fun and rewarding to fill up a bird feeder and watch the hungry flying machines gather for an easy meal, it is more important to provide life-sustaining nutrition in its most natural form all year long. Over the ages, astounding yet logical partnerships have formed; native plants, insects, and birds have their timing in sync. Through coevolution, they have worked out systems that coordinate a plant's budburst with a moth's nectar-hunger, with a caterpillar's emergence, with a bird's breeding instincts, and with nesting site availability. If one of these puzzle pieces is missing, there could be fewer birds next year or perhaps more caterpillars or no fruit.

Birds' lives are intricately woven into the ecosystem; they provide seed dispersal, population control, nutrient recycling, fertilizer, and, in some cases, pollination. Birds are important scavengers and predators. When birds go looking for food, they look for holes in leaves as a sign that caterpillars are nearby. Spraying insecticides may keep your leaves free of holes, but it will also leave your garden without birdsong.

Provide food sources and amenities that encourage birds to stop by and even stay awhile.

The information in this chapter covers a wide range of topics that will bring birds into closer focus for gardeners, including selected articles from experts who share insights into making your wild-bird gardening experience the best it can be.

The ABCs of ID—From an article by Clay and Pat Sutton

When we begin backyard birding, most of us feel a need to put names to the feathered visitors attracted to our yards. My husband, Clay, and I don't recall the first "yard bird" recorded at our home of thirty-plus years, but the last one was as puzzling as any bird during our career—and we wanted to put a name to it. From the backyard, we heard a high-pitched, long, thin whistle high overhead in the dark. We agonized for a week over this nighttime transient until a friend suggested the obvious: Black Scoters migrating through the night.

We'd heard these sea ducks many times but just couldn't place their call in such an out-of-context setting, miles from the ocean. Even after thirty-five years of birding, we still appreciate the satisfaction of identifying an unexpected avian visitor!

Clay grew up in a family that recognized and enjoyed the common birds around its Jersey Shore seaside home. His mother pointed out Northern Cardinals, Blue Jays, Baltimore Orioles, and the like, giving Clay a head start on bird identification. When he was thirteen, his grandmother gave him a copy of naturalist Roger Tory Peterson's *A Field Guide to the Birds*. He remembers feeling bewildered by the book at first; it contained so many birds. There's no way I can see or ID so many birds, Clay thought. A few days later, however, he used the guide to ID his first "life bird" (a bird seen for the first time): a black and white warbler in a neighbor's backyard.

To ID the warbler, Clay did what most of us do the very first time we are confronted by an unfamiliar bird: he frantically paged through the guide until the picture matched the bird in front of him. There is nothing wrong with this method (we even used it a couple of times when daunted by the tropical birds we saw while visiting Costa Rica), but it has huge shortcomings; for example, it works only for boldly marked birds at which you get a good, lengthy look. Had Clay's first "life bird" been a female Blackpoll Warbler—a bird often very difficult to identify in its drab fall plumage—this story might have had a different outcome.

Read Up

There are alternatives to merely thumbing through a field guide and looking for a match. One of the most important parts of any field guide, the introductory material, covers how to

Blue Jays are common to backyards in the eastern and central United States.

use the guide and how to ID birds. We all want to skip to the pictures, but a key part of birding is to understand the various types or groups of bird, how they appear similar, and how they differ.

The guide's introductory section describes plumage (the covering of feathers) and how it changes through the seasons, altering the look of a bird. It also explains how to learn bird songs and calls not only for pure enjoyment but also for help in identification because every bird species has a unique song. For example, once learned, the Carolina Wren's exuberant "tea-kettle, tea-kettle, tea-kettle" is unforgettable. Numerous individual and regional variations in bird song do exist, however.

Bird topography (the parts of a bird) is particularly important. A key feature in separating groups of birds is the bill, sometimes called the beak. Bills vary in length, thickness, and shape. Sparrows have thick, conical bills, for example, while warblers' bills are thin and pointed. While tail length, leg length, and body shape play important roles in ID, the size, shape, and color of the bill offers a good starting point when categorizing a bird.

The overall size and the general shape of the bird remain important aspects of identification. For example, jays appear far larger and sit more upright than sparrows and some (but not all) jays have a crest, which is a prominent semi-plume of feathers on the head.

Once you have an idea, or at least a guess, as to which group of birds your mystery bird belongs to, color and pattern will play a huge role. Many birds have unique coloration and diagnostic patterns; these are highlighted in field guides and classically known as "field marks."

Identifying birds by field marks was popularized by Peterson, the "father of American birding," with his 1934 field guide. Since that publication, all popular bird guides have used arrows to highlight the features to look for when identifying a bird—features that will confirm the ID of any species.

Write It Down

Your field guide might not be handy at the very moment when you encounter an unfamiliar bird. In such instances, a photographic memory helps. Try to commit to memory the bird's size, shape, colors, patterns, and bill size and shape. Sketch the bird, however crudely, using your own arrows to highlight colors and patterns. Drawing the bird forces you to look at it more closely, which enables you to notice many more details. Your sketch will give you something to compare to the pictures in the field guide.

After the bird leaves your view, it's important to consult the guide ASAP; memory fades, but sketches remain and will jog your memory. Even highly experienced ornithologists use field sketches when confronted with unfamiliar birds. Don't worry about your drawing ability; focus on highlighting key

Online Ornithology

Check out All About Birds (www. allaboutbirds.org), Cornell Lab of Ornithology's amazing website of birding know-how. You can find information about the behavior and life history of just about every North American bird, and you can learn about interesting research, watch and listen to high-quality video and sound recordings, and see how your backyard observations can contribute to a vital pool of knowledge through projects like eBird and the Great Backyard Bird Count.

colors, patterns, features, and proportions.

Beyond size, shape, and color, you should also note behavior because each group of birds exhibits distinctive behavioral traits. Sparrows scurry on the ground and through dense vegetation when

feeding. Flycatchers generally perch conspicuously and sally forth to chase flying insects. Nuthatches frequently hang upside down on tree trunks or under tree limbs.

Some individual species have highly specific traits. A Palm Warbler might look very similar to other warblers, but it is often found on or near the ground, bobbing its tail constantly. Similarly, an Eastern Phoebe might, at first glance, look like other flycatchers, but it uniquely flicks its tail constantly while perched. Some birds remain mostly silent except during the early morning and in springtime; other birds are highly vocal all year. Wrens might even sing during all seasons and at all times of the day.

Even given all the aforementioned methods and advice, many birds are "look-alikes," subtly patterned and somewhat devoid of obvious field marks. To a beginner, most sparrows

1. An Eastern Song Sparrow with the typical thick, conical bill.

2. A white eyebrow with a thin, dark stripe through the eye are among the small and stocky Red-Eyed Vireo's field marks.

look alike and can become exasperatingly difficult to identify. Remember that an experienced birder who can distinguish a Lincoln's Sparrow out of a flock of Song Sparrows doesn't have better vision or more special skills than you; an experienced birder simply has more experience.

As in sports, nothing takes the place of repeated practice and dedication. The more familiar you become with Song Sparrows and their subtle plumage variations, the more likely it is that a Lincoln's Sparrow will stand out as different from other species. Study the common, everyday species, and you will become better prepared to pick out and identify something new and different. Another recommendation is that you study your field guide leisurely and often, not just when you head outdoors or see a new bird in front of you.

There is an old saying that experience only comes from making mistakes, and this remains somewhat true of birding. You can accelerate the learning process by venturing beyond the backyard, however. Jump-start your birding skills by attending organized bird walks, bird watching courses, and other opportunities taught by longtime local birders. These offerings are available throughout the United States at nature centers and through bird clubs. During one bird-filled spring

The proper tools, such as a binocular and a good field guide, increase your chances of successfully identifying the birds you observe.

bird walk, you can learn and absorb more than you could in several years by yourself in your backyard.

Add It Up

Learning to ID birds feels much like putting together the pieces of a jigsaw puzzle. It can feel overwhelming at first, but with practice comes speed and skill. Make sure to note the pieces of each bird puzzle: size, shape, color, pattern, behavior, habitat, season and so on. Add together all of those pieces, and you form a picture—a picture of a new bird!

One time during a nature outing, our nephew asked his uncle, "How can you identify so many birds? They all look the same to me." He asked this question after he'd just finished identifying every passing car and truck on the highway, announcing each one's make, model, year, and, often, engine size. His nephew used the same set of skills that we used for bird identification: noting size, shape, pattern, and unique features; deciphering clues; and making choices until a solution became possible. We all do it every day, whether we're recognizing actors, logos, or brands or collecting rare coins or stamps.

Some people might have their very first birding adventures while on vacation, while on a cruise, or during a school field trip. For most of us, however, that first spark of interest occurs in our backyards. Do not let difficult-to-ID birds dampen your enthusiasm. There are many, many tools available—field guides, birding basics or "how-to" books, DVDs, Internet resources, and local nature centers—to help you get over the initial identification hurdles.

Essential Reading

Until the mid-twentieth century, birdwatchers struggled to ID birds. Learning tools were limited to black-and-white photographs, specimens, photos of dead birds, or drawings, which were often highly stylized. Roger Tory Peterson's landmark 1934 book, *A Field Guide to the Birds*, changed everything. For the first time, a bird book depicted similar birds side by side and in corresponding stances to allow for ready comparisons. The Peterson guide revolutionized bird identification and enabled bird-watching—and even bird conservation—to become what it is today. Nowadays, many bird ID guides are available. There are universal guides that cover bird species all over the world as well as specific guides for every group of birds.

Sparrows

Sparrows are notoriously difficult for novices to ID. At first glance, many species seem to exhibit look-alike plumage, but a number of sparrows have highly specific habitat preferences and would rarely, if ever, be seen in backyards or at birdfeeders.

Even a novice backyard birder should own a field guide to increase his or her understanding and enjoyment of birds. Seeing a "life bird" is always a thrill, whether you began birding yesterday or seventy-five years ago. Many birders document the date and location of each new bird in their field guides, ensuring that they remember the time, place, and pleasant memories of each new bird.

Peterson's venerable field guide remains a highly respected favorite. David Allen Sibley's *The Sibley Field Guide to Birds* is often regarded as the most advanced and state of the art, and Jon Dunn and Jonathan Alderfer's *National Geographic Field Guide to the Birds of North America* is also well respected. Kenn Kaufman's *Kaufman Field Guide to Advanced Birding*, a photographic guide, is also popular. Many avid birders use more than one of these guides. We recommend avoiding simplified guides.

1. The male Northern Cardinal is vibrantly colored in red while the female has just a hint of red on her head.

2. The Black-Capped Chickadee, pictured, is nearly identical in appearance to the Carolina Chickadee.

Season and Location

Many birds can look totally different at different times of the year. A male Northern Cardinal appears bright red during all seasons; on the other hand, a male Scarlet Tanager appears bright red only during breeding season, roughly from March to August. The rest of the year, male Scarlet Tanagers look greenish-yellow.

Also, females of some bird species can appear very different from males. A female Northern Cardinal is more grayish-brown than the male, and youngsters or juveniles can appear quite brownish.

As a group, warblers show marked differences between seasons. Many spring warblers have bold, bright, and unique colors and patterns; by fall, most lose their bold colors and distinct patterns. Seasonality is an important factor in bird ID. Variable plumage is an important reason to use one of the more advanced field guides, even if you are a beginner or rarely venture beyond your yard to look at birds.

Volunteer Your Skills

By Peter Stangel

Every person reading this book has something to contribute to bird conservation, and every conservation organization needs your help. One of the most important ways you can conserve birds is to help the organizations that help birds. Volunteering for a few hours a month can work wonders for conservation—and for your soul! The easiest way to get started is to contact an organization that you care about and offer your services. You might choose to help a nature center, wildlife rehabilitation facility, state park, or national wildlife refuge. Be prepared to tell the organization a little about yourself, such as what you like to do and what your skills include. Whether you want to help install software, work in the gift shop, clear trails, or build birdhouses, you can make a difference. You'll meet some great people along the way, too!

Field guides also contain important information that goes beyond depictions of plumage. Most field guides include habitat preferences, which remain an important component of bird ID. The American Robin, widespread in North America, is known as a bird of open lawns to some, but robins are found in many habitats, from tundra to forests. Other birds are far more specialized.

The Bobolink makes an unlikely backyard bird unless your yard includes a sizable meadow or grassland habitat. Meadowlarks are found only in fields and grasslands. Wood Thrush and Hermit Thrush are normally found only in deep woods.

Finally, range maps are an important feature of field guides. For example, the Carolina Chickadee and the Black-Capped Chickadee can look nearly identical, even to experienced birders. Recently, a novice birder told us about the Black-Capped Chickadee that she'd identified in her southern New Jersey backyard. She hadn't taken note of the range maps in her field guide, which told her that the Black-Capped Chickadee is found no farther south than north-central New Jersey, with virtually no overlap in range. In this case, studying the range map would have cemented the ID as a Carolina Chickadee.

While many birds are resident and sedentary, the range maps of other species can change by season because breeding birds migrate south in fall and north in spring. One man shared that he had narrowed down identification of the mystery hawk frequenting his backyard to either a juvenile Broad-Winged Hawk or a juvenile Red-Shouldered Hawk. We didn't even need to see the bird to make the ID. It was January, and all Broad-Winged Hawks from throughout the United States and Canada were in their winter quarters in Central and South America—a fact clearly shown by range maps in field guides.

Bird Sounds: Listen Closely—by Michael L. P. Retter

You might enjoy a perfectly good view from your kitchen window of the birds that visit your backyard feeders. The ducks that stop over on the neighborhood pond aren't very difficult to identify. During spring, colorful warblers appear obvious enough as they hop about in leafless trees. Why, then, should you learn about bird vocalizations? Because it increases your enjoyment of birding, that's why!

Who, What, Where?

If you learn your common birds' different vocalizations, you will open up a new world of information for yourself. Bird vocalizations tell us not only who's around but also what they're doing. Spring brings with it a deluge of birdsong, as male American Robins and Red-Winged Blackbirds vocally vie for the best territories before their potential mates arrive. A flock of Blue Jays or American Crows screaming their calls around your home serves as a pretty good sign that a hawk or owl sits nearby, while the incessant, begging calls of baby birds tell us that hungry mouths are in need of food.

There's a difference between a bird's song and its call. Typically, songs are complex, distinctive, relatively long sounds that (mostly) males use to establish and defend nesting territory and (usually) to attract a mate in the breeding season. The "*tsee-ew tsee-ew whoit whoit whoit whoit whoit*" of a Northern Cardinal and the "*chur-ee, chur-eet, tsee-ew, tsoo-ee?*" of an American Robin are their songs. In some species—such as woodpeckers, the Ruffed Grouse, the Wilson's Snipe, and the American Woodcock—even a nonvocal sound might function as song. Most songs are fairly easy to learn if you put your mind to it and listen to recordings.

Birds' calls usually are simple, nuanced, short vocal sounds used by both sexes for multiple reasons at any time of year. Reasons include denoting location, alerting to the presence of a predator, and scaring away a potential threat. The "*tik*" of a Northern Cardinal and the "*tuk tuk tuk*" and "*siiiiiii*" of an American Robin are calls. The "*chick-a-dee-dee-dee*" of a Chickadee is also a call. Generally speaking, calls can prove more difficult to learn than songs. You can find more information about the distinctions between songs and calls in the opening sections of many field guides.

Discoveries by Sound

As a child, I tracked down every unfamiliar bird sound. Most of the time, they were the calls of birds that I knew: the descending trill of a Carolina Wren or the buzzy "*dzrrt*" of an Eastern Meadowlark. One day, while birding with my grandmother, I heard a new, unique, repetitive sound that was somewhat musical

1. The Red-Winged Blackbird is visually and vocally distinctive.

2. A chatty Eastern Meadowlark.

3. The Black-Headed Grosbeak is familiar to birders in the Western United States.

The Veery is found across the northern United States and is known for its complex song.

and rather complex, so I guessed that it was a male's song. The sound led us to my first-ever Dickcissel, a rather handsome and proud bird singing from a fencepost. That memory remains very dear to me.

We also can use the vocalizations of species that we know to find birds that we don't know. One fall day, I heard an immense flock of Sandhill Cranes overhead. I rushed outside to see if there was a rare and endangered Whooping Crane flying among them. There wasn't—and I later learned that a whooper flew over my neighborhood an hour later—but knowing the Sandhills' bugling call made it much more likely that I'd find a whooper that day.

There's another way that familiar bird songs can help you with unfamiliar birds. Most birders from the West know the whistled song of the Black-Headed Grosbeak. Now imagine a Western birder visiting Magee Marsh in Ohio for spring migration. The array of new sounds almost feels overwhelming, but the person hears something familiar. Could it be a Black-Headed Grosbeak—here? It sure sounds like it, but it's very unlikely, and it doesn't sound exactly right. The song sounds a bit fuller. The out-of-state birder is hearing a Rose-Breasted Grosbeak, a closely related species with a very similar vocal repertoire. In many cases, knowing your local songs can help when dealing with unfamiliar yet related species, whether they're on your property or on different continents.

Use Technology to Learn

How do you go about learning all of these sounds? You can track down birds when you hear an unfamiliar sound. Believe me: after you spend forty-five minutes trying to locate a high-pitched whistle only to find that is a juvenile American Robin, you won't soon forget who makes that sound.

Technology, however, has made knowledge much more accessible. Cassette tapes and compact discs with birds' song and calls became all the rage in the 1990s and the early 2000s, and many of us still depend heavily on them today. They help you learn the vocalizations of the more common birds in your region and teach a little about the physiology of a bird's Y-shaped syrinx, its voice box. Not all birds use this structure, but it is put to fine use in the small passerines we call songbirds. If a Veery's song already sounds complex to you, wait until you hear it slowed down on a recording: the bird actually sings in harmony with itself using the two forks of its syrinx.

A number of online sources of bird recordings also are available, such as xeno-canto and Cornell Lab of Ornithology's Macaulay Library. The latter is the compilation of decades of scientific audio and video recordings, digitized and available at macaulaylibrary.org, but you can't download the files. That's where xeno-canto (www.xeno-canto.org) helps. There, you will find a compendium of digitized vocalizations ready for free download. We owe this resource to volunteers who offered their time, generosity, and personal recordings. Recordings are organized by species, location, and vocalization type (songs vs. calls). Furthermore, the advent of the iPod and other handheld devices brought about products preloaded with bird vocalizations as well as with field guide information, including illustrations, identification notes, and territory range maps.

Finding an Oasis—By Pete Dunne

You've probably noticed that the birds in your yard have a "now you see them, now you don't" quality—a temporal pattern linked to season. You likely know that central to this seasonal occurrence is a phenomenon called *migration*, which means that many species spend part of the year in one place and the rest in another. Your yard is just such a place and thus plays an important role in supporting bird populations in migration, a strategy for survival that allows birds to use food resources that our planet provides seasonally.

Winter Wonders

Take White-Throated Sparrows and White-Crowned Sparrows, two common species that are backyard and feeder regulars across much of the United States—during winter! During warmer months, these handsome sparrows breed, for the most part, in Canada. These birds remain in their breeding territories for only a few months—just as long as it takes to nest and fledge their young. Then, in September and October, the populations shift south, where warmer temperatures and limited snowfall offer these mostly ground-feeding birds the foraging conditions that they require. During summer, insects make up much of their diet. In winter, the birds' seed-crushing bills come into play, and they become birdfeeder regulars.

Come April and May, the migratory pendulum shifts. Our "winter residents" ride the migratory wave north at just about the time that birds like swifts, hummingbirds, swallows, warblers, and orioles return from the more temperate and tropical regions where they wait out the colder months.

Migrant Workers

Although many people view migration as a retreat from harsh conditions, it is more accurate to think of it as a strategy that allows birds to take advantage of the unclaimed territory and ample resources that summer

Bohemian Waxwings crowd around a fresh water source in winter.

brings to northern regions. Migration becomes a seasonal reenactment of the pioneering surge north staged by birds (and other animals) as the glaciers of the most recent Ice Age retreated and opportunity beckoned.

Without migration, species diversity in your backyard would be limited to those birds able to tolerate the seasonal extremes found where you live and able to outcompete the competition for limited resources. It also would mean that many more of the planet's bird species would remain clustered in the tropics, and areas subject to harsh winters would be very bird-poor. If you like to see a lot of birds of many different species, migration is a good thing. It shuffles the avian deck and deals birdwatchers a new hand almost every day. Yes, almost every day.

Migration actually occurs year-round. The first southbound Arctic breeders reach the lower forty-eight states at the end of June while summer is just getting started in the Arctic. In January and February, the first Purple Martins return to the United States from winter territories in Brazil.

Some nomadic species, such as Redpolls, move throughout the winter nonbreeding season in search of food. Other species make altitudinal rather than latitudinal shifts, breeding high in mountain ranges and then retreating to lower altitudes before or after heavy snowfall.

This shuffling process is multifaceted and ongoing. What most people think of as migration is really just "rush hour" in the migratory timetable, with peak migratory periods falling between April and early June and then again in late August into early November. What timetable birds keep, what routes and how far they travel, whether they migrate alone or in flocks or during the day or night—these all differ from species to species.

Because your backyard is part of this global strategy for survival, you have the opportunity to take the pulse of migration by noting species' arrival and departure dates. You'll probably find remarkable consistency (birds tend to keep regular schedules), and you'll notice that certain conditions "trigger" your birds to make their arrivals or departures.

1. A female Purple Martin. East of the Rockies, this migratory species lives mainly in man-made houses and nest boxes.

2. The Northern Waterthrush has a particular affinity to water.

3. Built for long journeys, the Arctic Tern migrates the farthest to find warm beaches in the winter.

You might discover that your yard is not only an important breeding area for some species and a wintering area for others but is also an important temporary waystation on the panhemispheric highway. In the strategy of survival that is migration, your yard is critical habitat, and birds depend on it. They'll thank you if you manage it that way.

Short-Term Residents

Most of the birds that take advantage of the habitat and hospitality of your yard do so for only a short time. These opportunity-seeking migrants might linger just a few minutes or hours. They might spend the night—or, in the case of migrating owls, the day—or they could remain for several days if what they find is to their liking.

Consider the Northern Waterthrush, an abundant and widespread northern breeder that spends winters in the tropics. In August and September, countless backyards harbor this surreptitious, tail-wagging warbler. If you have a dense flower patch, ample shrubbery, or understory-lush woodlands, it is almost certain that the Northern Waterthrush is on your "yard list" whether you have recorded it or not.

Don't forget to look up. The airspace over your home is right on the flight path for many migrants. The first hour after sunrise is the best time to see nocturnal migrants dropping in or "falling out." Midmorning and late afternoon become prime time for migrating hawks, gulls, and other high-flying birds.

Sometimes migrating birds appear visible on weather radar, shown as a circular flash around radar installations or a line tracing coastlines. Online, you might find other birdwatchers who post snapshots of weather radar to alert other aficionados to upcoming flights.

Migration Facts

Every autumn, more than 200 species of bird leave North America to relocate to Central and South America. The number of individual migrants numbers in the billions. In Veracruz, Mexico, more than 2.5 million hawks have been recorded in one fall season. The Arctic Tern is the long-distance migration champion, covering 15,500 miles (25,500 kilometers) between its Arctic breeding grounds and its wintering areas in the oceans of the Southern Hemisphere.

Birds that migrate long and short distances are built to play the part. Long-distance migrants, such as the American Golden Plover, whose journeys vault continents, have long, narrow wings. Northern Saw-Whet Owls, which breed and winter in North America, have shorter, blunter wings.

Welcoming Visitors

If you'd like to attract the Northern Waterthrush, a birdbath is a bonus. Although these birds might not be true thrushes, as the name implies, this northern bog-breeder does like water.

Now consider the Orange-Crowned Warbler, the Palm Warbler, or the Yellow-Rumped Warbler. Abundant northern breeders, all these favor semi-open habitats offering woody or weedy edges, as do many yards. In September and October, hordes of these birds sweep across the North American continent. Just look for them.

The fuel for migration is subcutaneous fat. Blackpoll Warblers, which fly nonstop from the northeastern United States to South America, nearly double their weight—from .4 to .8 ounces (11 to 21 grams)—to fuel up for their flight over the Gulf of Mexico.

Migrating birds use a number of navigational aids to keep their courses. They can navigate by the sun and the stars and, when clouds obscure the sky, by orienting themselves along the Earth's magnetic field.

Bird Behavior—By Brian L. Sullivan

For many of us, the first question we want to answer when we see a bird is "What kind of bird is that?" After we name the bird, we usually move beyond basic bird identification to other questions, such as "What is the bird doing?" and, perhaps more importantly, "Why is the bird behaving that way?"

Much of what a bird does throughout its day—and, indeed, throughout its life—revolves around two major events: finding food and producing viable young. Food obviously remains a requirement during the breeding season, although other behaviors add to the daily routine of finding food. Even migration, one of the most spectacular and interesting aspects of bird behavior, stems from a species' ability to move great distances in search of abundant food resources.

With these two major factors in mind, let's look at some of the most frequently observed behaviors during each season. Then we can try to better understand why birds do what they do.

1. Male birds large and small often have territory disputes with other males.

2. An Eastern Phoebe returns to the nest with food for the babies.

3. Singing is a big part of avian courtship. Pictured here is a Swainson's Thrush.

The Breeding Season

During the breeding season, birds engage in some of the most interesting and demanding aspects of their lives: song, courtship, begging, copulation, territorial aggression, tending a nest with young, and then feeding fledglings—we might see all of these behaviors during breeding season, and some occur only at this time. During this all-important part of a bird's life, it must establish a territory, protect itself and its territory from potential predators and competitors, attract a mate, and successfully raise young.

Song: This activity might rank as the most readily observable, familiar, and beautiful aspect of avian behavior. During the spring, it's well known that birds sing more frequently. The purpose of song is to attract a potential mate. In many species, like the Blackpoll Warbler, only the male sings. Song lets a male tell prospective females that he has a territory and is open for business. It also alerts neighboring males to his presence and identifies the boundaries of his territory. In some species, the male and the female both sing, and, occasionally, the sexes actually perform duets.

Courtship: As a general rule, male birds appear more brightly colored than females. The male has to impress the female, who likely has many suitors, and she decides on her mate. If she doesn't like one male's looks or behavior, she moves on to the next Casanova. Courtship displays vary greatly from species to species, ranging from quite simple to amazingly complex. A simple and frequently observed courtship behavior involves the male offering a food item to the female. More involved courtship behavior can include incredible feats of aerial agility, "dances" or performances, or the construction of fantastically adorned bowers.

Territorial aggression: It's important for a male bird to protect his investment from intruders. In certain long-lived species, such as Red-Tailed Hawks, many birds do not breed during their first year of life. Instead, they spend the summer wandering, mostly focused on food but also stumbling into the territories of established pairs and established older males.

It is the job of the territory-holding male to chase out the potential interloper. To do this, the older bird performs an aerial flight display. It consists of a rollercoaster flight performed high overhead, rising to the top of the peak on closed wings, dropping down on spread wings, and repeating the process a number of times.

If this fails to get the attention of the intruding individual, the older male might start an all-out tail-chase, with the established male beating up on the newcomer until the latter leaves the territorial boundary. While this kind of interaction appears most obvious in larger birds, such as the raptors, it plays out again and again in various ways in many species, even the smallest landbirds in your backyard.

Copulation: Once he secures territory and finds a female mate, the male focuses on the next order of business. Avian copulation is brief, noisy, and obvious, and you're bound to see it if you watch birds during the nesting season. In most cases, the male

A Carolina Chickadee (1) brings food home for the youngsters, while an Eastern Bluebird (2) removes a fecal sac from the nest.

offers food to the female, after which he jumps on her back. Noisy calling and wing flapping ensues, and a few seconds later, it's done. At the beginning of the nesting season, birds copulate frequently, and this behavior generally needs little explanation when seen.

Carrying food: Birds carry food for many reasons, but, more often than not, they aim to provision a female that is incubating eggs or to feed a nest full of young. Nestlings generate fecal sacs, and the parents remove these from the nest, carrying them far away from the area before dropping them. Sometimes it's difficult to determine if the bird is carrying food or a fecal sac, but both indicate that birds are nesting near your home.

Begging: About halfway through summer, you might hear noisy, unfamiliar sounds in your backyard trees. These are the fledglings of various species, now out of the nest and noisily begging for food. Typically high-pitched and relentless, the calls of begging fledglings let the parents—who are searching for food—know the youngsters' location. The noisiest time occurs, however, when the parents return with food, and the fledglings compete for attention.

The Nonbreeding Season

When birds are not breeding, they focus almost solely on finding food to sustain themselves, especially during migration or the cold nights of winter. Birdwatchers often use the term *foraging* to describe the feeding activities of shorebirds as they probe in the mud or of a warbler as it actively searches out insects high in the treetops. We often reserve the term *hunting* for the higher level predators, such as hawks and owls, but they are actually foraging, too.

Because the search for food plays such a big part in birds' lives, it remains complex and highly variable among species; however, here's an important general rule: when you see birds during nonbreeding season, watch their activity and try to determine what they are up to. Birds' specially adapted bills, feet, and body structures often reveal clues about their search for food. When you watch birds closely and look at their structure, much of what was once a mystery soon makes sense.

Favorite Backyard Birds—By Rob Fergus

About 600 bird species nest in North America, but most of us are familiar only with the dozen or so that appear near our homes. Although backyard birds might be fairly common, they are far from ordinary. Each has a distinctive anatomy and set of behaviors tailored to fit its unique lifestyle.

Birders and nonbirders across America are familiar with the "Robin Redbreast."

American Robins

While the famed "Robin Redbreast" is widely considered a harbinger of spring, and many do migrate, individual robins actually spend the winter across most parts of the United States. During those cold months, they trade in their worm-hunting tactics to specialize in eating berries and other fruit.

   Now found in almost every neighborhood with lawns (for worm hunting) and ornamental trees (for nesting), American Robins actually took a while to adapt to living near humans. American Robins on the East Coast hopped throughout yards and gardens in the 1800s, but most of those on the West Coast didn't move to suburbia until several decades into the twentieth century.

Chickadees

Named for their "*chick-a-dee-dee-dee*" scolding calls, these tiny gray and white birds with black caps and bibs are conspicuous and pugnacious visitors to bird feeders. In winter, roaming individuals join flocks centered around a resident pair of breeding birds, which dominate the flock.

   Black-Capped Chickadees are common across northern states, while the nearly identical Carolina Chickadee frequents yards and woodlands in the Southeast. Other species are found in the Pacific Northwest, the Rocky Mountains, and Canada's boreal forest.

Dark-Eyed Juncos

Sometimes known as snowbirds or mistakenly called chickadees, these small birds with dark hoods are a type of sparrow. In the

Three varieties of Dark-Eyed Junco, (1) Oregon, (2) Gray-Headed, and (3) Red-Backed.

summertime, Dark-Eyed Juncos nest in forests and woodlands. In the winter, they show up in yards and neighborhoods across the country as small flocks scatter widely to feed on grass and weed seeds. When startled, they flash white feathers on the sides of their tails as they fly off to seek shelter in thick bushes and shrubs.

Doves

With their easily recognizable long tails and "coo-coo-coo" calls, Mourning Doves are seen and heard in even the most urban of neighborhoods. In many areas, they are now joined by Eurasian Collared Doves, which appear larger and gray with black neck collars. After colonizing in Florida from the Bahamas in the 1980s, Collared Doves spread across the country. The Rock Pigeon, the common park dove native to Europe, might breed year-round in warmer parts of the United States.

Over thousands of years, doves have adapted their cliff-dwelling habits to nesting on building ledges. Long necks and small heads make doves adept at picking up tiny seeds from the ground. At your birdbath, you might notice that while most birds gulp water and then lift their heads to let it flow down their throats, doves are among the few species that can drink while keeping their bills in the water.

Goldfinches

Closely related to the true canaries native to Europe, these bright yellow and black birds are known by many Americans as wild canaries. American Goldfinches make winter visits to bird feeders in the southern states, but they live year-round across the rest of the country. In the Southwest, both Black-Backed and Green-Backed Lesser Goldfinches are frequent visitors to many yards.

Unlike most songbirds that feed insects to their young, goldfinch parents feed their young on regurgitated weed seeds, and they specialize in eating seeds still on plants. This adaptation makes them more likely to perch on and feed at birdfeeders.

Jays

Members of the crow family, jays originated in Australia and immigrated to the Americas millions of years ago. These intelligent and adaptable forest birds specialize in finding, storing, and eating acorns and other tree seeds. Jays live in social groups that usually consist of extended families; they communicate continually through a variety of loud calls.

In the West, the Western Scrub Jay, which lacks the head crest, is a common species, along with the darker blue Steller's Jay. The Blue Jay, the most famous member of the jay family, is more widespread in the eastern United States.

Northern Cardinals

In the eastern United States, few songbirds are as beloved as the Northern Cardinal, or "redbird." Its "cheer-cheer-cheer, chuck,-chuck,-chuck" song rings out across yards and neighborhoods wherever thick bushes and shrubs provide shelter in which to nest. Males appear all red with a black mask;

females are brownish with red crests, wings, tails, and bills. Young males look like females, but they have black, instead of red, bills.

Northern Mockingbirds

From California to New England, Northern Mockingbirds remain highly regarded as amazing songbirds. They mimic the songs and calls of many species as well as the sounds of cell phones and car alarms. When males are full of hormones in the spring, they might sing late into the night and start up again a few hours later in the darkness of predawn. Northern Mockingbirds also attract people's attention by aggressively protecting their nests from cats or nosy humans and by defending their preferred winterberry patches from other birds.

Nuthatches

Famous for walking down tree trunks, nuthatches are named for their habit of wedging nuts or hard seeds into the bark of trees and then hammering them open with their bills. Watch where a nuthatch goes when it leaves your birdfeeder with a sunflower seed, and you will witness this action firsthand.

Although most nuthatches do not migrate, Red-Breasted Nuthatches might move about during winters when seeds and other food sources become scarce, appearing farther south than in years when food remains plentiful in the north.

Orioles

Closely related to blackbirds and meadowlarks, these colorful songsters nest in large baskets that they hang from tree limbs. In the East, black and orange Baltimore Orioles sing noisily from the tops of tall shade trees. Across most of the West, however, they are replaced by the similar Bullock's Oriole. Several other yellow and black or orange and black species nest in the Southwest.

1. The bright-yellow and black American Goldfinch.

2. A Northern Mockingbird feeds on berries in the winter.

3. The Baltimore Oriole is striking in black and bright orange.

4. Pileated Woodpeckers are mainly forest dwellers.

Orioles thrive on berries and other fruit. You can attract them with jelly, raisins, or sliced fruit placed on a birdfeeder or by nailing half an orange to the side of a tree.

Phoebes

These tail-pumping birds are named for their "*fee-bee*" calls. Specialized in catching insects, they fly out from their perches and grab their prey in midair with their short, wide bills—quite a sight to behold. Although they originally preferred building their nests on cliffs and under rocky overhangs near water, phoebes now find bridges and buildings acceptable nesting sites.

Sparrows

Mostly brown and inconspicuous, fifty species of sparrow live in North America. The brown-streaked Song Sparrow and the white-breasted Chestnut-Capped Sparrow nest in yards and gardens across most of the United States. In the winter, flocks of sparrows often forage on the ground under birdfeeders for the smaller seeds spilled by other birds. Like most songbirds, sparrows learn their songs by listening to the adults of their species and through practice.

Woodpeckers

With long, barbed tongues that actually wrap around the inside of their heads, most woodpeckers specialize in boring holes into trees and spearing beetle larvae and other insects that they find inside. To balance on the sides of trees, they use their specialized feet and short, stiff tails for support.

Woodpeckers nest in holes that they excavate in trees, and these holes later provide nesting sites for dozens of other bird species. Instead of singing, most woodpeckers announce their territories by drumming loudly on hollow trees or other resonant sounding boards, including gutters or metal flashing on homes.

Bird Lovers Unite

A survey by the US Fish and Wildlife Service revealed that nearly 48 million Americans enjoy watching and feeding birds. That means that at least one in six of your friends and neighbors shares your interest! Backyard birding remains the most popular activity, with nearly 42 million Americans participating, but many birders also have wanderlust. Almost 20 million Americans travel to watch birds. Birders also make a whopping contribution to the economy. This same survey suggests that wildlife watchers, of which around 90 percent are focused on birds, spend about $46 billion annually on equipment, feed and feeders, travel, and other necessities.

Wrens

When European colonists came to America, these small songsters were among the first birds to nest in and around their homes and gardens. Wrens will nest in almost any small, sheltered spaces, including hats or coats left outside!

Wrens can seem fearless, so if you have one nesting on a porch or somewhere else where you are worried about it, rest assured that it will probably be OK. Nesting won't take long: the eggs hatch in about two weeks, and the young will be ready to fly off two weeks after that.

Beyond Basic Birds—By Don Freiday

More than 950 bird species have been documented in North America, north of Mexico. Some of them have strayed from other parts of the world, but more than 600 species build nests and raise young here. At least 300 species appear in each state, and California and Texas have more than twice that many, so you might see new birds without leaving the comfort of your home.

Brown Creepers

Brown Creepers raise their young in forested parts of northeastern United States and Canada, as well as in the western mountain states and forested areas of the northern West Coast. Creepers build their nests in large dead or dying trees, making such trees an essential habitat requirement for this species. Anywhere that there are large trees, look for migrant birds across the country in April and September to October.

Creepers select loose sections of bark behind which to build their nests, mirroring their habit of living close to tree trunks. With the cryptic feather patterns on their backs matching the trees' bark, creepers spiral upward—and only upward—on tree trunks, gleaning insects from crevices in furrowed bark with their sharp, curved bills. After climbing high, creepers swoop to the base of another tree in a flight often too fast to follow, and then they begin to spiral upward again.

Cedar Waxwings

Birders almost anywhere south of the Arctic are likely to spot Cedar Waxwings in their yards someday, especially if fruiting trees grow nearby. Waxwings like sugary fruits, and flocks often descend en masse on holly, juniper, and cherry trees. Indeed, it is unusual to see just one waxwing.

Waxwings often choose bare branches as perches, clustering around fruiting trees and often hovering briefly to pick berries.

1. The Brown Creeper's colors blend with those of the's tree bark.

2. Cedar waxwings rarely travel alone.

3. Cheerful in coloration and song, the House Finch can be found across America.

4. Indigo Buntings are eye-catching in their bright-blue jewel tones.

Somewhat nomadic, the birds might build their nests in your area one year but not the next, depending on the availability of fruit.

Only the adults produce the red, waxy tips on their inner wing feathers, leading ornithologists to speculate that the wax serves as a social signal for dominance or breeding readiness. Other identification marks are the obvious crest atop the head and the yellow tail tip.

House Finch

Originally native to the Southwest, the House Finch now appears coast to coast in the United States, thanks to releases of illegally sold and kept caged birds in the first part of the twentieth century. House Finches generally live amid human habitation, such as in the suburbs, on farms, or in towns, and they readily visit feeders, preferring black-oil sunflower seed.

Outside the nesting season, House Finches almost always move in small flocks. Males sing enthusiastically, mainly in spring and summer, but they might erupt in bouts of song on nice winter days. House Finches sometimes migrate, especially in the cooler parts of their eastern range, but most western populations inhabit the same areas year-round.

Indigo Bunting

Bright blue jewels of spring and summer, Indigo Buntings build nests in the eastern and southwestern United States, disappearing during the cold months to their wintering grounds in Central America and Mexico. Eastern Indigo Buntings migrate across the Gulf of Mexico, and the landfall of bunting flocks on the Gulf Coast wows American birders in April, when lawns sometimes appear blue.

Note that when not directly lit by the sun, male Indigo Buntings look black. The females appear drab brown, among the drabbest of all songbirds.

Red-Eyed Vireo

Think of the Red-Eyed Vireo as a basic bird that most people go through life never seeing. This species builds its nests in woods throughout eastern North America as well as in the Northwest and far up into Canada. If woodlands thrive near your home, Red-Eyed Vireos nest there.

Certainly one of the most common forest birds in the United States, Red-Eyed Vireos sing their simply whistled song persistently in spring and summer. Birdwatchers seldom see the birds because they most often look for food high in trees, where their small size and drab colors make them invisible to anyone who is not looking intently for them.

Like many common birds, Red-Eyed Vireos will not visit a backyard feeder—but they very definitely visit backyards. Particularly during May and September, carefully watch the trees as they migrate through their range.

Red-Winged Blackbird

Most people know the male Red-Winged Blackbird, often perched conspicuously near marshes or wet meadows in spring and summer, flaring his red epaulets and calling vigorously. Not so the female redwing, however, whose main color is dark brown with thick streaks on the chest.

Red-Winged Blackbirds build their nests coast to coast, and, during winter, they form large flocks and feed in farmlands and pastures where they consume seeds and grain. Redwings migrate quite early in spring, making them a seasonal harbinger in the northern parts of their territory range.

Watch the behavior of male redwings at backyard feeders. Their red shoulder patches signal dominance, but when many males gather to feed, most want to avoid a fight. They then shroud the red feathers with their black scapular, or shoulder, feathers so that only a small yellow stripe appears.

Sharp-Shinned Hawk

The Sharp-Shinned Hawk and other predatory birds can sometimes be found where small songbirds gather.

Inevitably, backyard birders will see a small songbird pinned to the ground, struggling in the talons of a hungry Sharp-Shinned Hawk. One species of bird preying on another reminds us that nature has no favorites. While I consider all backyard birds fair game for hungry hawks, you can give the smaller birds an advantage by providing protective cover near feeders in the form of planted shrubs.

As skilled hunters, adult Sharp-Shinned Hawks combine stealth, speed, and lightning-fast maneuvering to capture prey—almost exclusively small birds. The streaked-looking immature Sharp-Shinneds often miss their prey, thus a high percentage of young hawks do not survive their first year.

Highly migratory, "sharpies" breed in deep forests across the country, and they spend winter partially in that same range but also as far south as Panama.

Hawk-Watching

The term *hawk-watching* often conjures images of fall days at places such as Hawk Mountain in Pennsylvania; Cape May, New Jersey; or Marin Headlands, north of San Francisco. These places remain concentration points for migrating raptors, and, in favorable conditions, observers can expect many sightings. Hawk-watching can be done in many other places, too, because raptors move across the continent on a broad front. During migration, hawks can be seen just about anywhere if you're patient enough and have a sharp eye.

The same is true in your yard. In most cases, these birds are high-flying migrants as opposed to feeder visitors. During the fall (September through November) and spring (March through May), try sitting in your yard and looking skyward, scanning the edges of puffy clouds with your binoculars, searching for soaring birds. Chances are you'll see some migrant raptors to add to your yard list.

Unidentified Flying Objects

What a thrill—a bird you've never seen before! For many birdwatchers, a big part of the hobby is observing "new" species. Here's what to do if a new bird appears in your yard.

Don't look it up in your field guide—yet. Why not? Because you don't know enough after just a glimpse. Some birds are easy to identify, but some are not. The one critical detail you need might be the one that you failed to notice.

Birds have a habit of flying while you page through your field guide to look for a matching picture. Instead of immediately researching it, study the new visitor and maybe take notes. Use the field guide once you think that you could draw the bird from memory or at least describe it in detail.

Never identify a bird using less than three field marks. This tip keeps the experts out of trouble—if they remember to use it. For example, quite a few birds appear mostly yellow, fewer yellow birds also sport a light-colored bill, and only one yellow bird in North America has those characteristics plus a black cap and wings: the male American Goldfinch.

Note the fundamentals. Birding experts often skip the plumage details and begin their identification by looking at a bird's size, shape, and behavior. Most important are a bird's overall size and the precise shape of its bill. Remember that the way a bird is built and the way it acts offer much information about its identity.

When in doubt, aim at the head. Bird face patterns are often distinctive. If you think that you are going to get only a brief look, focus on knowing the new bird perfectly from the neck up. Note the shape and color of its bill. Does it have a dark line through the eye? A light eyebrow? A solid cap or a stripe through the center of the crown? A dark or pale throat?

It never looks just like the picture in the field guide. When someone claims that the bird he or she saw exactly matches a field guide picture, you can be sure that person didn't look carefully at the bird. Part of identifying birds is learning how differently the one in front of you can appear from the field guide picture. If it seems close but not perfect, keep looking in the guide until you find a better match.

Is it even possible? Never identify a bird without asking the basic question: "Is it supposed to be here?" This question contains several components. Is the bird known to occur in this region and at this time of year? Does it like this type of habitat? The answers to these questions appear in field guides and range maps as well as in bird-finding guides and regional checklists.

Nothing is impossible (almost). Use probability, but consider possibility. After all, birds have wings. Every birder makes mistake—something that your local experts know all too well because they've made them, too!

You can draw the Spotted Towhee out of hiding with vocalizations.

Towhees (Eastern and Spotted)

Like Eastern and Western Yellow-Rumped Warblers, this species pair once was considered a single species, combined as the Rufous-Sided Towhee, the name that birdwatchers will find in older field guides. One or the other of the pair builds its nests almost throughout the United States, missing only in the lower Midwest and most of Texas. Towhees winter across the southern two-thirds of the country.

Both members of this pair behave similarly but make different vocalizations; the Eastern Towhee commonly is called *chewink*, a phonetic representation of its call. Towhees feed almost entirely on the ground and are noted leaf-diggers, performing vigorous and humorous double-legged scratches in leaf litter. The scuffing unearths insects and seeds, and you might hear the resulting racket from the thickets where towhees feed.

Their thicket-loving behavior keeps these birds out of view, but they respond well to a bit of "spishing": try making vocal noises, such as "*spish-spish-spish*," to draw the birds' attention and lure them into sight. During nesting season, the males sometimes sing from open perches. Occasionally, towhees visit seed feeders, remaining below them on the ground and digging persistently.

Yellow-Rumped Warblers

Some backyard birdwatchers are startled to discover the warbler tribe, those fifty-odd species of brightly colored sprites so central to spring and fall migration. Yellow-Rumped Warblers—often called "yellow rumps"—build their nests in habitats from New England across Canada, well up into Alaska and south into the western Mountain region.

One of the first tricks in identifying a yellow rump is to realize that the rump, or the area above the tail, lies invisibly under the folded wings of a perched bird, and it appears only if the bird lowers its wings or flies. In the spring, male yellow rumps provide a spectacular introduction to the warbler tribe, showing blue, yellow, black, and white feathers.

The most common warbler, the yellow rump, is widespread across the United States during migration. You might see them almost anywhere there is vegetation, and because they can feed on berries as well as insects, unlike many other warblers, they can spend the winter months in the East as far north as New England and on the West Coast. Western Yellow Rumps sport yellow throats, whereas Eastern birds have white throats. The two types, or subspecies, once were considered separate species.

Birds of Prey—By Brian Sullivan

For birders, encountering raptors in the field offers a special treat. We usually see them at a distance, and their dramatic stoops and aggressive behavior are compelling to watch. There's even an entire group of birders called "hawk watchers,." whose passion is observing birds of prey, particularly during migration. These avian hunters appear in residential yards, too, when attracted by the bustling action of birdfeeders.

During the winter, most birds' daily activities revolve around food. The sparrows, doves, and finches frequenting your yard are there because you've created a ready supply of seed, and when resources are abundant, birds abound. The birds flitting noisily about your feeders create quite a spectacle, drawing the attention of a host of surrounding predators.

Just as finches and sparrows must hunt to survive during the winter, so do birds of prey. In the natural cycle of avian life, raptors sit at the top of the food chain, feeding on rodents, birds, and a surprising number of insects (although the latter are consumed mainly in the summer). Hawks, eagles, and falcons play an important role in our ecosystem by keeping prey populations healthy through natural selection. When a raptor sees dozens of small birds at a backyard feeder, it sees the scene as the perfect invitation to a meal.

Accipiters

The term *accipiter* collectively refers to the North American hawks that share this genus, the three most common being the Sharp-Shinned Hawk, Cooper's Hawk, and the Northern Goshawk. Accipiters are woodland hawks, usually breeding in forested areas. Because they prefer the confined spaces of forest and bramble, they are especially well adapted to hunting birds at backyard feeders.

Distinguishing accipiters remains one of the toughest identification challenges in North American birding. Most accipiters spotted in backyards are perched, making their characteristic flight styles and shapes impossible to discern. Each species, however, has its own set of features to look for when perched. Furthermore, there are significant sex-related size differences among the accipiters; females are typically much larger than males. This sexual dimorphism, as it is known, creates confusion. For example, a big female Cooper's is a large bird, and a small male Sharp-Shinned is a tiny raptor, but male Cooper's Hawks and female Sharp-Shinned Hawks appear similar in size, so much so that getting an impression of size can prove impossible.

Buteos

The term *buteo* describes the group of hawks that share this genus, the most familiar of which are the Red-Shouldered and Red-Tailed Hawks. Many buteos are open-country predators, seen hovering over fallow fields or perched stoically in roadside trees. Backyard sightings are relatively rare, but a few species have adapted to woodland environments. Built to live in more wooded areas, these buteos do not often feed on birds, and they are rarely seen lingering around feeders.

Spectacular woodland buteos, Red-Shouldered Hawks are seen mainly east of the Mississippi River, through southern Texas, and along the West Coast. Red-Shouldereds can be quite tame; they are often seen in suburban or backyard settings, but they don't typically prey on birds, preferring reptiles, amphibians, and small mammals. Adult Red-Shouldered Hawks are virtually unmistakable with bright rufous-barred underparts, brownish upper parts, and boldly patterned black-and-white flight feathers.

1. The Cooper's Hawk has the sharp, hook-shaped beak of a predator.

2. A Red-Tailed Hawk watches for prey.

3. Peregrine Falcons are often seen in urban settings.

Red-Tailed Hawk sightings are common across the contiguous United States; they usually are associated with open country, especially fallow fields and roadsides. Juvenile Red-Tailed Hawks rarely take feeder birds; they more often prey on small mammals. Backyard birders should become familiar with this species and use it as a basis for comparison for all other buteos.

Falcons

Observers frequently misidentify particular falcons at their feeders. Found across the contiguous United States in winter, Merlins are small, dark falcons with brownish upper parts and streaked brownish under parts. Does that sound familiar? Juvenile and female Merlins resemble juvenile Sharp-Shinned Hawks, which are common backyard-feeder visitors. Unlike most falcons, Merlins sometimes spend winter in small towns, feeding on the abundant nonnative birds that overwinter, such as European Starlings and House Sparrows. They often sit atop ornamental spruce trees or any towerlike structures, patiently searching for prey before taking off at full speed.

Falcons are birds of open country, built to chase prey at high speeds using their long, pointed wings. Surprisingly, Peregrine Falcons and American Kestrels can be found in urban environments; if you live in a city, it's likely that a Peregrine nests on a skyscraper or bridge overpass nearby. Nonetheless, these species are uncommon in suburban backyard settings.

Owls—By Rick Wright

The natural world doesn't shut down at dusk. As the familiar *diurnal* (daytime) birds and squirrels leave our gardens and lawns for their overnight roosts, a new cohort of animals emerges from daytime slumber. Katydids, moths, and cockroaches begin their nocturnal

Conserve for Birds: Develop a Raptor Rapport

We've come a long way from the days when raptors were shot for sport, but plenty still perish at man's hands. Given the popularity of bird feeding, many conflicts occur right in our own yards. One example is the avid participant on a birding field trip who practically bragged about shooting a Sharp-Shinned Hawk that invaded his feeders. This bird is listed as a species of concern in many parts of North America, but that birdwatcher thought that he had done a good deed.

Witnessing a raptor grab one of your small feeder birds remains a sobering experience. Your responsibility as a backyard birder is to provide the feeder birds with as much cover as possible so they can find safety quickly when a bird of prey appears. Dense clusters of shrubs and trees near your feeders can make all the difference for a songbird when danger arises.

In a natural animal system, birds forage for food and conduct their daily activities with an eye out for predators. They tend to stay in areas where they feel safe or can reach safety quickly. It's our responsibility as bird lovers to provide them with the same options in our yards.

Other Feeder Visitors

As much as we love to feed birds and enjoy their presence in our lives, putting out a ready food source creates the possibility of attracting everything from squirrels to rodents to neighborhood cats.

Squirrels can truly test a backyard birder's patience at feeders. Using impressive agility and determination, they'll keep birds away from the seed and ravenously ingest the expensive food. Dome-topped feeders or feeders with weight-triggered closures are great for keeping squirrels at bay.

Your feeder also might attract mice and rats. They rarely get into the feeders themselves, but they can be active where seed falls. Try to keep your feeders away from woodpiles and other piles of refuse where rats and mice can hide, and be sure to clean up seed hulls underneath the feeders.

Cats remain a special problem because many of them are neighbors' pets. Unfortunately, they also can make the biggest pests, often hunting birds at feeders. Cats tend to stalk prey while hidden and then pounce, so placing feeders in areas that have open ground below can help. Also, talk to your neighbors about the safety benefits of keeping their cats indoors. For more on the subject, learn about American Bird Conservancy's Cats Indoors! program at abcbirds.org/abcprograms/policy/cats/index.html.

1. An Eastern Screech-Owl brings food to the nestbox.

2, Great Horned Owls are prolific across America, from woodlands to cities.

courtships, and rodents scurry from one hiding place to another. The edible detritus beneath the birdfeeders offers a treasure trove for these and other creatures of the night. In turn, they attract predators, such as foxes, bobcats, snakes—and owls.

A few sunflower hulls lying on the grass is a small price to pay for having owls in the neighborhood. More mystery and mystique surround these nocturnal raptors than perhaps any other group of birds, and seeing an owl makes a red-letter day for just about any birder.

Owls seem somehow wilder than other birds, and some species are very difficult to find: the huge and majestic Great Gray Owl (*Strix nebulosa*) is the very emblem of undisturbed wilderness, while the tough, little Boreal Owl (*Aegolius funereus*) epitomizes scarcity for hopeful American observers. Not all owls shun human-influenced habitats, however, and not all owls are rare. A few species are surprisingly common and surprisingly tolerant of people—so much so that there might be an owl in your yard right now.

The Eastern Screech-Owl

Throughout most of the eastern United States, the most frequent "yard owl" remains the Eastern Screech-Owl (*Megascops asio*). A small but chunky species, the average Eastern Screech-Owl is only about three-quarters of the length of a Blue Jay but weighs twice as much at 6.5 ounces (180 grams)—about the same as a medium-sized potato.

In spite of their diminutive stature, Eastern Screech-Owls make ferocious predators. According to *Birds of North America* online (www.bna.birds.cornell.edu/bna), nearly 150 vertebrate species—mammals, birds, reptiles, amphibians, and even fish—number among the Eastern Screech-Owl's prey. The range of insects and other creepy crawlies eaten by these owls is even wider, including such noxious and well-protected species as cockroaches and crawfish, which are typically spurned by other predators.

These owls mostly eat animals smaller than they are, but they regularly kill young rabbits and large rats. In New York in 1885, one of these fierce little birds soundly drubbed a 9-pound (4 kg) Plymouth Rock rooster. The impressive encounter was witnessed and reported on by the bemused chicken farmer.

Looking for pellets piled on the ground beneath a dense evergreen or a tree full of cavities is perhaps the best way to find a roosting Screech-Owl. In theory, all you have to do is look up, carefully checking the darkest areas for something besides a tree. In practice, it's often much more difficult. The incredibly intricate patterns of a Screech-Owl's feathers do an unequaled job of mimicking tree bark, lichens, and dappled sunlight. Plus, it's ridiculously easy to look right past a bird, viewing it as a continuation of the branch or hole that it occupies.

The Great Horned Owl

Much larger and heavier than an American Crow, this "tiger of the sky" will eat just about anything it can overpower. Very few animals can escape this bird—it weighs more than 3 pounds (1.4 kg)—and its huge talons. Everything from large insects to rabbits to birds as big as ducks and Great Blue Herons falls prey Great Horned Owls. They swallow smaller animals whole and often decapitate larger ones before consumption. In fact, the first indication of the presence of a Great Horned Owl in the neighborhood might be the sudden appearance of headless squirrel or rabbit carcasses.

Its geographic range offers evidence of this magnificent species' success. Among the most widespread of all birds in the Americas, Great Horned Owls breed from north of the Arctic

Owl Pellets

Most of what we know about the food habits of owls comes from their obliging habit of casting pellets after each meal. Lousy in their table manners, most birds don't chew their food at all before swallowing. For owls, that means ingesting a great deal of indigestible bone, scale, and fur. Owls retain the rough material high in their digestive system, where it becomes compacted and ejected through the mouth several hours after eating. It's not the behavior that one hopes for in a dinner guest, but it's far better than harrowing the digestive tract with all that debris, and the pellets are a windfall for owl researchers.

Most owls return to habitual roosts day after day. Pellets often accumulate under these roosts in impressive numbers, and carefully dissecting and identifying their remains provides a better picture of the owl's food habits than even the most painstaking field observation. On numerous occasions, pellets revealed researchers' aluminum identification bands that had been attached to songbirds' feet.

If you come across a pellet and aren't sure which species you've found, the clue is in its size. Screech-Owl pellets tend to be about 1 inch long and half as thick. Bigger specimens (3 or even 4 inches long) offer a sign that you've stumbled across the lair of one of North America's most daunting predators: the Great Horned Owl (*Bubo virginianus*), also known as the Tiger Owl.

Circle through all of North, Central, and South America to the southernmost islands of Tierra del Fuego. In North America, very few wooded habitats remain unexploited by this species, and it is a common, if secretive, resident of urban parks and neighborhoods.

This species' young—usually two but at times as many as four or five in a clutch—hatch about a month after the females lay eggs. Although they are capable of flight and hunting on their own by two months of age, young birds receive some food from their parents for another five or six months, making their adolescence remarkably extended.

The Barred Owl

The Chocolate-Eyed Barred Owl (*Strix varia*) is a large species in which individual birds are mostly feathers. Named for the strong horizontal pattern along its upper breast, this forest-loving bird was long considered a characteristic inhabitant of southeastern swamps, but its range has expanded dramatically north and west

1. The Barred Owl is known for its horizontal pattern and abundant feathers.

2. Young barn owls in a nest box.

3. Despite population declines in other regions, the Western Screech-Owl is still abundant in the Southwest.

Attracting Your Local Species

It's more difficult to attract owls than chickadees or woodpeckers to your yard, but some general practices can make your land more appealing to these nocturnal visitors. Like all animals, owls need food and shelter. In addition to providing nest boxes, resist the urge to trim your trees and bushes. As creatures of the night, owls prefer those dense, dark tangles that we might be tempted to tidy up. As long as dead trees don't immediately threaten your roof and eaves, leave them as perches and potential nest sites.

Even if owls don't move in to roost or breed, they may be hunting on your property. Leave any messy corners of your yard as they are. Owls seek bugs and rodents; the more small nocturnal animals moving about, the more likely that owls will come to investigate. Try refilling your birdfeeders in the early evening to draw mice and large invertebrates that are irresistible to owls.

Build It, and They Will Come

There's no need to be fancy when constructing nest boxes; choose unpainted, untreated scrap lumber. To create your own nest box, cut slats of wood to the rough dimensions and nail or screw the pieces together. Cut the entrance with a jigsaw or build the front of the box out of two pieces. Make the roof larger than the floor to provide an overhang for shade and protection from rain.

Research the owls in your neighborhood before making your box; larger species require larger nest boxes. Barred Owls are unlikely to move into anything smaller than 15 inches long by 15 inches deep by 30 inches high (38 × 38 × 76 cm), but Barn Owls' boxes can be cubical at 15 × 15 × 15 inches (38 × 38 × 38 cm) all around.

The most important variable is the size of the entrance. Eastern, Western, and Whiskered Screech-Owls prefer the entrance hole to be 3 inches (7.6 cm) in diameter, whereas the tiny Elf Owl will accept an entrance as small as 1½ inches (3.8 cm) across. Barred Owls require an 8-inch (20cm) diameter circle for access. Great Horned Owls will accept large boxes, but they are more likely to use simple platforms about 2 feet (61 cm) square; if you build one, be sure to add a low railing to keep the eggs from rolling off.

Regardless of the species you hope to attract, add a couple of inches/centimeters of wood shavings to the bottom of the box to cushion the eggs. Carefully install your box at an appropriate height, ideally with a southeastern exposure to let the occupants enjoy a sunbath. To get up-close views, you can mount small cameras—"nest cams"—inside the boxes to monitor the birds. Don't otherwise disturb them, though.

since the mid-twentieth century. Now it is perhaps the most reliably seen of all breeding owls in British Columbia and Washington.

Although they retain their preference for heavily wooded habitats, Barred Owls also happily colonize treed suburbs and large parks. When humans planted trees across vast stretches of once-inhospitable regions, they probably enabled the westward movement of this species. Unfortunately, the species' arrival in so many new areas has resulted in some significant problems for other owl species, including the rare Northern Spotted Owl and the once-abundant Western Screech-Owl.

The Western Screech-Owl and the Elf Owl

Nature's balance remains somewhat more intact in the American Southwest, where the bubbly voiced Western Screech-Owl is common and familiar in many yards. A virtual twin of its eastern cousin, the Western Screech-Owl spends its days roosting in abandoned woodpecker holes in trees and giant cacti, venturing forth at night to dine on insects and mice. This cryptically colored species shares the saguaro deserts with the aptly named Elf Owl (*Micrathene whitneyi*).

Neither species shies away from inhabited areas. The Elf Owls' chips, barks, and cackles are among the characteristic nighttime sounds of residential neighborhoods in southern Arizona. The tiniest owl in the world, the average Elf is significantly outweighed by the Red-Winged Blackbird, and its diet remains accordingly dainty; moths and crickets comprise more than three-quarters of its food. It sometimes captures them at porch lights in the desert night.

Made in America

Nineteen species of owl breed in the United States. The Southwestern desert boasts the greatest diversity, with eleven nesting species in Arizona. The Pygmy Owl, barely larger than the little Elf

Owl, is a partly diurnal species of lowland and mountain habitats; northern and mountain Pygmy Owls commonly breed from western Canada into Mexico, whereas Ferruginous Pygmy Owls remain a scarce resident of Arizona and Texas's Rio Grande Valley.

Very common in the Rocky Mountains, the equally small Flammulated Owl, named for the flame-shaped spots on its wings, is so secretive that it is almost never seen. The Long-Legged Burrowing Owl is unique in its terrestrial habits: a bird of the Great Plains and far West, with a smaller population in Florida, it nests and roosts in holes in the ground, often expropriating prairie dogs and ground squirrels.

Closely related and very similar to the Western and Eastern Screech-Owls, the Whiskered Screech-Owl inhabits oak woodlands along the Mexican border. Sadly, the rare Spotted Owl's numbers are decreasing in the Pacific Northwest and in the mountains of the Southwest.

Four other owls—Long-Eared, Short-Eared, Northern Saw-Whet, and Barn—remain widespread across the continent. Long-Eared and Northern Saw-Whet Owls are reclusive woodland birds most often seen in winter, when they migrate south to roost in conifers.

The Short-Eared Owl is a species of open country, nesting on the ground and feeding in marshes, prairies, and large farm fields. It can often be seen hunting low over fields during the day. The ghostly white Barn Owl also inhabits open areas but nests in caves and abandoned buildings.

Among the most desired species of North American birds are the so-called "northern owls," which don't always migrate south in winter but sometimes travel in great numbers. The longest North American owl is the Great Gray Owl, an uncommon species of the boreal forest. The small Boreal Owl is both scarce and secretive; it breeds across the northern portions of the continent and the Rocky Mountains. The Northern Hawk Owl is a long-tailed tundra species that's often active during the day. A white beauty the size of a Great Horned Owl, the Snowy Owl's periodic incursions into the United States are always noteworthy.

Hummingbirds—By John E. Riutta, Noah Strycker, Stephen Kress, and Elissa Wolfson

Often heard before they are seen—their brilliant jewel-toned feathers glinting in the sun as they whir through the garden—hummingbirds remind an observer more of some exquisitely wrought mechanical toy than a living bird. Hummingbirds have captured hearts and captivated minds as far back as history records.

Different Types

Hummingbirds—along with swifts, treeswifts, and, according to some authorities, Owlet-Nightjars—belong to the taxonomic order

Apodiformes. It means "those without feet," an unfortunate name that likely gave rise to the "hummingbirds have no feet" myth. The family of hummingbirds itself is named Trochilidae (very appropriately meaning "small bird") and contains the second highest number of individual species of any bird family in the world. The family Trochilidae is split into two subfamilies: the Phaethornithinae, or "hermits," a small group of species found in areas of Mexico and Central and South America, and the Trochilinae, or "typical," which encompasses all of the rest. Ornithologists don't agree on exactly how many different genera and species of hummingbirds exist. Current lists record between 328 and 338 species grouped into between 102 and 108 total genera.

1. A Costa's Hummingbird.

The Black-Chinned (2) and Ruby-Throated (3) Hummingbirds are appropriately named.

Hummer Homes

Hummingbirds live exclusively in the Western Hemisphere. Collectively, their ranges span from the southernmost tip of South America to Alaska and northern Canada. Within this vast expanse, however, some species are highly migratory, with breeding areas that are thousands of miles from their wintering habitats. Other species are highly localized to areas perhaps as small as an individual forest or mountainside.

According to Operation RubyThroat (www.rubythroat.org), a prominent hummingbird conservation organization, twenty-seven species have been recorded in the United States and Canada. Of these, eighteen species could be considered commonly seen, with sixteen species breeding in this geographic area. Arizona and Texas lead the list of states recording the most hummingbird species within their borders (eighteen species each), with New Mexico right behind (seventeen species). Among Canadian provinces, British Columbia has recorded the most hummingbird species (eight). Only the state of Hawaii and the provinces of Nunavut and the Northwest Territories have no hummingbird records at all.

Hummingbirds:
What Am I Doing Wrong?

—By Sharon Stiteler

You have a hummingbird feeder out, but you haven't had any takers. You might wonder, "What gives?" Instead, one of the questions you should ask yourself is, "When was the last time I cleaned out my hummingbird feeder?"

Sugar water can ferment quickly, especially during warm weather. In a feeder in direct sunlight, it can ferment in as little as two days; in the shade, five days. You usually can tell when the solution ferments because it appears cloudy. Hummingbirds won't visit a feeder filled with fermented, moldy nectar. Would you want to drink a soda that's been sitting in a can in direct sunlight for a week? Hummingbirds don't like it, either.

Even if your sugar water is fresh, make sure that the feeder itself is not dirty. When you bring in your feeder to refill it, look it over. If you see little black patches of mold, clean the feeder with bleach and rinse it very thoroughly.

The time of year and where you live also can determine your hummingbird traffic. During migration, more hummingbirds might pass through your yard, as opposed to the few locals that may set up breeding territories in the summer. Remain patient and keep your feeders clean; hummingbirds eventually will show up.

Sometimes, unexpected guests will show up at your sugar-water feeder. Some species in particular don't realize that it's a "hummingbird feeder" and will partake of the sweet water themselves. These other birds include warblers, woodpeckers, orioles, and House Finches.

Apart from getting a hummingbird feeder with absolutely no perches, there's not much you can do. Birds are determined. If big birds won't allow hummingbirds to feed, consider placing an oriole feeder a few feet away. An oriole feeder's larger openings make it easier for bigger birds to perch and drink the sugar water. Also try offering a small dish of grape jelly to attract orioles; they tend to prefer jelly over sugar water.

Despite filling it daily, you might wake up to an empty feeder every morning. You might find it on the ground or, in some cases, completely gone. Generally, the most likely suspect is a raccoon, although black bears are possible culprits, too. If you live in the Southwest,

fruit bats might drain the sugar water from your feeder at night. If this becomes a problem, you can bring the feeder inside at night.

Wasps and hornets also can make unwelcome visits to hummingbird feeders, especially during late summer. Some hummingbirds can feed around the insects, but too many wasps can become a deterrent. You can help by purchasing feeders without any yellow coloration; yellow tends to attract more wasps and hornets than red does. Also, place a small amount of salad oil around the feeding ports. It will feel too slippery for the wasps and hornets to land on, and the hummingbird's long bill enables him to feed easily without being exposed to the oil.

Also, hang wasp traps near the feeder. Fill the traps with a heavy sugar solution, such as equal parts water and either sugar, maple syrup, or soda, to attract wasps' attention. Hummingbirds won't become attracted to the traps because they aren't red.

Ants also enjoy sugar-water feeders. The best way to deal with that problem is to purchase an ant moat. Many feeders have this feature built in, but you can purchase them separately and hang the moat right above the feeder if necessary. When filled with water, the moat will prevent the ants from crossing the moat to get to the sugar water.

Another problem that you might encounter at a hummingbird feeder is the aggressive nature of the species. In some yards, especially in urban areas, only one or two hummingbirds might show up at the feeder, and one hummer will take it over, not allowing others to share the food source.

Believe it or not, hummingbirds are naturally aggressive. Even after male and female hummingbirds mate, the female goes to her own territory, builds the nest, and raises the young on her own. In an urban area with fewer insects and nectar-rich plants, a single bird will guard a feeding station fiercely.

Hummingbirds might seem a little high maintenance, but it's worth the work to bring them over, especially when you catch sight of their iridescent feathers flashing all the colors of the rainbow.

Humdingers

—By Sharon Stiteler

The next time you watch a hummingbird glide gracefully through your yard to sip at your sugar-water feeder, consider these interesting facts about the various species:

- A hummer's heart can beat about 500 times per minute when foraging or perching. It can reach as high as 1,200 beats per minute when chasing a rival from a food source.
- Hummingbirds flap their wings about 60 to 80 times per second. During a courtship, a ruby-throated hummingbird male can beat his wings as fast as 200 times per second!
- According to bird-banding records, the oldest hummer was a Broad-Tailed Hummingbird that lived to twelve years and two months of age. The species' average lifespan is typically three to four years, however.
- Hummingbirds cannot walk. Their very small toes and feet are used strictly for perching. If a hummingbird wants to turn around on a branch, it must flap its wings, fly up, turn around in midair, and then land on the perch.

Physical Differences

In many ways, hummingbirds look like most other birds. They have feathers and wings, and they lay eggs. In some aspects of their anatomy, however, they are quite different, and these differences help to give them some of their most fascinating abilities.

Length and Weight

Perhaps more so than any one other single physical feature, hummingbirds are known for their small size. Most adults measure between 2.3 and 4.7 inches (6 and 12 cm) in length (bill included) and weigh between .1 and .2 ounces (3 and 6 grams). The smallest hummingbird species, the Bee Hummingbird of Cuba (also the smallest bird species in the world), has an average adult length of only 2 inches (5 cm) and weighs less than .07 ounce (2 grams).

1. A Rufous Hummingbird in an adult's hand gives some perspective on the bird's size.

2. The tiniest of the tiny, Cuba's Bee Hummingbird.

3. Hummingbirds need their long bills and tongues to reach the nectar deep in tubular flowers.

Bill and Tongue

The long, thin bill of a hummingbird, another well-known feature of its anatomy, is particularly well adapted for retrieving nectar from flower blossoms and for capturing tiny insects in their hiding places. Many species of hummingbird have evolved bills specially suited for particular shapes of flower varieties.

Likewise, the hummingbird's tongue is superbly suited to the task of retrieving nectar by a rapid lapping technique. To increase the amount of nectar retrieved, the tip of the tongue is divided and covered with tiny bristles that capture and hold liquid for return to the bill, where the nectar is squeezed out and swallowed.

Skeleton

Among all of the superb fliers of the avian world, few can rival hummingbirds when it comes to having a skeleton perfectly adapted for flight. Like most birds, the majority of a hummingbird's bones are pneumatized (porous rather than solid, a weight-reducing adaptation for flight).

To provide a sound foundation for their powerful pectoral flight muscles, hummingbirds have rib cages made up of eight pairs of ribs rather than the six pairs found in most birds. They also have very large breastbone keels to which those muscles attach that extend nearly the entire length of their bodies, from their shoulders to their tails.

Hummingbird skeletons also differ from those of most other birds in their ball-and-socket shoulder joints, which allow a range of rotation as wide as 180 degrees (an essential element in their ability to hover in place). Unlike almost all other birds, the "wrist" and "elbow" joints in a hummingbird's wings are fused, making the wings rigid in flight and able to most efficiently use the force exerted on them by the powerful flight muscles located in the chest.

The Broad-Billed Hummingbird displays jewel tones of green and blue on its head and body.

Feathers

Of course, the feature of the hummingbird that attracts so much attention remains its plumage. Despite having the least average number of feathers of any bird family, hummingbirds more than make up for this lack of quantity through quality. It often surprises many hummer aficionados to see that, when viewed under indirect light, hummingbirds' vividly colored feathers are actually rather flat, often dark, colors. The brilliant jewel-like and flashy metallic colors that make their feathers so noticeable come from melanin pigment arranged in flat platelets. These platelets contain tiny air bubbles that serve as reflectors and cause the feathers to appear iridescent. When light shines directly on a hummingbird feather from a particular direction, some wavelengths of that light are absorbed while others are reflected. Thus, the feather appears to the observer as a vibrant, sometimes even metallic, color.

The most iridescent of hummingbird feathers appear on males in their gorgets (throat patches) and, in some species, on their crowns. These feathers are arranged in a way so that the hummingbird can position them and reflect in the same direction all at once, producing the seemingly electric flash used in courtship displays.

Frequent Fliers

Thanks to its ball-and-socket shoulder joints, unusual wing structure, and strong flight muscles, a hummingbird's wings can move in a figure-eight motion. Because of this, hummingbirds

can fly forward, straight up, straight down, and backward. Hummingbirds also can hover in place, which is something that no other bird species is capable of doing and is a crucial ability for obtaining nectar from hanging flower blossoms.

Anyone watching hummingbirds in flight might assume that they are exceedingly fast fliers. In fact, their small size and ability to rise vertically and depart instantaneously without needing to pick up speed gives the illusion of exceptionally fast flight. The actual flight speed of a hummingbird is seldom more than 25 miles (40 km) per hour, although a bird might more than double this speed during escapes and short aerial courtship dives.

Feeding Frenzy

Hummingbirds feed mostly on the nectar of flowers. Of course, they visit feeders containing sugar water, too. While providing tremendous energy, natural nectar and sugar water cannot supply

1. The unique ability to hover in place enables hummingbirds to feed on nectar.

2. Sugar water is a ready source of energy for calorie-burning hummers.

3. A Ruby-Throated Hummingbird provides for her young.

What Is Torpor?

Hummingbirds experience a rapid loss of body heat when the air turns cold. The challenge of keeping warm during the day can be met through a continual cycle of feeding. At night, however, when sleep becomes a necessity, hummingbirds have evolved a remarkable adaptation called *torpor* to allow them to survive chilly nights.

In torpor, the hummingbird slows its metabolism to a mere fraction, perhaps as little as 5 percent, of its normal rate. In doing so, its body temperature falls to a level barely above what is necessary to stay alive—a sort of self-induced hypothermia. The dramatically reduced metabolic rate, combined with a much lower body temperature, requires significantly less energy, allowing the bird to survive until it can resume foraging.

Torpor is not unique to hummingbirds and is better known by a more common name when it occurs over a long period of time: hibernation. Unlike hibernation, torpor in hummingbirds lasts only a few hours, and it might occur on any night of the year, whenever it is needed. Hummingbirds likely emerge from their periods of torpor at the call of their internal alarm clocks. Vibrating their wings and slowly shivering raises their body temperature, heartbeat, and respiration to normal levels. Within about half an hour, the hummingbird becomes fully alert and ready to begin foraging.

the proteins, fats, and other nutrients that hummingbirds need, so they also eat many types of small, soft-bodied insects and arachnids.

Unlike many birds, hummingbirds feed more or less constantly throughout the day. The primary reason for this is that their metabolic rate is astonishingly fast, especially when in flight. With a body temperature averaging 105 degrees Fahrenheit (40.5 degrees Celsius), a flying hummingbird has a heart rate of roughly 1,200 beats per minute and might burn calories at a rate as high as eight times its normal resting rate.

Because of this, hummingbirds must consume between three and seven calories each day in order to survive. It may not seem like much, but to put that into human perspective: a person who eats 2,000 calories each day would need to consume more than 88,570 calories, given the differences in body size and weight.

Reproducing and Raising Young

Just like all other modern birds, hummingbirds lay eggs. A typical hummingbird clutch contains two eggs, each roughly the size of a pea and laid a few days apart. Unlike most other birds, in hummingbirds, only the females perform the tasks of building the nests, incubating the eggs, and feeding the young. Female hummingbirds select their nesting areas and build their nests before mating occurs. Nesting locations can be as low as 6 feet or as high as 50 feet off the ground.

Most hummers build open nests roughly the size of half a walnut shell and made of bud scales held together with spider silk. The outsides of nests are camouflaged by lichen, moss, and other natural materials, making them among the best hidden of all birds' nests. Thistle, cattail, or dandelion down pads the nest interiors.

Hummingbird Feeders

—By Sharon Stiteler

Before purchasing a feeder, the first question you should ask yourself is, "How easily can I open that feeder?" A clean feeder proves essential to attracting hummingbirds. Fermented sugar water and mold can be lethal, and most hummingbirds avoid a dirty feeder. If you cannot open the feeder easily, you probably won't clean it very often.

My personal favorite feeder design is the saucer style. The dish shape has a lid with feeding ports that fit over the top of the dish. Hummingbirds can dip their long bills and tongues into the dish to get the sugar water. The top cover comes off easily, making cleaning a cinch, and it prevents the liquid from spilling.

Many people like the traditional hourglass-shaped hummingbird feeder, but cleaning the tube can become challenging. Also, this style of feeder has a tendency to drip when the wind blows.

Speaking of dripping, some people like dripper feeders, which are usually are made of hand-blown glass and have a plug and tube on the bottom, from which the hummers sip the sugar water.

Sugar water is a subject of great debate among hummingbird experts. The recipe that most closely resembles natural plant nectar is four parts water to one part sugar (only sugar—do not use any other type of sweetener). You can store the excess in your refrigerator for up to two weeks.

Another way to provide food for hummingbirds is to set out a tray of slightly overripe fruit. When your bananas become too ripe for you to eat or the melons grow old, set them out, and fruit flies will follow, providing an additional source of protein for hummingbirds. This also can encourage a female hummer to build a nest in your yard.

If one hummingbird takes over your feeder, try setting out two feeders far apart. Another option is to hang more feeders than one hummer can defend, say, four or six feeders on a single deck. One hummingbird won't be able to guard them all, and others will have a chance to feed on the sugar water.

1. A backyard pond should provide an area for easy entry and exit.

2. Some hummingbirds prefer semi-open areas on the edges of gardens or woods.

3. Hummingbirds love to bathe in very shallow depths.

The female will incubate the eggs for 12 to 22 days, and the length of time it takes for the eggs to hatch varies by species; however, it is strongly influenced by how much time the female spends on the nest each day and the weather in the nesting area (cool temperatures delay hatching). Once hatched, the hummingbird chicks feed on insects regurgitated by the female. The young develop rapidly and, by roughly twenty days of age, have outgrown the nest and leave it. Even when they are fledglings, the female continues to tend them for a few more weeks.

Bathing—By Susan Day

If you think hummingbirds at feeders look adorable, you haven't seen anything compared to watching them when they get around water! These tiny acrobats dip, dive, dance, and frolic like crazy when they bathe. Because hummingbirds are so small and their habits are so different from other backyard birds, you need to think small when planning water sources for them in your backyard.

Bathing helps hummingbirds maintain their feathers, which must remain in tip-top condition to keep up with the frenetic pace of foraging and feeding. A hummingbird typically will bathe in a stream, in the splash or mist of a waterfall, or during a light rain. Hummingbirds flutter their wings and dart through the mist, or they stand along a stream or on a wet rock, using their heads to flick droplets of water over their backs so it runs over their bodies. They also rub their bodies against wet grass or foliage.

After bathing, hummingbirds preen by using their bills to collect oil from a gland located underneath the base of the tail. They spread the oil onto their feathers, forming a waxy surface that protects the feathers so they don't become dry and brittle. A hummingbird's daily routine includes several preening, fluffing, scratching, and oiling sessions.

Hummers have short legs and can't walk or swim, so they need very shallow birdbaths—only about a quarter inch deep. Hummingbirds don't wade into a bath like other birds do; instead, they perch on the edges of the bath and flutter their wings in the extremely shallow water. Small saucer birdbaths or even little plates will work for hummingbird bathtubs. Place them a couple of feet off the ground, because hummingbirds typically don't like to fly to the ground to drink or bathe.

Mold and algae grow quickly in warm, shallow water, so birdbaths should be cleaned frequently. A quick daily scrub with a brush or squirt of a hose is usually all it takes. If that doesn't do the trick, try eco-friendly products that contain natural enzymes. Another reason to keep birdbaths squeaky clean is that stagnant water attracts mosquitoes.

If you want or already maintain a large pond, you most likely can modify it by adding showers and tubs for hummers. Include a waterfall that creates mist, or arrange rocks to form hummer-sized puddles. Landscape around the rocks with nectar flowers such as cardinal flowers, salvias, or penstemons, and hang a few hummingbird feeders nearby. As long as a pond is shallow and accessible, the birds probably will find and use it. Sometimes, hummingbirds will dip down to the water in a pond and surf on their breasts along the surface.

Identifying Hummingbirds

Hummingbirds can be difficult to identify. To identify a hummer, you have to go beyond passive admiration to actively noticing what you see and hear. The finer points of hummingbird identification challenge even the experts. Even so, most hummers can be separated relatively easily. To make things easier, hummingbirds are fearless and attracted to backyard feeders, allowing plenty of opportunities for close study.

Step 1: Location

One of the simplest ways to identify a hummer is to consider its location. Remember, fewer than thirty species of hummingbirds have been recorded in North America, and most of those have restricted ranges or are extremely rare. Just one species—the Ruby-Throated Hummingbird—regularly appears over the entire eastern half of the continent.

At your feeders and nectar plants, you probably won't see a South American hummingbird. You shouldn't expect to see a Black-Chinned Hummingbird if you live in the East, and you're unlikely to see a Ruby-Throated Hummingbird in the western states. Hummers, like other species, stick to home ranges, rarely venturing far from their territories.

1. The Blue-Throated Hummingbird is found mainly in a small area of the Southwest.

2. Anna's Hummingbirds are year-round residents of the temperate western states.

Before you look through your binoculars, consult the range maps in your field guide, colored to show the ranges where species might appear. Cross out all of the species that do not occur in your area, and you've eliminated most possibilities. Once you figure out which hummingbirds to expect in your region, you'll be well on your way to identifying the ones at your feeders and plants.

Step 2: Season

The season of the year might help you. Hummingbirds don't hang onto the backs of geese, according to a popular myth, but most North American hummingbirds migrate incredible distances between their summer and winter habitats.

But wait! Take another look at those range maps in your field guide. In western states, Anna's Hummingbirds stay in the same areas year-round. If you live in the West and see a hummingbird in the winter, it's almost certainly an Anna's. Anywhere else in the United States, examine hummingbirds very closely because they should have moved south to warmer climates by that time of year.

Step 3: Visual Features

Carefully observing a bird's physical characteristics is the only way to make an absolute identification. Location, season, and other attributes provide valuable supporting evidence, but you must examine the bird to identify it.

Like other birds, hummers have helpful markings, but not every field mark is created equal. Do a little homework in your field guide to figure out which features are most important. When studying a hummingbird, look at the big picture first, considering location and season. Overall coloration and size are more important than the shape of the fifth tail feather. The five most important field marks of North American hummingbirds are gorget color and shape, body coloration, bill color and shape, tail pattern, and overall size and structure.

1. The Calliope Hummingbird is streaked rather than solid.

2. The Buff-Bellied Hummingbird has a red bill with a dark tip.

3. The tiny Calliope Hummingbird at a sugar-water feeder.

Gorget Color and Shape

Adult male hummingbirds have a unique patch of iridescent feathers on the throat called a *gorget*. When angled toward the sun, these feathers catch the rays and shine with unparalleled brilliance. If you're observing a hummingbird with a gorget, consider yourself lucky because adult males are the easiest to identify. If you see patchy or scattered iridescent feathers on an otherwise dull-looking throat, it's either a young male or a female.

Males of different species show various combinations of gorget color and shape. For instance, a Ruby-Throated Hummingbird sports a blackish-purple iridescence confined to the throat, whereas Anna's and Costa's Hummingbirds have elongated lower corners on their gorgets. A Calliope Hummingbird's gorget runs in parallel streaks down the throat, whereas Rufous and Allen's Hummingbirds have reddish-orange gorgets.

Body Coloration

Most hummingbirds appear green, at least to some extent. Males are decorated with bright gorgets, but females can be entirely iridescent green. Look for any patches that aren't green.

Rufous and Allen's Hummingbirds look distinctively reddish-orange, with limited green on the back and head. Broad-Tailed and Calliope Hummingbirds show a variable orange wash on the sides and flanks. Black-Chinned, Anna's, and Costa's Hummingbirds completely lack rufous (reddish) coloring.

Bill Color and Shape

Hummingbirds have very long, slender bills, adapted to suck nectar out of deep flowers. Take a closer look, and you'll see that some species have unique beaks, especially in southeastern Arizona; for example, Broad-Billed and Violet-Crowned Hummingbirds have reddish bills. If the bill is not straight and black, you might be onto something special.

What's Not a Hummingbird?

In desert regions of North America, insects such as sphinx moths (sometimes called hummingbird moths or hawk-moths) mimic a hummingbird's flight, size shape, and color. Sphinx moths, which fly during daylight hours, even confuse experienced birders. Best known among the look-alike sphinx moths is probably the white-lined sphinx, which is intricately striped with cryptic colors and often seen feeding on flowers in suburban gardens. Insect look-alikes fulfill the same ecological niche as hummingbirds, pollinating flowers by hovering to gather nectar, but don't let them fool you.

Certain butterflies and bees might resemble hummingbirds. How can you tell them apart? Butterflies usually fly with a much slower wing beat and are unlikely to confuse you for long. Large bees—such as carpenter bees—might briefly fly by a flower, but upon closer observation, you should detect their true identity.

Hummer How-Do-You-Do

When the female hummingbird's nest is nearly complete, she goes in search of a male. She will leave her nesting area and fly to a nearby neutral area or to the established territory of a male of her species. Once she meets a male, he will make introductory greeting displays that involve vocalizations and diving. If the female finds the male unappealing, she will leave the area or respond with aggression.

If, however, she is impressed with his initial overtures and remains in the area without attacking him, the male will move closer in a series of shuttle displays: swinging back and forth while doing his best to flash his throat feathers to assure her of his virility.

Actual mating generally takes place in the male's territory or somewhere nearby, and it is assumed that coupling takes place on a tree branch or on the ground. After mating, the two birds part ways. The female returns to her nesting area in final preparation for egg-laying, and the male resumes his feeding and awaits the arrival of another female into his territory.

Tail Pattern

In tricky cases, experts sometimes examine a hummingbird's tail. In flight, the tail feathers spread like a fan; experts scrutinize flight photos to determine the tail pattern. Although most hummingbird species can be identified without using this feature, the amount of rufous coloring on the tail is especially helpful in distinguishing between female and young male Calliope, Broad-Tailed, Rufous, and Allen's Hummingbirds, which overlap in parts of their western ranges. Some Rufous and Allen's, in particular, remain impossible to accurately identify in the field. To tell those individuals apart, you'd actually have to measure the width of specific tail feathers.

Overall Size and Structure

Always important but often somewhat subjective is the physical shape of the hummingbird. Is it small? Large? Elongated? Size and structure require some experience to interpret correctly, and relative size is easiest to judge when two species appear side by side at a feeder or nectar plant.

The Calliope Hummingbird is the smallest bird in North America and appears tiny even next to other hummingbirds. The Magnificent Hummingbird, a regular in southeastern Arizona, is sometimes big enough to perch and tilt the feeder. Black-Chinned Hummingbirds look relatively lanky compared to compact Costa's Hummingbirds.

Step 4: Other Factors

In your observation, you might discover important clues that are barely touched upon in field guides. For instance, voice is rarely used to identify hummingbirds, even though each species makes unique vocalizations. The squeaky song of an Anna's Hummingbird is quite distinct. Even the sound produced by a hummer's wings varies by species; for example, male Broad-Tailed Hummingbirds hover with a high-pitched, whirring trill.

The male Broad-Tailed Hummingbird (right) makes a whirring noise with his wings when he hovers.

Behavior can provide clues to identification. In spring, most male hummingbirds perform flight displays in specific patterns to defend territories and attract females. For example, the male Rufous Hummingbird starts high, descends quickly, and pulls up at the last second in a J-shaped dive. Flight displays alone can clinch an identification.

Observing the habitat is also useful. Calliope Hummingbirds nest in high-elevation riparian zones, whereas Rufous Hummingbirds congregate in montane meadows in late summer. Anna's Hummingbirds are common year-round in lowland suburbs.

Furthermore, some hummers are attracted to particular types of flowers, while others prefer coniferous forests. Experts have hypothesized that some hummingbirds prefer to set up territory in the vicinity of hawk nests, which affords them protection from predators.

Step 5: Rarities

For some reason, hummingbirds occasionally show up far from their normal ranges. A Ruby-Throated Hummingbird in the eastern United States is common, but it's newsworthy on the West Coast. When a hummingbird shows up far from home, this causes quite a stir in the birding community.

If you believe that a rare hummingbird is at your feeder or nectar plant, study it carefully and take notes and—if possible—many photographs. Before you decide to call the bird a rarity, try to eliminate all usual and unusual variations of a common species. Sometimes, individual hummers show odd plumages, and albino hummingbirds lack pigment on their feathers and appear totally white. Also consider that hummingbirds could have pollen on their foreheads, making them appear yellow, or an individual could have lost several feathers in a run-in with a housecat, giving its wing a different shape.

On the following pages, you'll become acquainted with twelve fascinating hummingbird varieties.

Allen's Hummingbird (*Selasphorus sasin*)

The genus name of this scarlet-throated hummingbird means "flame-bearing." Allen's is a close relative of the Rufous Hummingbird, and females and immature birds of the two species are nearly impossible to distinguish. Allen's and Anna's are the only two common nesting hummingbirds in Northern California's gardens.

Length	3¾ inches (9.5 cm)
Wingspan	4¼ inches (10.8 cm)
Migration	Moves north from Mexico up the Pacific coast in late winter. Nonmigratory populations live in Southern California.
Habitat	Nests primarily in California and prefers brushy hillsides, canyons, parks, coastal gardens, and mountain meadows.
Field marks	Reddish-orange flanks, rump and tail; metallic-green mid-back and cap; flame-red throat; relatively long bill.
Voice	Its call is a high, hard chip: "*tyuk*." Males' wings create a high, buzzy trill.
Nesting	Nests sit in trees up to 90 feet above ground, usually in dense shade. The female lays two pure white eggs and then incubates and feeds chicks.
Feeding	Prefers red, tubular flowers, including Indian paintbrush, penstemon, and California fuchsia.

Anna's Hummingbird (*Calypte anna*)

Anna's is the most widespread hummingbird on North America's Pacific slope. This adaptable species often lives in human habitats. During courtship, a male stakes out territory over a flower patch with a rich nectar supply. A female enters the male's territory, mates, and then leaves to build a nest. Unlike similar hummingbirds, Anna's is not migratory.

Length	4 inches (10 cm)
Wingspan	4¾ inches (12 cm)
Migration	Lives year-round on West Coast and either does not migrate or travels only short distances for food.;
Habitat	Open woodlands, shrubby areas, backyards and parks.
Field marks	Flight: Tail held stationary and aligned with body; gray-edged tail feathers. Sitting: Short, straight bill; long, sloping forehead; dark head with pale eye-ring. The male has an iridescent rose-red crown and throat; the female has a gray breast and red throat patch.
Voice	The call sounds squeaking and grating, and the feeding call is "*chick*."
Nesting	The female builds a nest using plant down and spider webs, camouflaged by lichens. She lays one to three pure white eggs and then incubates and feeds chicks.
Feeding	Eats tiny insects, spiders, and flower nectar from red-flowering currant and fuchsia.

Black-Chinned Hummingbird (*Archilochus alexandri*)
Named for the male's black throat, this species is widespread over much of the West during nesting season and almost entirely absent in winter. Courting males perform "pendulum" displays, whirring back and forth in a wide arc.

Length	3¾ inches (9.5 cm)
Wingspan	4¾ inches (12 cm)
Migration	From the western United States to Mexico each fall and back each spring.
Habitat	Low-elevation, semiarid river groves; chaparral, parks, and suburban gardens.
Field marks	Slender, small-headed, and long-billed. Males have distinctive black throats with purple and white bands below and iridescent green above. Females have grayish-green backs and crowns.
Voice	The call sounds like a husky, soft "*ti-up*" or "*ti-pip*." The song is a high warble.
Nesting	Its nest is a deep cup of plant fiber and spider webs, camouflaged with lichen, built in a deciduous tree. The female lays two white eggs and then incubates and feeds chicks.
Feeding	Ocotillo, desert honeysuckle, and tree tobacco in arid regions. This species repeatedly flicks its tail while feeding.

Blue-Throated Hummingbird (*Lampornis clemenciae*)
The Blue-Throated has the largest wingspan of any breeding hummingbird in the United States. This bold, aggressive bird uses size to its advantage, vigorously chasing other hummers from favored flowers or feeders. Its range is limited to a few mountains near the Mexican border.

Length	5 inches (12.7 cm)
Wingspan	8 inches (20 cm)
Migration	Most American birds depart in fall; Mexican birds are permanent residents.
Habitat	Shady canyons in lower mountains, typically near wooded streams.
Field marks	Often fans its long, broad tail. Males have subtle blue throats and black tails with flashy white corners.
Voice	The call is a monotonously repeated, high, clear "seek," and the song is a soft, repeated, rattling "*situ-tee trrrrrr.*"
Nesting	Its nest is a plant fiber cup, often sheltered by an overhanging limb or eaves, distinctively covered with green moss. The female lays two white eggs and then incubates and feeds chicks.
Feeding	Feeds heavily on small insects and spiders, enabling survival during dry seasons, and favors penstemon, cardinal flower, and tree tobacco.

Broad-Billed Hummingbird (*Cyanthus latirostris*)

The Broad-Bill's name stems from the relatively wide, flattened base of its bill. Within their limited US range in the Arizona, New Mexico, and southwestern Texas lowlands, these hummers are abundant in summer, rarely venturing to high elevations.

Length	4 inches (10 cm)
Wingspan	5¾ inches (14.6 cm)
Migration	From southwestern United States to Mexico each fall.
Habitat	Low oak woodlands, desert canyons, wooded streamsides, and mesquite thickets.
Field marks	Stocky body; reddish-orange bill; broad, bluish-black tail. Males have iridescent green and blue bodies, blue throats, and notched tails. Females have gray undersides and dark cheek patches.
Voice	The call is a dry, sharp "*seek*" or "*tek*," and the song is a high, crackling, and tinkly "*situ ti ti ti ti ti ti zreet zreet zreet.*"
Nesting	Nests are built in deciduous shrubs up to 9 feet high. Unlike other hummers, a Broad-Bill uses no lichen to camouflage its nest. The female lays two white eggs and then incubates and feeds chicks.
Feeding	Favors insects and nectar from ocotillo, desert honeysuckle, tree tobacco, and bouvardia.

Broad-Tailed Hummingbird (*Selasphorus platycercus*)

The Broad-Tailed male creates high, metallic trilling sounds with its wing feathers as it flies; this is a characteristic summer sound in the western mountains. Courting males fly high and dive repeatedly. These hummers hover at flower masses, often darting and chasing one another from choice blossoms.

Length	4 inches (10 cm)
Wingspan	5¼ inches (13.3 cm)
Migration	North through lowlands in early spring; south through mountains to Mexico in late summer.
Habitat	Mountain meadows and forests more than 10,000 feet high.
Field marks	Long body; long, broad tail; white eye-ring. Males have bronze-green backs and bright, rosy throats. Females have whitish underparts and reddish-brown flanks and tail sides.
Voice	The call is a high, sharp "*chip.*"
Nesting	The female makes a nest using spider webs and plant down, camouflaged with lichen, on horizontal branches about 20 feet high. She lays two white eggs and then incubates and feeds chicks.
Feeding	Nectar from red, tubular flowers, such as columbine and bouvardia.

Buff-Bellied Hummingbird (*Amazilia yucatanenesis*)

Residents of Mexico, Belize, and Guatemala, Buff-Bellied Hummingbirds are part of the tropical element in southern Texas, where they summer. They are the only hummingbirds to nest there regularly.

Length	4¼ inches (10.8 cm)
Wingspan	5¾ inches (14.6 cm)
Migration	Some remain in Texas throughout the winter; others fly north along the coast to upper Texas and Louisiana.
Habitat	Woodland edges, brushy areas with scattered trees, citrus groves, and suburban gardens.
Field marks	Overall dark color, bronze-green back, emerald green throat and breast, buffy cinnamon belly, red bill, reddish tail. Males and females look similar.
Voice	The call is a sharp, metallic, high "*smack*," given in short series of two to four notes.
Nesting	The female might reuse an old nest or will build a new one in a small tree or large shrub up to 10 feet high. She lays two white eggs and then incubates and feeds chicks.
Feeding	Prefers flower nectar from Turk's cap, mesquite, red yucca, and anacahuita.

Calliope Hummingbird (*Selasphorus calliope*)

The smallest bird in North America, the Calliope Hummingbird's previous genus name, *Stellula*, means "little star." Despite the birds' tiny size, they survive frigid mountain nights and migrate 3,000 miles annually. Males are recognizable by distinctively streaked, rosy throats.

Length	3¼ inches (8.2 cm)
Wingspan	3¼ inches (8.2 cm)
Migration	Some migrate from Canada to southern Mexico, mostly via the Rocky Mountains.
Habitat	Lives in high-elevation forest glades, meadows, and canyons.
Field marks	Short tail with short, thin bill. Males appear green above and white below, with unique reddish- and purple-streaked throat patches.
Voice	The call is a high, musical "*chip*," while the song is a very high, whistle-like "*tseee-ew*."
Nesting	Usually on conifer twigs, the nest is built to resemble part of the cone. The female lays two white eggs and then incubates and feeds chicks.
Feeding	Often feeds at lower flowers, avoiding aggression from larger hummers, and prefers orange and red tubular flowers, such as Indian paintbrush and lousewort. Calliopes also eat tiny insects.

Costa's Hummingbird (*Calypte costae*)

Male Costa's Hummingbirds perform daring aerial courtship displays, plunging downward with a continuous shrill whistle and then pulling up sharply and rising. The birds nest in the deserts of California, Arizona, and northwestern Mexico in late winter, avoiding the hot summer by migrating to the cooler West Coast in late spring.

Length	3½ inches (8.9 cm)
Wingspan	4¾ inches (12 cm)
Migration	Southwestern deserts to the coast.
Habitat	Sage scrublands; dry desert canyons with cactus, yucca, and ocotillo plants.
Field marks	Small, stocky body; short tail and neck; round head. Males have iridescent violet crowns and violet throat flares on either side of their necks. Females have green backs and brown crowns.
Voice	The call is a dry "*tink*," and the song is a thin, high, buzzy, rising and falling "*szeee-eeeeeeew*."
Nesting	The female builds a nest in sparsely leafed shrubs, including yucca. She lays two white eggs and then incubates and feeds chicks.
Feeding	Nectar from native desert flowers, including ocotillo, agave, desert honeysuckle, and chuparosa.

Magnificent Hummingbird (*Eugenes fulgens*)

One of the largest hummingbirds, the Magnificent's wing beats are slower than those of smaller hummers. Its species name, derived from the Latin *fulgere*, means "to gleam" or "to glitter." Some vigorously defend flower patches or feeders.

Length	5¼ inches (13.3 cm)
Wingspan	5¼ inches (13.3 cm)
Migration	From the southwestern United States, birds migrate a short distance south to Mexico each winter.
Habitat	Coniferous, high-elevation southwestern forests; pine-oak woods; and sycamore canyons.
Field marks	Large body, long bill. Males have purple crowns, emerald-green throats, and dark bellies. Females have green backs; pale, spotted throats; and pale tail edges. The slow wing beats might be discernible in flight.
Voice	The call is a sharp "*chip*," ranging from high to low.
Nesting	Nests are built on horizontal tree branches up to 60 feet high. The female lays two white eggs and then incubates and feeds chicks.
Feeding	In addition to nectar from agave and penstemon, the species forages in woodlands, picking insects from foliage and bark and spiders from webs.

Ruby-Throated Hummingbird (*Archilochus colubris*)

Named for the male's dazzling red throat, the Ruby-Throated is the only hummingbird regularly found in eastern North America. Despite their tiny size, these birds perform a marathon fall migration, traveling from southern Canada to Central America. Their wings beat an incredible eighty times per second. Males perform aerial displays in front of females during courtship.

Length	2¾–3½ inches (7–9 cm)
Wingspan	3–4¼ inches (8–11 cm)
Migration	Across Gulf of Mexico to Central America in winter. Some northern birds stay in North America and spend the winter along the southern Atlantic or Gulf.
Habitat	Sips nectar from flowers in open woods and gardens.
Field marks	Flight
Voice	Squeaky, high-pitched calls. The wings produce a faint, high buzz.
Nesting	The female uses plant fiber and spider webs to build her nests on forked branches. She lays two white, bean-sized eggs and then incubates and feeds chicks.
Feeding	Tiny insects and spiders; prefers tubular red flowers and nectar from impatiens and trumpet honeysuckle.

Rufous Hummingbird (*Selasphorus rufus*)

Although Rufous Hummingbirds weigh less than a American quarter, they can fly 500 miles without stopping. These compact dynamos have hearts proportionally larger than other hummers and vigorously chase rivals from feeding areas. They conserve energy by roosting at lower elevations with warmer temperatures and by feeding during the day in higher, colder areas. Rufous Hummingbirds' migration coincides with that of sapsuckers, whose nestholes provide an important source of sweet sap in early spring, when few flowers are available. The name *rufous* denotes the color red.

Length	3½ inches (8.9 cm)
Wingspan	4½ inches (11.4 cm)
Migration	Around 3,000 miles from Mexico to Alaska nesting sites.
Habitat	Streamsides, forest edges, and mountain meadows
Field marks	Relatively short-winged, it is the only rufous-backed North American hummingbird. The upper parts are red-brown, and the throat is flaming orange-red.
Voice	The call is a high, hard "*chip.*"
Nesting	The female lays two pure white eggs and then incubates and feeds chicks.
Feeding	Flower nectar, including native columbine, bleeding heart, Solomon's seal, and salmonberry.

5
Birds:
Part II

Birdscaping Basics—By Carole Sevilla Brown

Imagine that you are a very small bird about to make the incredible journey from Canada to your Central and South American wintering grounds. You spent days feeding constantly, and you added a nice layer of fat to fuel your travels. Even so, you weigh less than an American 25-cent coin.

One day, as dusk falls, you take to the skies. You fly all night, hearing the calls of thousands of other birds all around you. As dawn breaks, you need to find a safe place to sleep and refuel so that you can continue your journey that night. As you look down in the early-morning light, you cannot see a place to rest or food to eat. Below you are city skylines, parking lots, shopping centers, and housing developments.

It's a fact: habitat loss due to human activity remains the leading cause of bird population declines. Fortunately, landscaping for birds, or birdscaping, creates oases amid human development.

What Is Birdscaping?

Birdscaping involves much more than putting up a few bird feeders. It means arranging your property—whether a patio or expansive acreage—to create welcoming habitats for birds. It means planting a variety of plants to provide rest stops for migrating birds, safe places for breeding birds to raise their young, and food and shelter for winter residents.

Douglas Tallamy explains the importance of your birdscaped garden as follows in his book Bringing Nature Home: "Now, for the first time in its history, gardening has taken on a role that transcends the needs of the gardener. Like it or not, gardeners have become important players in the management of our nation's wildlife. It is now within the power of individual gardeners to do something that we all dream of doing: to make a difference."

Birdscaping is one of the very few activities that exemplifies the motto "If you build it, they will come." It also grants immediate gratification. I've seen proof of it many times in my work of designing and installing wildlife gardens. One day, I was putting a long waterfall into a pond because my client wanted to provide a water source for the birds. I was smoothing the liner into the trench when a Black-Throated Green Warbler suddenly appeared, hopping along the waterfall, even though there was no water yet.

Believe me: I got that liner installed, inserted the rocks to create the waterfall, and got the water running in record time. You, too, can experience this kind of moment after you choose to birdscape your garden.

Many birdscaping experts advise going for a more natural look rather than pristine and perfectly manicured.

What Birds Require

The philosophy behind birdscaping involves four aspects of wild birds' needs.

1. **Food:** Providing food entails more than setting out feeders. Landscaping your garden with native trees, shrubs, and perennials provides berries, seeds, fruits, and, most importantly, insects. While many adult birds eat seeds and berries, almost all land birds feed insects to their young. Over time, insects have developed mutually beneficial relationships with the plants native to your region, so the more native plants you keep in your yard, the more at home the birds will feel.

2. **Water:** Birds need year-round access to fresh water. In addition to traditional birdbaths, you can provide this necessary resource by adding a rain garden, wildlife pond, and storm-water bioswales (landscaped biofilters) to your property.

3. **Shelter:** Birds require safe places to hide from predators and avoid weather extremes. You can do more than just hang a few birdhouses: you can provide shelters similar to the ones that they'd find in natural areas by planting evergreen trees, shrubs, and hedgerows; leaving tree snags; and creating brush piles.

4. **Space:** Birds need room to move around and places to raise their young. Many birds prefer to raise their young in tree cavities, dense shrubs, leaf litter, and tree branches instead of birdhouses. While landscaping, add these elements to your yard to increase your land's appeal and the variety of birds that will choose to raise their young there.

Get to Know Your Space

Birdscaping begins with a good look at your property. Pull up a chair and get to know your property. Really discover what's going on there. Where is it sunny most of the day? Where are the shady spots? Where does the water collect when it rains? Which areas seem to dry out more quickly? What kind of soil do you have?

A well-birdscaped yard provides natural and man-made places for birds to build nests and take shelter.

Be sure to provide yourself with a spot to relax and observe.

The answers to these questions will help when you start choosing the best plants for your bird garden. Move your lawn chair to all of the different areas of your yard. Take time to observe how the birds already use your garden so you'll have an idea of how to enhance the various spaces.

Next, draw a rough map of your property, including property lines, your home and other buildings, paved surfaces, and existing trees, shrubs, garden beds, pathways, and lawn areas. Grab a tape measure and calculate your home's distance from each side to the property line. Also measure buildings, driveways, paths, and other elements of your space, including existing garden elements. Add your lawn, seating areas, barbecue area, compost pile, and other areas. Include driveways, paved spots, garden sheds, and patios.

Add all of these measurements to your map; they can help you choose the appropriate plants for each area of your yard. You don't want to plant a shrub with an 8-foot spread in a place where you have only 3 or 4 feet of available space, especially near pathways.

Another easy way to take inventory is to take a series of photographs of your garden through the seasons. Use a felt-tip marker to identify the plants in each picture. Mark the shady areas and the sunny spots as well as the likely puddle sites after rainfall. From your lawn-chair observations, draw in sunny areas, shady spots, wet places, and very dry areas.

Remove Invasive Plants

Before considering the best plants for birdscaping, you need to know what not to plant. Invasive, or nonnative, plants are destroying habitat across the country. If you drive through Cape May, New Jersey, you will see the porcelain berry covering the trees and shrubs. In the mid-Atlantic states, paulownia, Bradford pear, and Norway maples are outcompeting native plants in woodland ecosystems. In the South, kudzu spreads like a plague. In the Southwest, tamarisk is sucking the water out of riparian streams.

Do not purchase or plant anything considered invasive in your area. Consult your local cooperative extension office (www.csrees.usda.gov/extension). Do an online search for the phrase "invasive plants + your state" and print that list. Carry it with you while shopping for your garden. Avoid any species on that list.

If you have invasive plants in your garden, remove them. You'll gain valuable space to add native plants, and you'll earn the rewarding opportunity to provide resources for birds.

Stop Spraying

While the invasive eradication plan may necessitate a short-term use of herbicides to kill off the toughest of the tough, transition your garden as if it were becoming a certified organic farm. Toxic chemicals like pesticides, herbicides, and chemical fertilizers are dangerous to birds, accumulating in their tissues with every contaminated bug that they eat. These chemicals can interfere with reproduction and might even cause death.

The best gift you can give to the birds and other wildlife in your garden is to discontinue the use of chemicals. When your garden overflows with a wide variety of native plants, you should not need to use these substances.

Create an Ecosystem

When deciding what to plant in your garden, consider the overall landscape. Don't let your birdscape become a "plant zoo"—just a collection of single specimens from all over the world with no relation to each other or to your local birds and other wildlife. Rather, seek to create an ecosystem with a community of plants that work together. Your yard should resemble the plant communities of the natural areas nearby. This is called *ecosystem gardening*.

You can get a feel for these natural ecosystems by exploring the parks and preserves close to your home. Your local native-plant society can become a great resource, providing information about specific plants that might work in your garden as well as field trips and workshops that you can participate in to explore and learn more about the native flora of your region. Plus, you can meet people with experience in growing many of these plants in their own gardens and discover what works best for your specific conditions.

To mimic your local ecosystem in your yard, select plants for the roles they play in the environment, the benefits they provide to wildlife, and the biodiversity and protection they offer toward sustainability. Each of us is a steward of our land; the choices we make on our properties can prove helpful or harmful to the ecosystem. The goal of ecosystem gardening is to make the choices that become most beneficial to wildlife and natural resources.

1. With its red flowers and sweet nectar, cardinal flower appeals to hummingbirds as well as depends on the tiny birds for pollination.

2. Visit local parks or wooded areas to get a feel for your area's native plants.

Plant groups of at least three to five plants of the same species, especially when selecting plants that attract hummingbirds. A large clump of cardinal flower (*Lobelia cardinalis*) or bee balm (*Monarda*) successfully feeds these perpetually hungry birds better than a single plant can.

Plant Locally Native Plants

Get to know your native plants because they prove essential to supporting local food sources. Native plants stand out as the best choices in your habitat garden for birds. Native plants and insects have co-evolved over thousands of years, and most birds—no matter what they eat as adults—need insects to feed their young. With native plants, you'll create an insect buffet for your feathered visitors.

As a plant develops some kind of defense to protect itself from insect predation, most insects succumb to those defenses and move on to another plant. Alternatively, some insects overcome those protective measures and can feed on specific plants that others cannot eat. As a result of this evolutionary process, most insects can eat only specific plants or families of plants. Research the bugs that certain plants attract, and keep these in mind as you select your landscape species.

Why would you want to encourage insects in your garden? To attract birds, of course! Native plants and insects form the base of the food web that supports all other wildlife. Without those insects, we wouldn't have birds. Ninety-six percent of our land birds feed insects to their young, no matter what those birds eat as adults.

Birds have adapted to eat the fruits, berries, seeds, and nuts of locally native plants. While some

exotic plants grow fruits that tempt birds, these fruits are often too large for birds to swallow. Also consider that some invasive plants are spreading out of control because birds eat the berries and then deposit those seeds far and wide as they fly.

Your best bet for creating the habitats that support the largest number of birds is to plant a wide variety of native plants appropriate to your region. The more natives in your garden, the more birds you will see. It really is that simple.

1. Planting to attract insects provides your backyard's birds with a ready source of food.

2. Berries can be both helpful and harmful to the ecosystem.

To begin choosing the best plants for your bird-friendly habitat garden, talk again with your local cooperative extension office. Utilize online resources such as PlantNative (www.plantnative.org) and Wild Ones (www.wildones.org). You will find lists of trees, shrubs, perennials, ferns, and grasses that will suit your local area. These sites may also connect you with local native-plant nurseries as well as community gardening resources.

Native plants surrounding a water feature give birds easy access to both food and drink.

Make a Plan

Putting plants in the right places will save money and time. From your inventory map, you can see which conditions occur in each area of your landscape. You've identified the sunny and shady spots. Add native plants to each area of your garden based on the conditions in which they thrive. Place plants that need wet roots in the areas where the rain pools after a storm, place sun-loving plants in the spots that receive the most sun, introduce understory plants into your shady spots, and add plants that don't require supplemental irrigation to the locations that seem to dry out the quickest.

Can you enlarge your planting area by reducing your lawn? Lawns provide very little in the way of habitat for birds, and they often require the use of toxic chemicals and lots of water. Consider making your lawn smaller or even eliminating it.

Take some time now to sketch out your new bird-friendly garden. Remember that you do not have to implement this plan all at once. Start with one area. Next year, do a little more. The important thing is just to start somewhere!

Keep in mind that you want to mimic the structure of the native ecosystems near you. For example, if you live near wooded areas, you want a tall tree layer, an understory tree layer, a shrub layer, a flowering plant layer, and a ground cover layer.

Rather than fight against the conditions in each area of your garden, the object is to work with them. Gardening should not feel like a constant struggle to pamper plants that don't thrive because of your yard's conditions.

Reduce Your Lawn

By reducing the sizes of our lawns, we can greatly help the local birds in our yards. Consider reducing your lawn area by 10 percent every year, adding more native plants in its place, and you will create habitat that can attract more birds and other wildlife.

Dead trees provide cavities and crevices for shelter and nesting.

Transform your yard into a place where you can relax in that lawn chair and watch the birds you attract.

Start with Trees and Shrubs

Trees form the foundation of your birdscape, providing structure and height to your garden, a view for your enjoyment, and a plentiful habitat for birds. Trees offer food, shelter, and nesting places for many species. When you choose trees for your birdscape, focus on those that provide the greatest value to your local birds.

Native shrubs form the secondary structures of your garden, providing food and habitat for birds. In *Bringing Nature Home*, author Douglas Tallamy compiled a list of the trees and shrubs used as host plants by the highest number of species of butterflies and moths. He states that if many Lepidoptera (the order of insects that includes butterflies and moths) use the trees, birds will have plenty of food, too. Check with your local native-plant society to learn which species of these trees thrive in your region. Here are the ten most popular types of trees and shrubs, listed by genus:

1. *Quercus*: The United States features about sixty native species of oak, which are divided into two groups: white and red. Oaks support an astounding 543 species of Lepidoptera, including polyphemus and imperial moths and hairstreak and duskywing butterflies.

2. *Prunus*: This genus includes almond, apricot, beach plum, cherry, chokecherry, peach, plum, sweet cherry, and wild plum trees. These plants support 456 Lepidoptera species, including eastern tiger swallowtail, hairstreak, and red-spotted purple butterflies; and cecropia, promethean, and hummingbird clearwing moths.

3. *Salix*: Willows are home to 455 species, including mourning cloak, red-spotted purple, and viceroy butterflies.

4. *Betula*: Birch trees are frequented by 411 species, including tiger swallowtail butterflies and cecropia, polyphemus, and luna moths.

5. *Populus*: Aspen, cottonwood, and poplar trees boast 367 species, which include tiger swallowtail and mourning cloak butterflies and twinspot sphinx moths.

6. *Malus*: Crabapple and apple host 308 species, including io and cecropia moths.

7. *Acer*: Maple and boxelder claim 297 species, including io, saddled prominent, luna, and imperial moths. Norway maples, however, are highly invasive; you should not plant them.

8. *Vaccinium*: Cranberry and blueberry host 294 species, including brown elfin, spring azure, and striped hairstreak butterflies.

9. *Alnus:* Alder supports 255 species, including orange sulphur, eastern tiger swallowtail, and giant swallowtail butterflies.

10. *Carya:* Hickory, pecan, pignut, and bitternut host 235 species, including io, polyphemus, luna, pale tussock, and American dagger moths.

Fill in with Perennials

Native perennials, grasses, and wildflowers provide at least three seasons of beauty in your landscape as well as seeds that feed many birds. Here are Tallamy's top picks for the herbaceous plants that will support the most wildlife.

1. *Solidago:* Throughout the United States, 125 goldenrod species occur, and they support 115 Lepidoptera species, which are used by many insects and spiders as well as birds that feed on the seeds and insects. They make a beautiful addition to the autumn garden.

2. *Aster: Aster* supports 112 Lepidoptera species. It is a huge family, with species that thrive in prairie, meadow, pasture, roadside, and woodland environments in spring- and fall-blooming varieties. You can choose a wide variety of species, but try to avoid the cultivars and opt instead for true native species. Asters provide abundant pollen and nectar for bees and butterflies.

3. *Helianthus:* Sunflower supports 73 Lepidoptera species. Although the large-headed, many-seeded annual cultivars remain most commonly known, many native perennial sunflower species exist, too. The plants provide ample

1. A cherry tree, *Prunus avium*, in bloom.

2. The common birch, *Betula pendula*.

3. Autumn leaves on a maple tree.

4. The shagbark hickory, *Carya ovata*.

5. Sunflowers attract wildlife for nectar and seeds.

nectar and pollen, and many birds and other wildlife eat the seeds. Try a mix of native perennial species with annual species.

4. *Eupatorium*: Joe Pye supports 42 Lepidoptera species. Joe Pye includes boneset, snakeroot, and many other species and offers one of the best native alternatives to the invasive butterfly bush. These plants produce a lot of nectar and pollen, making them excellent choices in a pollinator garden.

5. *Ipomoea*: Morning glory supports 39 Lepidoptera species. Do your homework before selecting morning glory for your yard; many introduced varieties become extremely invasive. Research your choice carefully and check with your state's native-plant society for guidance.

6. *Carex*: Sedge supports 36 Lepidoptera species. Many native sedges are considered threatened or endangered in the United States; planting them in your garden can help protect them and provide for wildlife. Sedges thrive in grassland, prairie, and woodland environments. Gardeners often neglect these species, but grasses and sedges play essential roles for wildlife.

7. *Lonicera*: Honeysuckle supports 36 Lepidoptera species. Choose *Lonicera* species native to your area; several invasive alien honeysuckles can wreak havoc in many ecosystems. Native species attract hummingbirds and butterflies.

8. *Lupinus*: Lupine supports 33 Lepidoptera species. Several endangered butterflies, such as the Karner Blue, rely on species in this genus.

1. A monarch on goldenrod.

2. Sky blue morning glories.

3. Abundant green sedge.

4. Blue lupines and yellow asters together support close to 150 Lepidoptera species.

5. Choose geranium varieties according to your location.

Choosing Multipurpose Plants

To get the most from your plant dollars, especially in limited space, choose native plants that provide more than one service to birds and create beauty for you. Many evergreen species, such as spruce, pine, and holly, provide the multiple services of food, shelter, and nesting places. Have you ever seen a flock of American Robins descend on a native holly in January, eat all the berries within a short time, then fly off in search of another? It's a beautiful sight and has warmed many a winter day for me.

Oak trees provide shelter, nesting places, and food in the form of acorns. Also, more than 500 species of butterfly and moth use oaks to host their eggs. Those caterpillars provide high-protein food for nestling birds. Other trees and shrubs with high insect value include *Prunus* species (cherry, chokecherry, beach plum, and almond), willow, birch, poplar, cottonwood, aspen, crabapple, maple, blueberry, alder, hickory, and pecan.

When you plan your birdscape, try to add as many multipurpose plants as possible. Your reward will be the sight of so many birds in your garden.

9. *Viola*: Violet supports 29 Lepidoptera species. Violets are host plants for one of my favorite groups of butterflies, the fritillaries, many of which are endangered. Choose several species for early spring color and wildlife habitat.

10. *Geranium*: Geranium supports 23 *Lepidoptera* species. If you decide to incorporate geraniums, seek the native species best for your location.

Add Water

You can provide clean water for birds in many ways: birdbaths, overturned trash can lids, rain gardens, a wildlife pond. You'll find that different sources will attract a wider variety of species.

In my yard, some will venture to the pond, where I've placed several tree branches and created shallow areas for the birds. Others will splash happily in the birdbath while the hummingbirds fly through the mister and the chickadees drink from the "cup" of my cup plant and the ant wells in my hummingbird feeders.

Access to water remains important during winter, when natural sources might have frozen. Consider offering heated birdbaths, covered water dishes, or even pans of fresh warm water every few hours. I use a heated dog bowl in which I place a brick so that the water is very shallow, and the American Robins, Northern Mockingbirds, and sparrows use it all winter.

It's essential to clean your water sources every few days with a scrub brush and then add fresh water, especially during mosquito breeding season. Also, the birds can foul the water, so you want to make sure that it remains clean.

Other Features

Build a brush pile by stacking fallen branches, sticks, and twigs that accumulate in your garden. Brush piles provide great hiding places, shelter, and food. Every spring, I watch Carolina Wrens, nuthatches, and warblers pick through my brush pile in search of insects. When the House Wrens return to nest in my garden, they create a constant stream of traffic from the brush pile to feed insects to their hungry offspring.

Plant a living fence—which could include small trees and shrubs such as elderberry, serviceberry, holly, cherry, dogwood, and blackberry—to provide food, nesting places, and shelter. Leave some snags or dead trees. Woodpeckers will excavate a new nest cavity each spring, while other species will use the old cavities. Insects will move in, providing a feeding bonanza for birds.

My neighbor's yard includes several dead trees. We've observed Northern Flickers as well as Red-Bellied Woodpeckers, Downy Woodpeckers, and Hairy Woodpeckers making nest holes every year. The trunk becomes a constant swirl of motion as White-Breasted Nuthatches, Brown Creepers, and many warblers glean for bugs.

Birdscaping Small Gardens

You don't need to have a large property to create a habitat for birds. In fact, you can even provide some habitat in a small urban courtyard or on a high-rise balcony.

Make your balcony a hummingbird haven by planting different salvia species in containers, with some cardinal vine climbing a trellis behind them. Your best bet on a balcony is to plant annuals unless you live in a warm climate where plants will not freeze in the containers during winter.

Urban gardens are perfect for small fruiting shrubs and seed-bearing plants like coneflowers and sunflowers. Hanging baskets also provide nesting places for small birds. The trick is to fill the available space with a wide variety of native plants.

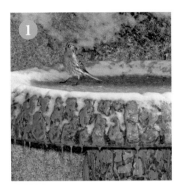

Look outside your window to your yard beyond. With some planning, research, and intentional design, you can add plants and flowers that invite more bird species to visit than ever before, and you'll be doing your part to conserve the environment for the greater good.

Keeping Birds Safe in the Garden

Converting your property into an oasis for local birds doesn't stop at landscaping. For a truly safe and successful birdscape, remember these safety tips.

1. Keep your cats indoors. In the natural environment, birds sometimes fall prey to cats and other wildlife. If you have cats, do everyone a service and keep them inside or under your very watchful eye if they spend time outdoors.

2. Consider location. Place your birdbath in the shade to avoid algae buildup, but keep it at least 3 feet away from the shrubs and wildflowers that provide hiding places for cats and natural predators.

3. Avoid head-on collisions. Place birdfeeders close to your windows so that birds cannot gain enough momentum to stun or injure themselves if they accidentally hit the window while trying to flee a predator. If displaying your feeders too close to the house makes you nervous, place them at least 10 feet away from windows to further prevent window-collision injuries.

Clean, clean, clean. Remain scrupulous about keeping your bird feeder clean so it does not harbor diseases that can be easily passed from bird to bird. After doing so much to create a space to share with them, the last thing you want to do is make the birds sick.

1. A birdbath in winter serves no purpose if the birds can't access the water.

2. Keeping your cat indoors is a safety measure for both your backyard visitors and your cat.

3. A nest box's opening should be large enough to let residents in but small enough to keep predators out.

4. A clutch of beautiful blue American Robin's eggs.

5. The female Robin incubates her eggs for twelve to fourteen days.

Feed Fruit for Fuel

To attract birds to your yard and keep them well-fed and healthy, landscape with fruit-bearing trees, shrubs, and vines. To make things exciting, plant fruit-bearing shrubs and trees in places where it's easy to watch birds up close. While you watch, take comfort that fruit provides much-needed nutrition for birds, especially during migration, when carbohydrates become necessary energy-providers for long-distance flyers.

Select fruit-bearing plants native to your area. Some berries and fruits attract species that might not come into your feeding stations. For example, the American beautyberry might lure Hermit Thrushes that otherwise rarely show up at bird feeders. Even insect-loving birds such as Eastern Phoebes drop in for some fruit on cold days when the bugs don't fly.

Encouraging Avian Visitors—By John E. Riutta

Nesting places for resident and migratory birds are always in high demand. This is good news indeed for bird aficionados who would dearly love to see bluebirds, warblers, or chickadees raise broods in their backyards. If you want to make sure that your property looks like prime real estate in the avian community, you should spend a little time learning how to be a good landlord for the local birds.

Fortunately, you already know that everyone in the market wants a suitable place for a young couple to bring up a family. As with all good parents, keeping the little ones well protected from the elements as well as from danger is the primary goal. The nest cavity or nestbox needs to be snug and secure, protected from rain, wind, and unhealthy temperature variations. For this reason, birds excavating nest cavities in trees or dirt banks generally dig fairly deeply to create a thick protective layer between the actual nest and the outside world, keeping the temperature of the nesting space fairly constant. Such deep excavation also creates a difficult angle for nest-robbing predators.

After protection and security, a ready supply of food becomes the next necessity. For birds, good sources of food usually mean a lack of developed land. Oh, sure, there is always the possibility of popping over to a well-stocked backyard feeder once in a while. Parents, however, prefer a much wider variety of available food to provide the well-balanced diet that a mother and a brood of growing little ones need. From fruit-bearing trees and berry-laden bushes to a weedy field border or a pond buzzing with insects, the more opportunities for hunting and foraging, the more attractive the property will look to the local birds.

"If I let the weeds grow and the pond gets 'buggy,' how does that create 'pleasant landscaping?'" you might ask. Admittedly, you can't let your entire yard

A tiny Anna's Hummingbird's nest.

just "go wild" (well, you could, but your neighbors might object), but you're bound to find a happy medium between what you can tolerate and what the birds need to nest, eat, and live. At the very least, you can hand-weed rather than apply chemicals around nest sites, refrain from spraying insecticides, and maybe let some of the blossoms, berries, and fruits remain after the time to pick them has passed.

Once a bird shows an interest in your property, the rest is fairly easy. Your previous efforts to ensure that the site looks attractive to birds are exactly what you should keep doing once they decide to take up residence. Try to give the birds a little "personal space," make sure that the feeders remain filled and fresh water is available, and consider keeping a journal of the parents' activities so you'll be even better prepared the following year.

Like any landlord, you're going to feel curious about who's living in your rental properties. Monitoring the comings and goings of your avian tenants—and even peeking in on them from time to time to see what they've been up to—is not only legally and socially acceptable, it's also one of the greatest benefits of inviting birds to your backyard.

As long as you do it properly, you can monitor a nest even to the point of checking inside a nestbox or natural cavity without disrupting the nesting cycle; however, if you aren't confident climbing a ladder or opening a nestbox, it is perfectly fine to observe from a distance. Whichever method you choose, keep a journal (a simple notebook will do) of what you did and what you observed.

A removable panel allows for easy observation, but once there are eggs in the nest, stop opening the box and observe only from a distance.

- Record the location of the nest site as soon as you notice a natural nest cavity. Allow plenty of pages to document your observations on each potential nesting site that you discover or establish.
- Check the site daily—using binoculars or a spotting scope, if possible—for signs of activity. Note each day that you check, even if you don't see any birds there.
- When you notice bird activity at the site, record the species, the number of birds you see, and their behaviors.
- Pay particular attention when the birds stop bringing nesting material, such as twigs and

Utilize Your Patio

Don't be afraid to plant a tree in a large pot on a patio for birds. There are various species of tree that grow well in pots and will be big enough to encourage birds to spend time on your patio or deck area while they stay safe from family pets.

Patio covers and eaves are also great places for birds. Place trelliswork near overhangs and eaves, and grow vines over a patio cover to automatically bring birdlife to the area. Birds will also be encouraged to stay and build nests on these structures.

grasses, to the site. This likely indicates that they have finished building the nest and soon will produce eggs.

- Note how frequently the parents bring food items to the nest and what those items are, when you can see the first juveniles in the nest, and when the young begin to move out of the nest in preparation for final fledging.

If you opt to peek inside the nesting site, remember to:

- Only open a nestbox that has an easy-access panel—nothing more than unlatch and lift.
- Open a nestbox no more than once per day.
- Consider using a small extendable mirror to look inside; often you can purchase these from naturalist-supply companies as well as local auto-parts shops.
- If you open or peek in a box and see a bird on the nest, close the box and back away quietly and quickly.
- Once you suspect that eggs are in the nest, switch to monitoring from a distance only.

By following these guidelines, you can create a thorough and informative record of your avian renters' sojourn on your property.

Nesting Nitty-Gritty

When it comes to the avian nesting cycle, things are as they have long been: strictly business. Female birds look for mates that will pass on the best genes to the next generation, and males do everything within their power to demonstrate that they've got "the right stuff."

First and foremost among the male's mating techniques is molting. While all birds molt yearly to replace worn and damaged feathers, many of North America's most colorful species undergo a prenuptial molt to prepare for breeding. Think of it as the male updating his wardrobe to impress the

females. In many birds, such as tanagers and warblers, the males who can show off the most vivid and brightly colored feathers must be the healthiest birds—thus the sources of the best genes.

The male often is responsible for establishing a territory that contains all necessary elements for a good nest site, after which he will vocally and physically advertise that he is not only healthy and available but also actively seeking a female to set up house. Should a passing female find that she likes what she sees and hears, things kick into high gear fairly quickly. Actually building the nest—or furnishing a natural cavity or a nestbox—falls to the female in most species.

Then, of course, there is copulation. The anatomy of birds is structured in such a way that copulation is relatively simple. The male usually needs to climb on the female's back, and their cloacae (reproductive organs) have to touch just long enough for his sperm to be transferred. If all goes well, the sperm finds its way along the oviduct to a place where it can be stored for fertilization of the eggs.

The female commonly lays one egg each day until the clutch is complete; the number of eggs varies by species. The eggs are then incubated, or brooded, in the nest until hatching. Once this occurs, species with altricial (i.e., naked and helpless) young increase their activity level because feeding a nest full of hungry chicks becomes a full-time job. Birds such as ducks, with precocial young that can move about soon after hatching, have it a bit easier.

Even once they are capable of flight, the young might remain close and continue to beg food from their parents. Some species, such as jays, remain with their parents long enough to help raise the next generation. At some point, regardless of species, they all strike out on their own to begin the entire cycle anew.

1. Make sure that monitoring the nest box does not disturb its inhabitants.

2. A Violet-Green Swallow brings food to her young in the nestbox. This species is seen in the western states.

3. Birds find their own natural cavities and crevices for nesting.

YardMap

The Cornell Lab of Ornithology and partners such as the US Fish and Wildlife Service and Roger Tory Peterson Institute of Natural History have developed a project called YardMap that will allow you to describe in great detail the habitat and conservation practices in your backyard. YardMap (www.yardmap.org) will let you paint habitat information about the places that you know best on top of a satellite map. From this citizen-science collaboration, scientists will get a wealth of data about bird habitat, and you will get a fun map of your yard that you can share with friends and family—and use to plan bird-friendly changes to your yard.

Year-Round Birds

It's always a good idea to offer birds additional shelters by setting up birdhouses in various places. This, along with water features and feeders to tide birds over in the lean food months, will ensure that your outdoor area is filled with birdsong all through the year.

Garden Specifics

Naturally, the types of trees, shrubs, grasses, and vines you can provide to attract a large variety of birds depend on the size of your property as well as what conditions prevail in your yard.

"Consider the natural shelter you are providing as a pyramid-styled tent, starting with trees, followed by shrubs, then lower-growing plants, and eventually ground covers that will create a thicket," says master gardener Nancy Matsuoka of Laguna Hills Nursery in Foothill Ranch, California. "If you have [a lot] of space, you can actually plant trees and shrubs in this layered formation to create a special area that backyard birds will consider home and use as base to visit other parts of your garden. And, if you add beds of perennials and annuals for seeds and nectar, they will appreciate the on-tap food source."

Create a Natural Canopy

Leafy trees provide natural protection from predators and the elements. "It's a good idea to limit the height of your trees to

1. Offer birds materials that they can take and use to build their nests.

2. If you find a nest with eggs in it, leave it alone!

between 15 and 20 feet," Matsuoka suggests. "Once you have achieved the height you want, prune them to create a nice, natural umbrella shape. Wild birds will automatically be attracted to this kind of foliage because they will be out of sight from larger predator birds circling overhead or sitting in taller trees nearby." She goes on to say that evergreen trees offer the benefits of cover from predators and protection from the elements year-round. "Once you've determined the prevailing winter wind direction in your garden, plant trees to provide protection from these winds."

Share Your Fruit Trees

"It's possible to share a fruit tree in your garden with wild birds," Matsuoka explains. "Place swinging deterrents in the lower branches so that birds will stay away from the lower fruit-bearing branches and gravitate to the top part of the tree. This way, the fruit on the lower branches can be kept intact for human consumption, and the birds can enjoy the fruit on the top branches as well as the shelter such branches provide." For example, apple and cherry trees are huge attractions to robins, woodpeckers, and Cedar Waxwings. She also cautions not to spray fruit trees with chemicals because they are harmful to birds that may hang out or even nest there.

Make Shrubs Attractive

If you are trying to landscape an area of your garden with shrubs for protection and nesting, a large variety of shrubs thrive in full and partial shade and can be placed in close proximity to your trees. With such an arrangement, birds can easily either crawl into a bush or fly up to a safe branch overhead if disturbed.

Using garden accessories, such as stake feeders, is an excellent way to attract birds to particular

If you don't have fruit trees, offering fresh fruit and even grape jelly will attract fruit-loving birds like the Baltimore Oriole.

Trees, Please

Among the species of tree that will entice birds to take shelter in your garden are:
- Cherry
- Crabapple
- Dogwood
- Hawthorn
- Holly
- Mountain ash
- Mulberry
- Oak
- Peach
- Plum
- Serviceberry
- Viburnum

Needle and broad-leaved evergreen trees and shrubs, such as arborvitae, cedar, holly, juniper, spruce, and white pine provide essential winter protection as well as food. Birds love pines because the cones provide an in-house source of food for many different species of bird, including Blue Jays, chickadees, finches, and nuthatches.

Note: Different species of many of these trees grow in the different climates around the country. Always check with a native-plants organization to ensure that you are not selecting invasive varieties.

Flowering Plant Factors

No matter where you live in the United States, you can plant flowering shrubs that will attract birds to your yard.

Northeast/Midwest (Connecticut, Delaware, Illinois, Indiana, Iowa, Kentucky, Maine, Maryland, Massachusetts, Michigan, Minnesota, Missouri, New Hampshire, New Jersey, New York, Ohio, Pennsylvania, Rhode Island, Vermont, Virginia, West Virginia, and Wisconsin):
- American elder
- Bayberry
- Black haw
- Highbush blueberry
- Native dogwood
- Native honeysuckle
- Native viburnum
- Pinxterbloom azalea
- Winterberry

These plants attract American Robins, bluebirds, cardinals, catbirds, mockingbirds, Purple Finches, thrushes, Tree Swallows, woodpeckers, and Yellow-Billed Cuckoos.

South (Alabama, Arkansas, Florida, Georgia, Louisiana, Mississippi, North Carolina, South Carolina, and Tennessee):
- American elder
- Arrowwood
- Bayberry
- Black haw
- Highbush blueberry
- Hybrid weigela
- Native cotoneaster
- Native dogwood
- Smooth sumac

These plants will attract American Robins, bluebirds, Brown Thrashers, cardinals, Carolina Chickadees, Cedar Waxwings, flickers, Hermit Thrushes, and mockingbirds.

Central (Kansas, Nebraska, North Dakota, Oklahoma, South Dakota, and Texas):
- Beauty bush
- Coralberry
- Fragrant sumac
- Native dogwood
- Winterberry

These plants will attract American Robins, cardinals, catbirds, Cedar Waxwings, Hermit Thrushes, Purple Finches, and Ruby-Throated and Rufous Hummingbirds.

Southwest (Arizona, Colorado, Idaho, Montana, Nevada, New Mexico, Utah, and Wyoming):
- American elder
- Black haw
- Native honeysuckle
- Native viburnums
- Red dogwood
- Serviceberry
- Snowberry

These plants will attract American Robins, Broad-Tailed Hummingbirds, Evening Grosbeaks, Lewis's Woodpeckers, magpies, Pink Grosbeaks, and sparrows.

West Coast (California, Oregon, and Washington):
- Beauty bush
- Blue elder
- Snowberry

These plants will attract American Robins, Black-Headed Grosbeaks, Rufous Hummingbirds, thrushes , and Wrentits.

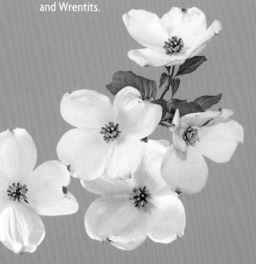

shrubs that will offer them sanctuary. Stake the feeder into the thick of a particular shrub so that only the saucer-shaped bowl protrudes, and then fill it with seeds or water.

It's also essential to keep shrubs pruned to allow birds easy access to the inner branches and foliage. It's a good idea to leave some of the smaller cut twigs lying around so that the birds can pick them up and use them to build nests.

Ornamental Plantings

Hanging moss-filled baskets and plants in trees will attract birds, too. Very often, they will use the structure for a nest or take bits of the moss and nest in one of the nearby trees.

Consider growing tall ornamental grasses, which offer great cover for birds that like to be low to the ground. This is ideal for gardeners who like to keep their lawns neat and don't want to let grass grow tall for birds to take refuge. There are many grasses to choose from based on your area's climatic conditions. "I also suggest planting grasses in clusters," Matsuoka says. "Then, apart from providing birds with cover, they make an attractive accent in your garden, too."

Add Garden Accessories

Garden accents—such as an arbor made out of metal, plastic, or wood—are an excellent idea in a smaller garden that would be overpowered by a large tree. When covered with a woody vine, an arbor gives birds a place to sit and duck down into the vine itself should the need arise. "Arbors work well on patios, too," Matsuoka says. She also suggests trelliswork set up against a wall for shelter, grapevines for shelter and as a food source, or any of the many woody flowering vines to attract birds and provide refuge and nesting sites.

Water Works—By John E. Riutta

Too often overlooked in the development and maintenance of backyard habitats, water remains the most important thing that you can provide to attract and provide for the well-being of your feathered visitors. Birds must take care of their feathers through regular preening and cleaning. Birds can preen almost anywhere using their bills and, for most species, an oil-producing gland called the *uropygial gland*. Located near the base of the tail, it produces a rich lubricating substance that helps keep feathers healthy and strong. Cleaning, however, proves a bit trickier. Nothing substitutes for a good, old-fashioned water bath to really clean the feathers and prepare them for preening.

An Avian Haven in the Los Angeles Suburbs

—By Catherine Waters

Most bird lovers know that birds, including hungry and thirsty migrants, benefit greatly from even the tiniest patch of open space that meets their needs for safe shelter, accessible water, and available food. With a bit of thought, research, planning, and planting, it's easy to create an at-home oasis for attracting birds.

My husband's and my primary goal in transforming our modest backyard garden into a bird sanctuary was to experience the joy of having a garden that attracted birds with a local, year-round range. We also hoped to entice more migratory birds and to retain for a longer period the overwintering birds known to use this region.

We studied the birds that lived around us, including which species overwintered in the region and which species could be expected to migrate through the area, and noted what type of habitat our target species desired. We read, talked to local birders, and visited local parks and gardens.

Next, we gave some thought to what these species consumed: insects, worms, seeds, fruits, nuts, berries, small mammals, or other birds on the ground? Finally, we considered the habits of these birds. Did they perch high or low, in dense foliage or in the open? Did they perch and then fly out to catch insects on the wing, or did they spend most of their time seeking food on the ground? Where did they nest and when?

We are lucky enough to have three distinct gardens on our urban lot: a Midwestern-type "tree-lawn" front yard, a vegetable and native plant garden in the side yard, and a traditional backyard. The first part of our transition was the backyard. We kept lawn, patio, barbecue, and storage areas exactly where they were, but we gave up our intrusive and noisy gardener in exchange for a less manicured, denser, and drought-tolerant lawn mowed by an amateur (me).

Next to go were the meticulously raked beds. We let inches-thick layers of leaves build up in the shrub beds, added shrubbery into any gaps, and moved shrubbery into the lawn area. We surrendered the annual flowerbeds to plants more attractive to birds and butterflies, such as verbena, yarrow, lavender, salvia, and butterfly milkweed.

Without a heavy mower to compact the lawn areas, earthworms began appearing nearer to the surface, and thrushes and Northern Mockingbirds were better able to feast. Buildup from leaf litter, fallen debris, and spent blooms quickly yielded the little succulent grubs, insects, and seed loved by wintering Fox Sparrows, thrushes, and towhees.

We let foundation and border shrubs grow thicker and nearer to the ground to form a denser green corridor for birds that like to immediately seek shelter when flying into a yard. Because birds like to move through cover when seeking water, we allowed a dense hedge to grow taller and thicker to provide shelter and safety. We added two modest running-water features and a few birdbaths immediately adjacent to vegetative cover, creating shelter for the birds approaching the water slowly for a drink or a bath.

These changes brought in local——but previously unseen in our yard—California Towhees, Spotted Towhees, and Dark-Eyed Juncos. Hummingbirds began nesting in the backyard, joining Black Phoebes, Bushtits, House Finches, Mourning Doves, and Northern Mockingbirds. As time passed, a few Hermit Thrushes, White-Crowned Sparrows, and Yellow-Rumped Warblers began to stay through the entire winter, and their migratory cousins started coming through in larger numbers.

Feeling encouraged, we stopped pruning our largest tree, a white sapote, on an every-other-year schedule, and the Pacific-Slope Flycatchers began turning up earlier and staying later. We left the dry twigs and branches in the same tree, and Western Wood-Pewees, which like to perch on bare branches, became yearly visitors in the spring and fall.

Planting a semi-dwarf almond tree and two smaller growing oaks attracted regional resident Western Scrub-Jays to seek nuts and acorns daily. Sweet gum trees gave us shade, a privacy screen, and fall color, and they provided migratory Pine Siskins, Lesser Goldfinches, and American Goldfinches with seeds. Putting low landscape lights on slender poles in the lawn brought the unanticipated by-product of attracting Black Phoebes that like to perch low to catch flying insects.

The single plant that gave us the biggest impact was the addition of a weeping white mulberry. Ungrafted mulberries become too large and messy for even a generous yard; grafted weeping mulberries stay much tidier and more compact. Western Tanagers, Hooded and Bullock's Orioles, Black-Headed Grosbeaks, and Swainson's And Hermit Thrushes all flock to this small tree to feast in the spring, and the year-round residents feed on it well into summer.

The steps we took translate to almost any part of the country, any size yard, and nearly any budget. We never used insecticides or pesticides, so we didn't have to worry about poisoning the animals we attracted. Cats, feral and pet, remain a problem, so we keep our water features off the ground and stay vigilant.

When it comes to hydration, most avian species drink by filling their bills with water and then raising them skyward and letting gravity take care of the rest. Although it's a simple enough process, it's not one that lends itself to taking advantage of just any source of water. The water that birds drink must be clean and from a source that allows them to approach it with secure footing. Then they need to lower their heads to reach the water, immerse their bills sufficiently to fill them, raise their heads to pass the water down their throats, and repeat the process multiple times.

When looking for water features to add to your yard, consider whether the design of a basin will properly accommodate your visiting birds' bathing and drinking requirements. Most birds don't care to bathe in water deeper than their legs' length, so look for a water basin that appears fairly shallow or that at least has a bathing platform within it. Birdwatchers with an existing pond can create such a platform easily by adding a few large, rough-surfaced, flat rocks near an edge, no more than 1 or 2 inches below the water. Even better is to angle a rock down from the edge so that it forms a shallow slope into the water, allowing different species to wade in to their own preferred bathing depth.

If you choose a stand-alone bathing vessel, place it on a pedestal to provide the bathers with visibility of any lurking dangers. Free-roaming cats are quickly attracted to the sound of wings splashing in water; they will take full advantage if given the chance.

Some of us prefer to take leisurely baths; others prefer quick showers. The same goes for birds. Fortunately, adding a shower option to your bathing facility is simple: just add a mister! A mister produces a fine, gentle, vertical or horizontal spray of water; many are designed to attach directly

1. An American Robin enjoys the view.

2. A bubbler creates appeal while and rocks provide a proper shallow depth.

3. A mister is particularly appreciated by hummingbirds

to birdbath basins, while others stand alone. A mister above a basin creates a gentle rain on the water's surface that keeps insect larvae from developing while making the water more noticeable to birds in the area. Positioning a mister near a leafy green shrub so that it coats the leaves with water also provides visiting birds—especially hummingbirds and warblers—the opportunity for leaf bathing. The birds rub against the wet leaves and then work the water through their feathers as though they're taking a sponge bath.

What About Winter?

Just as you winterize your outdoor faucets so they don't freeze during the cold months of winter, you also must make a few adjustments to the water features in your backyard habitat to ensure that visiting birds enjoy uninterrupted access to water. Because many natural sources of water freeze over in cold weather, providing bathing and drinking opportunities will make your yard a must-visit destination for any birds that spend the winter in your area.

If the temperature in your region only occasionally drops below freezing, a drip feature might keep the water from turning to ice. In areas where winter means "deep freeze," however, plug-in birdbath heaters might help. Never add antifreeze or glycerin to the water to prevent freezing because drinking it can sicken the birds, and bathing in it will gum up their feathers.

Maintaining Public Health

Keep the water in your basin or pond clean by cycling or changing it regularly. Beyond the commonsense reasons for keeping the water clean and fresh is an even more far-reaching argument for doing so: the prevention of diseases transmitted by water-borne insects, especially mosquitoes. The dangers of malaria are well-known, but mosquitoes also can transmit yellow fever, dengue fever, various forms of encephalitis, and West Nile Virus, the latter being the most important concern to people in the United States and Canada. The best defense against the virus is to prevent mosquitoes from breeding. Mosquitoes lay their eggs in shallow, stagnant pools of tepid water, making poorly maintained birdbaths and backyard ponds ideal mosquito incubators.

Fortunately, it isn't difficult to prevent mosquito larvae from becoming established, and certain maintenance techniques even attract birds. A simple drip-producing device or "water wiggler" added to a bathing vessel prevents the water from stagnating by breaking the surface tension and keeping the water in motion. The resulting water sounds also attract nearby birds to the bath itself.

Once you set up an outdoor water feature, plan to clean and change the water from time to time, particularly if you have shallow vessels in sun-lit areas. The combination of sun-warmed water with the assorted dirt and debris that birds wash from their feathers will quickly produce a breeding ground for a variety of botanical and microbial unpleasantries. Don't use bleach or other cleansers; simply empty the water and scrub the basin well using a brush.

A Yellow-Rumped Warbler enjoys a bath on a sunny day.

Optimal Placement

In many ways, deciding where to place bird-friendly water features is like deciding where to place birdfeeders. Many of the same issues come into play: accessibility, maintenance, and, perhaps most importantly, safety.

Water basins should be slightly elevated to allow for enhanced visibility of the surrounding area by the bathers but also relatively low. After all, few natural sources of fresh water occur high off the ground. They should not be located beneath ledges or terraces where something four-footed and furry might conceal itself until it's close enough to pounce on visiting birds.

Placing a water feature in the middle of a lawn is not recommended, either. Full sunlight will heat the shallow water quickly, accelerating the growth of undesirable plant and microbial life. Such placement does not provide nearby perching areas for birds waiting their turns or preening and drying after their baths.

A bird can perch on the side of the water basin to get a drink.

Place your water basin in a fairly flat and at least partially shaded area near some branching shrubbery. This will provide the bathers with some privacy as well as visibility of their surroundings and a selection of nearby areas in which to preen.

The Need for Seed—By Sharon Stiteler

If you are new to the art of attracting birds, deciding on a menu can feel overwhelming. Certain seeds will attract certain species, and you should know several basic rules. Look for the following key ingredients when purchasing seed.

Types of Seed
Black-Oil Sunflower Seed

If you use only one seed, make it black-oil sunflower seed, which is quite possibly the most crucial seed you can offer backyard birds. No matter what part of the country you live in, this high-fat, high-

No Starlings

A big advantage to feeding sunflower seeds in the shell is that European Starlings cannot eat it. These birds can act aggressively at feeders and will drive away native birds from nesting cavities while they raise their own broods. The muscles in European Starlings' bills are designed to push open, not crush, like Northern Cardinals' bills. Because of this, starlings are physically incapable of feeding on black-oil sunflower. Other blackbirds, such as Brown-Headed Cowbirds, Common Grackles, and Red-Winged Blackbirds can eat black-oil seeds, but the non-native starling cannot.

meat-to-shell-ratio seed attracts more species of seedeaters, from the urban House Finch to the rural Rose-Breasted Grosbeak, than any other. Wild birds that prefer black-oil sunflower include chickadees, finches, grosbeaks, jays, Northern Cardinals, nuthatches, titmice, and woodpeckers. You can offer sunflower seeds in any type of feeder.

Unfortunately, squirrels and raccoons also love black-oil sunflower seed. If you want to avoid squirrels and raccoons in your yard, try a weight-sensitive feeder that allows only lighter birds to feed, or place a squirrel baffle on the feeder's pole.

If you offer the popular black-oilers, empty seed shells will accumulate on the ground, and you must clean them up from time to time. The collection of shells can kill off the grass underneath the feeder, so a bare patch will likely develop in your yard where the feeder is located if you don't diligently clean up the shells.

Sunflower Hearts

The only seed that can rival black-oil sunflower seed in popularity is the sunflower heart itself. This seed goes by many different names, including hearts, sunflower pieces, sunflower chips, and hulled or shelled sunflowers. The chips can come in different sizes, including whole heart, medium-sized, and even extra-fine to fit through the tiny holes of a finch feeder.

Because the seed is out of the shell, it will not germinate. Many people like to offer sunflower hearts to avoid messes caused by the shells, making them ideal for people who live in apartments

From left to right: nyjer, striped sunflower, milo, and safflower.

Safe Seed Storage

Avoid storing birdseed in your home. Most seed contains some Indian mealmoth eggs and larvae, and there is no safe way to treat the seed without affecting the birds. If birds find mealmoth larvae in their food, it's just a protein bonus! However, an unused large bag of seed can allow the larvae time to pupate, hatch, and begin mating to create new moths in your home.

If you live in an apartment or condo and purchase seed in smaller quantities, store it in the refrigerator or freezer to prevent the moths from hatching. If this is not an option, store your seed in a large metal container with a tight-fitting lid, and place it outside in a dry, cool area, such as the garage or storage shed. Secure the lid with a bungee cord or even a chain with a lock to keep varmints from breaking in.

or condominiums. Species that like to eat sunflower hearts include buntings, chickadees, finches, grosbeaks, Northern Cardinals, nuthatches, and, on rare occasions, even warblers, orioles, and robins.

There are some downsides to offering sunflower hearts. First, seeds out of the shell cost more. Second, hearts quickly can get moldy after rainy weather or even in high humidity. It's a good idea to periodically check and possibly shake the feeder to make sure that the seeds don't clump. Birds usually have enough sense to avoid moldy seeds, but eating one can prove lethal. A final downside to the sunflower heart: it's very attractive to European Starlings because it is out of the shell. If starlings become a problem in your neighborhood, avoid this seed.

Safflower

Safflower is a useful bird-feeder addition when used properly. It's not a favorite, but some birds will eat it. Birds that eat safflower include chickadees, House Finches, Mourning Doves, Northern Cardinals, nuthatches, and Rose-Breasted Grosbeaks.

The big advantage to safflower is that Common Grackles do not care for the taste, and European Starlings can't crack it

1. Pine Siskins congregate at tube feeders.

2. A partial albino Tufted Titmouse stops by for a snack.

3. A mesh bag serves as a feeder for mixed nuts and a handy perch.

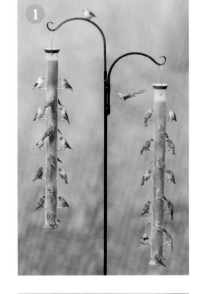

open. As native blackbirds, Common Grackles arrive in large flocks and quickly can empty a feeding station; therefore, birders often try to avoid attracting them. Many people offer sunflower seed until blackbirds become a problem, and then they switch to safflower.

Birds generally do not like a dramatic change in food, and a sudden shift from sunflower to safflower might cause birds to abandon the feeder for a few weeks. It's best to offer safflower gradually. If you are offering sunflower, start adding in a few safflower seeds, increasing the amount over time. Another option is to have a second feeder filled with only safflower. It might take a few weeks for the birds to become used to it, but once they do, it will offer a haven from the blackbirds.

White Millet

White millet remains a fine seed, but it is best used in moderation. It's great for sparrows, which prefer the size and taste. You might think, *Why do I want to attract those irritating brown birds?* Not all sparrows are as irritating as the nonnative House Sparrow, though, which can take over a feeder. Some less irritating native sparrows that enjoy white millet include White-Throated Sparrows, White-Crowned Sparrows, Fox Sparrows, and Dark-Eyed Juncos. Indigo Buntings and Painted Buntings like white millet, too. Handfuls of white millet scattered on the ground or in a feeder become a fun addition to any yard, especially during migration, when sparrows are on the move.

Pygmy Nuthatches enjoy suet, a type of beef fat.

Corn

Found in either cracked or whole-kernel form, dried corn is best offered in moderation. Cracked corn attracts Red-Winged and Yellow-Headed Blackbirds, Brown-Headed Cowbirds, Blue Jays, Juncos, and native sparrows. Less popular among songbirds, whole-kernel corn tempts wild Turkeys, Ring-Necked Pheasants, quails, and waterfowl.

Corn also attracts deer, raccoons, foxes, and squirrels. Keep in mind that offering large quantities of corn during the spring while Canada Geese are migrating and looking for places to nest might give the geese the impression that your lakeside home offers a great place to nest. If you don't want geese taking over your neighborhood in the summer, avoid offering dried corn during the spring.

Nuts

You might think that nuts are just for squirrels, but they tickle the fancy of many bird species, too. You can offer peanuts or mixed-nut combinations of cashews, almonds, pecans, walnuts, and pistachios. Birds that like nuts include woodpeckers, chickadees, nuthatches, jays, and Northern Cardinals.

If you offer nuts in a tray, crows and blackbirds might make off with the whole stash before other birds have a chance to find it. A mesh feeder made of ¼-inch hardware cloth forces birds to chip away at the nuts in small pieces, preventing other birds from vacuuming them up. Like sunflower hearts, peanuts can get moldy in rain or humid weather, so keep an eye on the feeder.

Unsalted nuts are best for birds. Although no known studies specify the effects of salted nuts on birds, it is best to err on the side of caution and offer only unsalted varieties.

The Cactus Wren is among the birds that prefer nuts to seeds.

Thistle/Niger/Nyjer

This seed goes by many names. It started out as niger (pronounced NYE-jer), a seed imported from Nigeria. Unfortunately, because the name occasionally was mispronounced, seed sellers started calling it by the folk name thistle. That name also caused controversy, however, since some people confused it with the noxious thistle weed. The Wild Bird Feeding Industry devised a way to spell the name phonetically: nyjer. Many sellers now call it nyjer or nyjer thistle. No matter the name, the bottom line is that this remains a great seed to offer finches.

Nyjer is best offered in finch-style tube feeders with tiny slits that keep out larger, more intimidating birds, allowing small birds access to the seeds and preventing the seeds from spilling on the ground. You also can purchase mesh bags for finches to hang from while getting the nyjer. To access the nut meat on the inside, finches must crack open the shell, so husks will collect on the ground beneath the feeder.

Always purchase nyjer in small quantities, and buy often. Finches avoid nyjer that appears wet or old (typically older than six months). On the rare occasion that they come to the feeder, a finch will hop to a perch and take a peck, hop to a second perch and take a peck, hop to a third perch and take a peck, and then leave the feeder altogether. If finches suddenly stop coming despite your full feeder, consider this as a sign that your nyjer has gone bad.

You can offer nyjer by itself or purchase it mixed with extra-fine sunflower chips, which finches also enjoy. Remain aware that sunflower chips might attract Downy Woodpeckers, which sometimes will peck open the feeder's holes for wider access to the food.

For the Birds?

Most of the food items found in our kitchens are not bird-friendly food fare. Following are a few exceptions:

- Eggshells: Crushed eggshells can provide a beneficial supplement to a female bird's diet during the breeding season, replacing the calcium lost during the egg-laying process. Sterilize them before setting them out by either boiling the eggshells for ten minutes, baking them at 250 degrees Fahrenheit for twenty minutes in a conventional oven, or microwaving them for six minutes. After the shells have been sterilized, crush them to the size of small seeds so that birds of all sizes can eat them. Place them under the feeder or on a tray mixed with seeds.

- Fruit (dried): Many birds will eat dried fruit, but they prefer fresh fruit.

- Fruit (fresh): Oranges attract blackbirds, Gray Catbirds, House Finches, jays, Northern Cardinals, orioles, American Robins, Thrashers, and woodpeckers. Old bananas and melons attract fruit flies which, in turn, will attract hummingbirds.

- Melon seeds: These are rarely used in bird feeding, but they can be attractive to quail, pheasant, and American Crows.

- Peanut butter: Mix it with cornmeal to create a dry dough and then place the dough in a suet cage, in clumps on a platform feeder, or on the side of a tree. Brown Thrashers, Carolina Wrens, chickadees, Northern Cardinals, nuthatches, and woodpeckers are among the many species that will thank you for it.

- Popcorn (unsalted and unbuttered): American Crows, geese, Grackles, and European Starlings might go for this, but the nutritional value is debatable.

Some birds that you can expect at nyjer feeders include American Goldfinches, Common Redpolls, House Finches, Indigo Buntings, Lesser Goldfinches, Painted Buntings, Pine Siskins, and Purple Finches.

Seed Mixes

Bird food also can be offered in mix form; the best mixes have a strong sunflower base. Look for mixes that appear mostly dark in color, a sign that the mix consists mostly of black-oil sunflower seeds. Avoid mixes sold in packages that don't allow you to see the contents, especially if they are available at an unbelievably low price. The mix could be full of filler seeds that won't attract a wide variety of birds. Also avoid mixes that appear mostly yellow or orange because it signals that the mix could be filled with less popular seeds to lower the price; these mixes usually attract only quail, turkeys, or waterfowl.

A good all-purpose mix will contain 75 percent sunflower seed, 10 percent millet, 10 percent safflower, and 5 percent peanuts or white millet. If you live in a condo or an apartment, consider trying "hulless" or "no-mess" mixes. These usually consist of seeds out of their shells, including sunflower hearts, peanuts, and cracked corn.

Some seed packagers sell high-end mixes containing sunflower seeds, mixed nuts, dried fruits, and, in some cases, dried mealworms. Birds will eat these mixes, but they are more expensive than the average songbird mix. They seem to work best in hopper-style or tray feeders because fruit sometimes becomes lodged in the feeding ports of tube feeders, blocking birds' access to the seeds. Some seed mixes are scented with a strong berry or citrus aroma, which is mainly for humans' benefit because most birds have a poorly developed sense of smell.

Alternative Foods

Suet (rendered beef fat) is a tantalizing high-energy treat for woodpeckers, chickadees, and nuthatches. You can purchase raw chunks or flavored cakes and plugs; the flavors range from peanut (birds' favorite!) to sunflower to fruit.

Suet is available in dough form, too, allowing it be offered in hot climates. Offer suet in cages or logs with holes drilled into the sides. During spring and fall migrations, you might find warblers, tanagers, orioles, and other insect-eating birds coming in for suet.

Sugar water offers another source of food. The best ratio for making sugar water is four parts boiling water to one part sugar. Wait until the mixture cools before setting it out for the birds. This will attract hummingbirds, orioles, and even a few House Finches and woodpeckers.

Replace the sugar water after three or four days, and store any extra in the refrigerator for up to one week. Never use honey or artificial sweeteners when making sugar water for birds. Birds wouldn't eat these products in the wild, and they could prove lethal. You can use a red feeder or tie a red ribbon around the feeder to attract hummingbirds, but never add red food coloring to the homemade syrup.

If orioles make regular visits to your yard, try offering grape jelly; they will love it! Offer this treat in small, brightly colored dishes. Orioles also enjoy eating live mealworms, available at most pet-supply stores and wild-bird specialty stores. Mealworms also attract American Robins, bluebirds, chickadees, Gray Catbirds, Northern Cardinals, nuthatches, thrashers, and warblers.

Feeder Facts —By Nikki Moustaki

When choosing feeders for your backyard, you can add several types to encourage backyard diversity or use just one type to discourage certain types of birds and feed only the species that you want hanging around.

Types of Feeders
Globe Feeders

Globe feeders, also called satellite feeders, are generally made from clear plastic or glass, allowing birds to spot a feeding station and you to see when the feeder needs refilling. A globe feeder attracts small songbirds, such as chickadees, finches, nuthatches, and titmice, as well as some woodpeckers.

Some globes are designed with a hopper inside that dispenses the seed on demand either through one or more holes in the globe

1. A roofed feeder with an overhang keeps the birds and the food dry.

2. A basin-style sugar-water feeder.

3. A Northern Cardinal and a Carolina Chickadee visit a dome feeder.

or with a feeding shelf. Those with feeding holes thwart larger species that can dominate feeders; small birds can cling to the bottom to feed. Most globe feeders are intended to withstand poor weather, especially rain, which is a nice feature in damp climates.

Because globe feeders work mainly for smaller species, you can place them close to your home (without the risk of being awakened on Sunday mornings by vocal jays or Northern Mockingbirds!) or use them as secondary feeding stations to keep bigger species away from the smaller birds' buffet.

Tube Feeders

Tube feeders are generally filled with small seeds that attract finches, buntings, and sparrows. Goldfinches and Pine Siskins are attracted to tube feeders filled with nyjer, which will blow away if used in another type of feeder. Tube feeders filled with sunflower seeds attract larger species, such as nuthatches and grosbeaks.

Some tube-style feeders come with more than one tube, so you can fill each with a different seed to attract a variety of species to one feeder. Some designs also can attract or discourage certain types of birds. For example, a tube feeder with the feeding holes below the perches will attract Goldfinches and Pine Siskins, which can eat while hanging upside down, but it will discourage nonnative House Finches. Some models include a cage around the feeder to thwart squirrels, and many come with rain guards.

Dome Feeders

Dome feeders attract an extensive variety of birds, and they generally consist of a platform with a domed top to keep out rain and squirrels. They are very flexible; you can add almost any type of seed, insect, or fruit to the feeder. Some dome feeders come equipped with a place to add a suet cake or thistle feeder. Some also include movable domes that allow you to adjust the dome height, locking out larger species and acting as a baffle against squirrels.

Platform Feeders

Platform feeders, also called fly-through feeders, encourage the widest variety of birds, even drawing ground feeders such as Mourning Doves. Platform feeders are the easiest type to use. Simply dump seed or other food onto the platform, and you're done. The problem with platform feeders, though, is that they can succumb to weather, squirrels, and domination by large species because everyone in the neighborhood will visit.

A platform feeder with a solid bottom requires more frequent cleaning than a feeder with a wire bottom, though both should be cleaned when soiled. With a solid bottom, birds can walk anywhere on the platform, so the feeder can become caked with waste. Some models offer squirrel-proof platforms; others come with a roof or rain guard.

Sugar-Water Feeders

Intended to attract hummingbirds, sugar-water feeders are designed with those species in mind. Hummingbirds are attracted to the color red, so these feeders often include red in the design, usually at the port where the birds feed.

Some hummingbird feeders mount to a window with suction cups; others hang from a mount near a window or in the yard. Offer only fresh sugar water and keep the feeder as clean as possible to ensure the health of the birds. Thoroughly clean your hummingbird feeder every three days, following the directions on the packaging.

If ants and other insects become a problem at your feeder, add a cup filled with water to prevent the ants from reaching the feeder. Many feeders include this as a built-in option.

Hopper Feeders

A hopper feeder usually resembles a quaint house, barn, or gazebo and is often a hobbyist's first feeder. You fill the hopper with seed, which releases on demand into a tray as birds eat. Most hoppers have clear sides so you can see when the seed needs replenishing.

Both small and large species can use hopper feeders. The size of the tray makes perching easy, so birds that normally seem reluctant to use other types of feeders might like the hopper. Ground-feeders will appreciate the spillover that picky birds kick out of the tray.

Feeder Hints

- During winter, place feeders on the south side of buildings to protect birds from cold northerly winds.
- To discourage squirrels, hang feeders at least 8 feet from the nearest tree trunk or limb. When using a squirrel baffle on a pole, place it at least 4 feet above the ground.
- To prevent birds from injuring themselves by flying into windows, place feeders 3 feet from windows. Birds taking off from this distance won't gain enough speed to hurt themselves if they mistakenly fly into windows.
- If you're beginning to offer food in a new yard, start in early fall, when birds seek reliable food sources to last them through colder weather. If you attract them in fall, you might keep them through the winter.

When buying a hopper, make sure that it's easy to refill; you'll have to do so often, and its placement in your yard can make refilling awkward. Also, a hopper feeder requires regular cleaning, especially during wet months when seed can become moldy.

Jelly Feeders

Some birds, such as orioles, bluebirds, tanagers, and Northern Mockingbirds, are attracted to jelly and fruit; some jays even feed on jelly. Jelly feeders often come with a fruit station or fruit spikes, making it easy to serve the fruit (such as apples and oranges) that attracts migratory birds. Orioles in particular like grape jelly; keep plenty on hand when they fly through your area. You also can offer mealworms to tempt songbirds to your jelly feeder. Some jelly feeders offer an area to place sugar water, making the feeder nearly irresistible to orioles. Jelly feeders require frequent cleaning because fruit rots, and jelly and fruit leave a sticky residue.

Suet Feeders

Suet feeders attract insect eaters, such as blackbirds, bluebirds, Blue Jays, chickadees, European Starlings, Northern Mockingbirds, nuthatches, orioles, warblers, woodpeckers, and wrens. You can mix the suet with various tasty treats, such as seed, insects, fruit, and pellets. Suet can be offered year-round, but it will melt and go rancid in warmer climates unless you purchase a "no-melt" commercial variety.

1. A Red-Bellied Woodpecker visits a jelly feeder that offers grape jelly and an orange.

2. Some birds, including woodpeckers, will hang upside down to eat suet.

3. A mounted window feeder often entices small birds.

4. The mesh on a woodpecker feeder allows the bird access to larger seeds.

Varying the Menu

During summer, consider switching up the feeders. Many birdwatchers remove suet from the menu during warmer weather and replace suet feeders with those meant to lure hummingbirds. Debate continues over the best way to place sugar-water feeders so that territorial males can't keep female and young hummingbirds from using them. Recent observations have shown that sugar-water feeders separated from one another might attract many territorial males. Some people suggest placing several feeders in a tightly clumped group because bullying males become tired and overwhelmed when numerous hummers keep trying to use these feeders. By late summer, when fledglings and females are all on the scene, it apparently becomes easier for males to let everyone sip sugar water in harmony.

Another change in hummingbird feeding strategies is the extension of hummingbird season, particularly east of the Mississippi River. Putting up sugar-water feeders earlier in spring and leave them out in fall does not keep resident hummers from migrating south in autumn when their internal clocks say it's time to go. Spring and fall feeding can, however, provide much-needed fuel to late or early migrants.

Suet feeders don't require constant refilling, and they attract a variety of colorful species. You can purchase suet feeders at wild bird-supply stores, garden-supply centers, or online retailers. If you want to feed only woodpeckers and other clinging species rather than European Starlings, use an upside-down suet feeder to prevent unwanted birds from feeding. Woodpeckers will appreciate a suet feeder with a "tail prop" at the bottom, making it easier for them to balance while they feed.

Do you want to keep squirrels out of your suet? Buy a squirrel-proof suet feeder and a commercial version of suet that includes hot peppers. It's great for birds but not so fun for rodents.

Window Feeders

Usually made of clear plastic or acrylic, window feeders attach to the glass using suction cups or by fitting inside the window frame. This type of feeder enables up-close viewing of feathered visitors, and birds easily can find the food because they are able to see it through the clear plastic. Some feeders include one-way mirrored backs so that movement inside your home won't interrupt the birds but you can still watch them dine.

Fresh or dried mealworms work great for window feeders, attracting bluebirds, chickadees, Gray Catbirds, Northern Cardinals, Northern Mockingbirds, thrushes, titmice, and woodpeckers, among others.

Nyjer Feeders

Nyjer (a.k.a. thistle seed) remains the preferred food of goldfinches, Pine Siskins, and other songbirds. Often served in a sock or bag feeder, it is easy for small species to pluck out the small, black seeds, which will blow away in most other feeders. Thistle socks are relatively inexpensive, usually less than $10 each. If you want to get a little fancier, try a tube-style thistle feeder. Finches will love it, and larger species won't be able to use it.

Woodpecker Feeders

Woodpecker feeders allow woodpeckers to comfortably cling vertically to the feeders, propping their tails for stability. For this reason, most woodpecker feeders are quite long. Some woodpeckers are content with upside-down feeding, keeping nonclinging birds out of the feeder. The mesh on a woodpecker feeder allows for suet and large, hulled seeds to be consumed easily—but not so easily that a raccoon or squirrel can squander the feast.

Woodpeckers are drawn to fatty nuts and suet, both of which can go rancid in warm weather, so use these sparingly in the summer. Instead, offer fresh fruit and smaller amounts of suet and nuts that can be consumed quickly.

Location Suggestions

The locations where you place your feeders can determine their popularity. If one of your feeders doesn't get much attention, try moving it to a different area with the following qualities:

- **Brightness:** The brighter the area, the better you'll be able to see your visitors. Find a place that receives some sunshine during the day.
- **Protection:** Place your feeders near shrubs or trees where birds can take cover. Songbirds will scatter there if a predator approaches while they eat, and sneaky cats or squirrels can jump nearly 10 feet up from a low-lying branch or fence post. Also, make sure that your feeders are placed in areas that will protect the birds from cold winter winds.
- **Convenience:** Make sure that you can see the feeders from your favorite chair and that they aren't in places that make it difficult for you to reach, clean, and refill.

Configurations —By Rick Marsi

By placing feeders properly—and filling them with varied food items—you will draw feeder birds like a magnet. Let's focus on a few location strategies.

Concentrated Feeders

One location strategy centers on placing several feeders in close proximity. For example, attach five bracket arms to a 6-foot-high 4×4 post and hang a different feeder from each arm; for example, a sunflower tube feeder, a hanging feeder filled with nyjer (thistle seed), a free-swinging suet basket, a mesh feeder packed with peanuts, and a dome-topped feeder with perches (to offer sunflower in a different way).

To attract birds that feed at different heights when foraging in nature, vary the heights of the bracket arms on this all-in-one station. Place the post in a clearly visible spot some distance from the side of your home. Once birds become comfortable feeding there, you can move the feeding station gradually closer.

Although you want the feeder to be easy to see, it needs to sit in an area with vegetation. Birds are more likely to visit feeders near brush piles, evergreens, or other sources of cover. If your yard doesn't have such cover, add a brush pile or a clump of used Christmas trees so the birds can land there before and after visiting a feeder, and where they will be safe from predators and sheltered from weather. If there's a pecking order at the feeder—and there usually is—protective cover gives birds that are low on the totem pole a spot to wait until their turn arrives.

1. A tray feeder permits easy access to birds as well as varmints.

2. A "feeder station" with different types of feeders offering different types of seed will attract a range of birds.

Spread It Around

While this concentrated set-up with cover nearby will attract birds in numbers, it shouldn't be the only feeder source in the yard. Offering other feeders, at spread-out locations, prevents overcrowding and increases the variety of species attracted to your backyard buffet.

A good example is a large tray or table feeder placed fairly close to the ground and stocked with cracked corn or a seed mix containing white proso millet. Most feeder birds prefer this type of millet to milo, wheat, and other ingredients that companies might add to seed mixes. Ground-feeding birds, such as juncos, Northern Cardinals, sparrows, and towhees will respond to a tray feeder's location.

Squirrels will come to a tray feeder, too, but that's not a bad thing. Access to a tray feeder at one end of the yard might keep varmints, as well as undesirable bird species, away from sunflower feeders at the other feeding station. Luring these creatures to an "all-access" feeder a bit out of the way might

Raptors at Feeders

A pile of feathers at the base of a bird feeder is a sobering sight: a sure sign that a predatory bird—likely a Cooper's or Sharp-Shinned Hawk— found a meal. Before humans offered bird feeders, these hawks haunted forests, and although they captured and consumed a steady diet of songbirds, their predation never caused a significant drop in the population of prey species.

Enter the era of backyard bird-feeding, with birds concentrated in numbers that a hawk can't resist. We truly can't blame the hawks. To survive in the best way they can, they're simply taking advantage of the songbird abundance that our feeders create.

What we can do is make sure that hawks cannot easily capture birds at our feeders by providing brush piles, evergreens, and other sources of shelter near feeding stations—not so close that predators can lurk in them, but close enough that a songbird can dash into one if a hawk sweeps in to attack.

keep them from being pests to the birds at the other feeders.

Ground-feeding birds will also like a lean-to feeder. This roofed feeder keeps seed rain- and snow-free and available in all weather. Put this type of feeder at the edge of a brushy area, allowing birds to enter it without leaving cover.

Consider adding more suet at multiple locations in different types of feeders; at least one feeder should be free-swinging and one should be solidly attached to a post or tree. Smaller woodpeckers, such as Downies, don't mind swaying about while chiseling chunks of protein-rich suet, but larger Hairy and Pileated Woodpeckers appreciate a stationary feeder.

Cleaning Tips

Most birdfeeders need cleaning about twice a month, although some—like sugar-water and jelly feeders—require more regular cleaning. A good rule is to clean the feeder before it becomes soiled. Moldy or rancid seed or suet can make backyard birds sick if ingested. Birds also can spread disease by gathering at feeders, so it's important to regularly clean the feeder area.

To clean your feeders:

1. Fill a plastic tub or utility sink with a solution of ten parts water and one part bleach.
2. Put on rubber gloves.
3. If the birdfeeder is easy to disassemble, take it apart and place each part into the bleach solution.
4. Using a stiff scrubbing brush (or a tube-cleaning brush for a tube feeder), remove the debris from the feeder, paying careful attention to the platform and perches. If the feeder appears very soiled or moldy, leave it in the bleach solution for about ten minutes.
5. Rinse the feeder very thoroughly; any bleach left behind can be fatal to the birds.
6. Dry the feeder with a towel. For a tube-style or wooden feeder, let it air-dry overnight before refilling it with seed or suet.

Squirrel Feeders

No discussion of birdfeeders is complete without mentioning squirrels. Many birders take great pains to thwart the squirrels in their yards, adding baffles and domes to their feeders, even trying mechanical feeders that spin when a squirrel tries to feed. Other backyard birders take an "if you

can't beat 'em, join 'em" attitude toward squirrels, installing squirrel-diversion feeders to provide the rodents with their own food and keep them out of the birdfeeders.

A simple squirrel feeder might consist of a spiral wire that holds a dried corncob; however, many feature more complex designs and are aimed at making the squirrels work for their food. Why not? These agile, acrobatic creatures will do anything for a peanut, and it's quite entertaining to watch them use their brains to solve a problem. Some squirrel feeders require the critter to lift a lid on a box, some look more like moving jungle gyms, and others employ bungee cords. If you're going to feed the squirrels, you might as well enjoy the show!

Backyard Bothers

If you feed wild birds, sooner or later you'll be visited by some unwanted visitors. "Many animals are attracted by the seeds in the feeders, while others are attracted by the birds themselves," says Howard Bishop IV, owner of the Wild Birds Unlimited location in Carlsbad, California. However, just because you like to feed songbirds doesn't mean that you also have to support the pests who may come along. "To eliminate many pests, make sure there is no seed on the ground," Bishop says. "Rats and mice are attracted to seeds that fall from the feeder or are thrown from the feeder by birds looking for a specific type of seed." He recommends using a large plant saucer under the feeder or a commercial seed catcher, or buying seed mixtures that are already hulled.

1. Squirrels go to great lengths to get to seed and suet.

2. A squirrel baffle placed above the feeder prevents the squirrel from climbing down to get food.

3. Squirrels like the sweet stuff, too!

Those Nutty Squirrels

Many people who feed birds complain about squirrels raiding their feeders, while other people admire these animals' intelligence and ingenuity. Squirrels spend a great deal of time eating because

they metabolize food quickly; they eat more than their body weight in food each week. They have sharp incisor teeth that enable them to chew through nutshells—as well as the sides of bird feeders. Tree squirrels can jump from 4 to 6 feet vertically and from 6 to 8 feet horizontally. Ground squirrels are athletic, too, but are more prone to climbing than jumping. However, their sharp nails make them proficient climbers.

To keep squirrels away from your feeders, Bishop recommends placing feeders on poles, preferably metal, at least 10 feet from any fence, tree, or sturdy shrub. Some commercially available feeders are marketed as squirrel-proof, but you can make just about any feeder safe from squirrels by using a baffle (a metal cone that the pole slides through) under the feeder on the pole that supports the feeder. If a squirrel is able to shimmy up the metal pole, it ends up inside the cone with no way to reach the feeder. Other baffles are dome-shaped and made for the top of the feeder, positioned with the rounded side up. The squirrel slides off the dome and cannot reach the feeder.

Hit the Road, Rodent

If seeds are present, especially seeds with high oil content, like sunflower seeds, rodents such as rats and mice will also show up. Ground rats, roof rats, and mice of all kinds willingly frequent bird feeders, and once they find food, their numbers increase rapidly. Rodents will also attract other predators, including cats and snakes, which may catch birds as well as some of the rodents.

Bishop advises using baffles above and below the feeders, but, he advises, "Never hang the feeders from the rafters of your house or from tree limbs. Not only can rats climb, but they will chew the feeder to pieces to get to the seeds inside. Plus, if the rats find feeders hanging from your rafters, they will move into your house."

As previously mentioned, placing seed catchers underneath feeders keeps seeds from falling to the ground. The US Fish and Wildlife Service recommends storing birdseed in metal containers

Cat Concerns

Domesticated cats are appealing when they lie on our laps, purring, and are amusing when they chase and bat at their toys. But they are still extremely capable hunting animals and are credited with killing thousands of songbirds in the United States every day. In addition, birds that are caught and escape with injuries usually die of those injuries within days.

In 1997, the American Bird Conservancy began a program called "Cats Indoors" to educate cat owners about keeping their cats inside—not only to protect millions of birds from predation by the cats but also to promote longer, safer lives for the cats themselves. Cats that spend their lives outside are prone to being hit by cars or killed by dogs and other predators, and they are more at risk of disease and other dangers.

Raccoons

Raccoons will eat just about anything and have been known to raid bird feeders. Furthermore, they are very intelligent and good problem-solvers, so it's tough to outwit these raiders. Raccoons are active at night, when songbirds are roosting, so one easy way to foil them is to bring feeders in at night. Large baffles also will stop most raccoons; small baffles, made for mice or rats, will not work.

1. Seed on the ground will attract rodents, who can be more than just an annoyance if they carry disease.

2. The ant moat above the feeder prevents ants from getting to the sugar water.

with tight-fitting or locking lids because mice and rats can chew into bags and even plastic storage containers. Bishop says that rats also like to find food sources near shelter, so don't put feeders near stacks of firewood, and clear up trash, debris, dense shrubs, and dead plants.

Going Buggy

Ants are common visitors to bird feeders, and once an ant finds a food source, other ants come in droves. Ants are especially attracted to sugar-water feeders, and once they begin swarming a feeder, the birds rarely return.

Stopping these insects is easy. Most stores that sell bird feeders also sell red cups that hang between the hummingbird feeder and the support for the feeder. When filled with water, this will stop all ants in their tracks.

Bees are also attracted to hummingbird feeders, but apparently hummingbirds are willing to share their food with bees. Since honeybees are having difficulty surviving in so many regions of North America, perhaps allowing them to share is a good policy!

Mosquitoes, however, are another story. Mosquitoes are attracted to water, where they lay their eggs. Bird baths with shallow, still water are perfect for these pests' needs. With mosquitoes able to pass along so many deadly diseases, including West Nile Virus, it's important that you deny them the ability to reproduce.

Adding chemicals to the water to kill mosquito larvae may harm the birds that use the water, so look to other options. Bishop recommends a contraption called a "water wiggler." Water wigglers run on batteries and agitate the water in a bird bath, discouraging mosquitoes from laying their eggs there. Birds are attracted to the reflections of moving water, so they in turn are more attracted to the bird bath. Even with a water wiggler, though, you should replace bird-bath water daily to keep it clean and reduce any chance of mosquito larvae.

Optics for Birders—By John E. Riutta
Binoculars

A birder's first optics purchase should be a binocular: a portable tool capable of greatly enhancing the experience of bird watching. To select the appropriate binocular, let's begin by decoding how binoculars are identified: by two sets of numbers separated by an "×." The number to the left of the × reveals the magnification level of the binocular, which denotes how many times closer (or larger) the bird will appear to you when viewing it through the binocular. The × itself is the symbol for magnification level, or power, so one might say, "I just bought a 7-power binocular." The number to the right of the × reveals the diameter of the objective lens (the one farthest away when using the binocular), measured in millimeters; the abbreviation "mm" may or may not appear after the number.

The entire sequence identifies the binocular. For example, a 7-by-42-millimeter (indicated as 7×42mm) binocular magnifies an image to seven times its actual size and uses a 42-mm objective lens on each side.

The type of prism and focus mechanisms also distinguish binoculars. The type of prisms used in the optical system will be either porro or roof, and the focus mechanisms will be either center focus or independent focus.

Porro prism, named after inventor Antonio Porro, is the older of the prism designs, characterized by objective lenses that do not appear in line with the eyepiece lenses. Roof-prism binoculars, named after the roof-shaped prisms they use, are identified by objective lenses directly in line with the eyepiece lenses.

Center-focus binoculars have a dial along the central hinge for simultaneously focusing both sides of the binocular, whereas users of independent-focus models must adjust each eyepiece separately. The time required to focus an image proves crucial in birding, so independent-focus models are rarely used.

When choosing a binocular, bigger isn't always better. Too many people purchase a high-magnification binocular because they assume that it will make birds easier to see and identify. Although a higher magnification level will increase the apparent size of the bird to the user, other factors prove less desirable.

First, the exit pupil (the aperture of light visible in each of the binocular's eyepiece lenses) is governed by the size of the objective lenses. Dividing the objective diameter by the magnification level determines the diameter of the exit pupil in millimeters. A larger exit pupil will present more light to the user's eyes, brightening the image seen through the binocular and, in many cases, making it clearer.

Between two binoculars of the same brand and model—one an 8×42mm and one a 10×42—the 8×42 model offers a brighter image to the user. Although some manufacturers use larger objective lenses in higher magnification binoculars to overcome the shrinking exit pupil, this also makes the binocular heavier and less pleasant to carry for long periods.

Does the ideal combination of birding magnification and objective diameter even exist? Not exactly, but some arrangements are quite popular. The 7×42, for example, generally provides a wide field of view and a large exit pupil. A wide field of view enables a user to observe flying birds, and a large exit pupil offers a bright image and helps stabilize the image even if your hands shake a little. The 8×42 is popular for the slight boost in magnification that it offers without sacrificing too much exit pupil diameter. The 8×32 finds favor with many because it is smaller and lighter yet still retains full-size binocular performance levels.

Whichever style you choose, always make sure that your interpupillary distance (the distance between your pupils) is compatible with the interpupillary range of the binocular. Check that you can adjust the hinge of the binocular to position both eyepieces directly in front of your eyes to offer a full and unobstructed field of view. If you always see little black crescents at the edge of the field no matter how you position the hinge, that binocular doesn't fit you properly.

Other highly desired features in a birding binocular include a focus distance (how close you can get to an object and still adjust it into focus) of 10 feet or less and a waterproof body filled with nitrogen or argon gas. Waterproofing and gas filling will help to prevent internal condensation from building up in the binocular—a condition known as *fogging*.

Most binoculars have a folding rubber eyepiece or retractable eyepiece guards. Birdwatchers who don't wear glasses should use these guards extended, but those with glasses will need to fold or retract them. Eyeglasses differ, but most binocular models with an eye relief distance of 16 mm or higher prove compatible with the majority of eyeglasses. (Remember this point with spotting scopes, too.)

Beyond Binoculars

A spotting scope is a telescope designed for use primarily when looking at objects on, or at least within, the atmosphere of the Earth. Unlike larger and higher-magnified celestial ("star-gazing") telescopes, a spotting scope can be a handy tool for birdwatchers. Spotting scopes have higher magnifications, so they require tripod mounting for a steady image. The highest magnification level that most people can keep steady without a tripod is 10×.

A spotting scope is a helpful tool for the backyard birder.

1. Whether we like it or not, the American Black Crow (*Corvus brachyrhynchos*) is abundant across the country.

2. Wild waterfowl can be backyard guests but never kept as pets.

Most spotting scopes use a porro-prism design and large objective lenses (generally 60 to 80 mm) and are made with straight or angled eyepieces. Unlike binoculars, the most common type of eyepiece used on spotting scopes is the zoom eyepiece. Settings range from 15× up to 60×, but with only one optical channel, a well-built eyepiece can be designed to change the magnification levels' dramatic loss of quality.

Choosing a spotting scope proves much easier than choosing a binocular; your main considerations are (1) whether you want a straight or angled eyepiece design and a built-in or interchangeable eyepiece and (2) whether you plan to use it for digiscoping (using a digital camera to capture still or video images through the spotting scope). Angled eyepiece models generally feel comfortable to use but are a little more difficult to master because the direction in which your eye looks is 45 degrees off the direction in which the scope points. With a bit of practice, however, you easily can overcome this challenge. An interchangeable eyepiece design allows you to extend the life of the scope as your skills improve and preferences change.

Advice for Backyard Birders

Birds in the garden open up a world of inquiry, observation, and inspiration that repays your efforts to provide them habitat. Food, water, shelter, and space take on deeper meaning if you turn a focused eye in the direction of our feathered friends. Like the proverbial canary in the coal mine, here are a few reminders of the powerful connections we may experience with backyard birds.

Find Beauty in the Familiar

Crows are everywhere. In the United States there exists, on average, one crow per family. Like pigeons, starlings, Canada Geese, and English Sparrows, crows are where they are because we've created a space for them. Now we have to deal with them, and that's where our attitudes can have a big influence.

Crow Planet by Lyanda Lynn Haupt explains her view as a result of her deep study of crows. "Certainly it is ironic, at best, that we remove forests, replace them with concrete and shrubbery, line the sidewalks with plastic cans full of food scraps and topped with ill-fitting lids, and then lament the presence and noise of so many crows. But no, if it were about deserving, we would have no bird at all. As it is, we have a shiny, black, intelligent, native, wild bird. Crows may not be the bird we deserve, but they are the bird we've been given."

Respect Boundaries

On a freezing cold morning in November, during the time I was writing this book, I found a dead duck under my car. I was both saddened and intrigued. I put on gloves and examined it for a few minutes. The beautiful green neck showed its iridescence. The pale feathers thickly covered a full, stout body. A bright blue patch was barely visible on the wing until I brushed my thumb across to see the rectangular band. I gave the foot a gentle squeeze, amazed at the tough, rubbery webbing. Not sure what else to do, I bagged and boxed it, adding a sprig of herbs from my garden as a token, wishing safe passage to the other side.

After finding out that this duck had been seen wandering in the busy street nearby, I was more curious about learning what happened. As a result of persistent inquiries, state wildlife biologists took an interest. They examined the bird, and the results bothered me: it had been a captive male Mallard with a clipped wing. Because it couldn't fly, it most likely was hit by a car and then dragged itself to a secluded spot to die.

It is illegal to keep any migratory waterfowl captive. I wondered if the people who kept the bird knew that. I wondered if they had been keeping it for food or as a pet. I wondered if, as children, these people had learned to appreciate wild birds by watching them from a distance, seeing them land in creeks full of clean water, and learning about why they migrate—and would that have made a difference? I will never know, but I know that keeping wildlife in captivity never ends well. Birds are meant to fly.

Do Your Best

On a lighter note, in the film *Dirt: The Movie*, Wangari Maathai narrates an inspiring traditional legend of how the littlest of birds, the hummingbird, can inspire all of our actions. The story of the hummingbird is about a huge forest being consumed by a fire. All the animals in the forest come out, and they are transfixed as they watch the forest burning. They feel very overwhelmed, very powerless. Except this little hummingbird. It says, "I'm going to do something about the fire." So it flies to the nearest stream, takes a drop of water and puts it on the fire. It goes up and down, up and down, up and down, as fast as it can. In the meantime, all the other animals, much bigger animals … they are standing there, helpless. They are saying to the hummingbird, "What do you think you can do? You're too little! And this fire is too big!" But, as they continued to discourage it, it turns to them, without wasting any time, and tells them, "I am doing the best I can."

Maathai concludes with the moral of the story: "That, to me, is what all of us should do. We should always feel like a hummingbird. I may feel insignificant, but I certainly don't want to be like the animals watching the planet go down the drain. I will be a hummingbird. I will do the best I can."

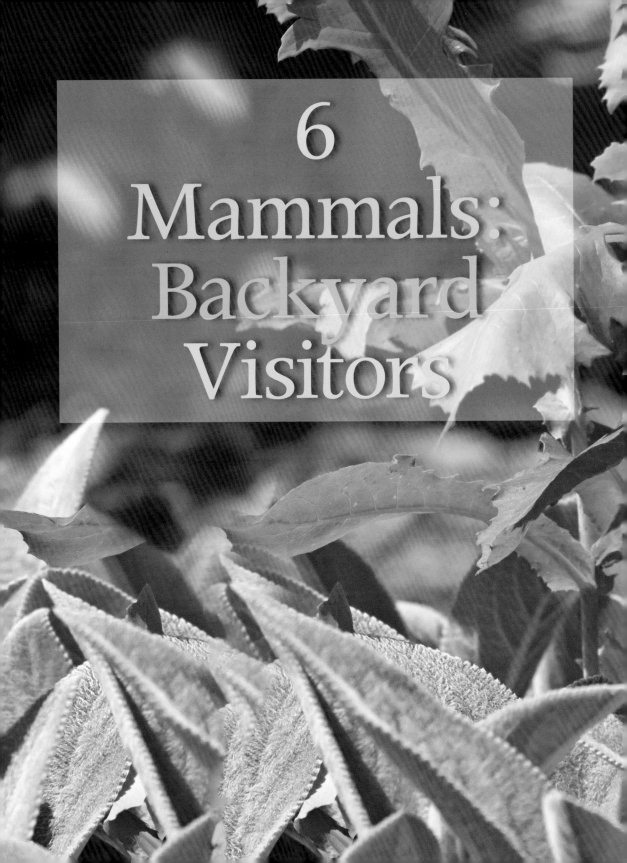

6
Mammals: Backyard Visitors

Your first thought when considering inviting mammals into your backyard sanctuary might be, *That's asking for trouble.* Good. Listen to that instinct. Be cautious about who might show up uninvited. Mammals can be helpful—or destructive—to your garden, so plan wisely. Consider attracting mammals that help in the same ways that birds and insects do: cleaning up, recycling, and regulating growth in the backyard habitat.

Mammals in Your Garden

In the existing literature on wildlife in gardens, we are generally encouraged to invite birds, bees, and butterflies but keep everything else out. People love seeing winged beauties of all shapes and varieties, but they consider ways to exterminate furry little critters. Conflicts with wild mammals in residential gardens often are due to misinformation, fear, or a lack of understanding that the animals are simply looking for opportunities to survive. However, sometimes there is a justifiable need to protect your property and plants. Following are some general guidelines for a peaceful coexistence with mammals and wildlife of all types.

Invitations

- Domestic and wild don't mix. Keep pets indoors unless you are specifically using a dog to establish dominance in the territory; for example, to warn deer or coyotes not to come close. Keep the pet food inside, too. Nothing says "welcome" to critters better than a readily available food supply.
- Garbage smells good. Just like pet food, your trash is an open invitation to get too close for comfort, and it will likely make wildlife sick. Not only will processed food—or worse, its packaging—do a number on wild animals' digestive systems, but their reliance on human handouts could lead to aggressive behavior.

The Garden's Ecosystem

I like the advice given in the book *The Wildlife Sanctuary Garden* by Carol Buchanan: "Making a backyard wildlife sanctuary garden, inviting nature in ... means we welcome all creatures, including the ugly and the creepy crawlies, the beautiful, the comical, and the cute. We don't exclude an animal from the sanctuary because we don't like it or we're afraid of it or it has some loathsome quality, such as its smell or its feeding habits ... We've worked to make an ecosystem with plant communities, but the animals are part of that ecosystem, too."

- Bird feeders make it easy for wildlife to get to food. If you put out food for one species, such as sunflower seeds for your favorite finches, you must acknowledge how attractive seeds are to rodents, too. There are many deterrents that make it harder for rodents to get the seed, but making tougher obstacles to food sometimes results in tougher animals.
- Limit the amount of food you put out, and store your seed supply inside metal garbage cans with lids. Many rodents can chew through plastic.

• Use plants wisely. Native plants will produce seed at the right time for the species that need it the most. The more you learn about the tastes of animals such as deer, the better you can disguise their favorite plants. Place less-appealing plants around your property as a border. Also, interplant the ones they avoid with the ones they love.

• Compost carefully. Vegetable scraps can be as appealing as fresh produce growing in the garden. Meats, fats, and bones will rouse interest from mammals, so these should never go into the compost pile. Keep compost far from any buildings in case it does attract rodents.

Prevention

• The enemy of your enemy is your friend. A balanced food web never lets one species get too comfortable. To an extent, providing habitat for snakes, owls, and other birds of prey will keep the population of small mammals under control. However, be careful how you use this tool, because it could lead to more wildlife than you've bargained for.

• Trapping is not recommended. Professional wildlife rehabilitators or relocators make house calls. They are trained to understand the life cycles of mammals and know how to handle them without undue stress. Focus on removing the attraction, not the animal.

• Secure the premises. Depending on the animal you want to keep out and the size of your garden, fencing may be the best type of prevention. For burrowing animals, you'll need to bury the fence or fan it out a good distance from the baseline. To keep out climbers, angle the fence at least 45 degrees outward at the top.

• Poisons are not an option. Every animal on your property is part of a food web that extends beyond your boundaries. Raptors, scavengers, or even pets could be your unintended victims, and pesticide use drastically affects beneficial insects.

1. Pet cats belong indoors to keep them from being predators or prey.

2. An unsecured trash can is an open invitation to all kinds of unwelcome, and even dangerous, visitors.

3. Fencing your property will work to keep some animals out.

• As a last resort, use scare tactics. Well-timed loud noises, fake dead animals, species-directed distress calls, and barking dogs are as annoying to wildlife as they are to humans. Such tactics can teach wildlife not to get too comfortable around humans, and that is for their own good. Shout, wave your arms, and appear large and aggressive until the animal is far from your sight, but make sure that it has an escape route. Never corner a wild animal.

Bats: Gardeners' Friends—By Samantha Johnson

If you're leery of bats, you aren't alone, but bats actually perform a variety of services— including pest control and pollination—that can prove immensely helpful to gardeners. If you haven't already welcomed these winged creatures into your garden, a pleasant surprise is ready to swoop into your life.

The Misunderstood Mammal

Unfortunately, negative myths regarding bats began long ago and remain deep-seated in the minds of some people. According to the 1925 book *Bats, Mosquitoes, and Dollars* by Charles A. R. Campbell, "From time immemorial, the bat has been considered a 'thing of evil.' The ancient poets and painters, while giving the benign spirits and angels the beautiful white, symmetrical wings of birds … gave to the malignant spirits and demons the dark and sombre [sic] wings of a bat; hence this truly valuable creature has always had a most unenviable reputation." Correlations between bats and vampires, and the bat's popularity in spooky Halloween décor, have done little to debunk the negative stereotype.

Thousands of bat species exist worldwide, but fewer than fifty are native to North America. Insectivores represent the vast majority of bat species, with a few classified as nectar-feeding. As the only flying mammal, the bat remains a unique creature with incredible abilities. Many of the insectivore species use echolocation (biological sonar) to detect their prey in the dark through vocalizations and sound waves.

Jamaican fruit-eating bats have a particular liking for figs.

Bats as Pollinators

Most people are familiar with common insect pollinators, such as bees and butterflies, and their importance is certainly undeniable. Fewer people are aware of the vital importance of bats as pollinators. "Bats play a key role in pollinating many plant species that are themselves integral parts of local ecosystems," says Victoria Wojcik, PhD, research director of Pollinator Partnership, a San Francisco-based nonprofit. Wojcik cites the saguaro cactus in the Sonoran Desert as a prime example. "The giant saguaro is a keystone species that supports life in this arid ecosystem, [and] countless other species depend on it for food and shelter, but the saguaro is incapable of self-fertilization, depending on the lesser long-nosed bat (*Leptonycteris yerbabuenae*) for pollination."

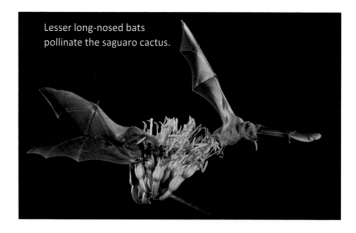

Lesser long-nosed bats pollinate the saguaro cactus.

The lesser long-nosed bat is one of only a handful of nectar-feeding bats found in North America. According to Wojcik, other nectar-feeding species include the Jamaican fruit-eating bat (*Artibeus jamaicensis*), found in far southern Florida; the Mexican long-tongued bat (*Choeronycteris mexicana*); and the Mexican long-nosed bat (*Leptonycteris nivalis*), found in the southern United States. "It is only the nectar-feeding set of bats that visit flowers and act as pollinators," Wojcik says. "Another fact about bat pollination is that many plants have specialized to be uniquely pollinated by bats."

Bats are most commonly associated with the pollination of fruit. The US Fish and Wildlife Service estimates that bats pollinate more than 300 types of fruit in tropical and desert climates. "Many bats are critical pollinators of plants such as bananas, figs, and guava," Mies says. "They are the only pollinators of agave." Bats also pollinate some nuts, such as almonds and cashews.

If you live in a southern region and want to encourage bats to visit your garden, you don't have to plant a banana tree in your yard. To attract pollinating bats, the best thing you can do is "plant the night-blooming species they feed on and protect the wildland habitats (desert caves) in which they live," advises Wojcik. By protecting the natural habitats of nectar-feeding bats, you'll help these species thrive in your area, regardless of your desire to grow figs, guava, or other types of fruit.

Give Bats a Chance

Rob Mies, executive director of Organization for Bat Conservation, says that bats are intelligent, docile animals that bite only if threatened. "Bats are not blind, will not make a nest in your hair, and will not drink your blood," he adds. Only vampire bats, which are not found in the United States or Canada, drink blood.

Always bear in mind that bats vastly prefer to keep to themselves. Encouraging them to visit your garden shouldn't increase your encounters with them or cause any alarm.

Bats and Rabies

The ever-present issue of rabies is undoubtedly a valid concern. According to the Centers for Disease Control and Prevention (CDC)'s website (www.cdc.gov), "most bats don't have rabies." The website also notes that any bat that is active by day or is found in a place where bats are not usually found might be rabid. "A bat that is unable to fly and is easily approached could very well be sick." The CDC also notes that because you can't determine whether a bat has rabies simply by looking at it, it's wise to take the safest course of action, which is to never handle a bat. Call a local wildlife rehabilitator.

1. Moonflowers are appealing to bats and can grow taller than 10 feet high.

2. Little brown bats are helpful insect-eaters in the garden.

Natural Pest Control

The idea of bats pollinating your garden might sound wonderful, but what if pollinator bats don't reside where you live? How can bats help you in your yard? For gardeners in the vast majority of the United States, bats are natural helpers in quite another way: eating nuisance bugs. According to Rob Mies, "Bats are the primary predators of night-flying insects. They consume large numbers of stink bugs, corn earworm moths, cucumber beetles, and tomato hornworm moths." Bats are also famous for their ability to effectively devour mosquitoes, which is an appealing trait. An individual bat is capable of eating hundreds of mosquitoes per hour. Some bats can eat up to 50 percent of their body weight in mosquitoes in a single night.

Attract that Bat!

If you'd like bats to "hang around" your yard, provide an attractive array of night-blooming flowers to entice them. Night-blooming flowers attract moths—and, consequently, bats—which makes these plants an ideal addition to a bat-friendly garden.

When planning a garden with an eye on attracting nectar-feeding bats, it's important to select appropriate plants. "Flowers pollinated by bats are predominantly open during the night, are light in color, are very fragrant, and provide large amounts of nectar," Wojcik says. This advice holds true even if you live in a region without nectar-feeding bats; insectivore bats will be attracted to the moths that visit the same type of pale-colored, fragrant, night-blooming flowers.

If naturally bat-friendly sites don't exist near your garden, never fear! It's easy to prepare artificial alternatives. Bat houses (also known as "bat boxes") offer an ideal way to invite bats to take up residence near your yard. Wojcik clarifies: "[Bat houses] are great, but the bats that inhabit them are not the species that pollinate." However, a colony of little brown bats (*Myotis lucifugus*) might decide to move right in.

Building a Bat House

You want to build a house (or two or ten!) for the bats in your garden? Bats are very particular about their housing and won't use anything that doesn't meet their instinctive specifications. Here's what you need to know:

Find a good plan. By constructing your own bat house, you can control all aspects of the project and create the house to your precise specifications. Bat Conservation International and the National Wildlife Federation offer plans for a wall-mounted single-chamber bat house, as does the Organization for Bat and possibly your state's department of natural resources.

Paint your bat house. You'll choose the color of your bat house depending on the average summer temperatures in your area. For cooler northern regions, it's recommended to use a dark color, such as black. Choose a medium shade or even a light color in a hotter region in which temperatures regularly reach 90–100 degrees Fahrenheit during summer months.

Choose the right location: In most regions, full sun is the ideal location for a bat house. Bats typically avoid shady locations, so choose a spot that receives several hours of direct sun each day. Place the bat house within easy distance of a water source, and attach it to the side of a building. Install your bat house early in the spring for the best chance of encouraging bats to use the house immediately.

You can mount bat houses on a sturdy tree, but the side of a building is a better location.

While the plants in your garden play an important part in attracting bats, you also can increase your yard's appeal by creating a small pond. A nearby water source is important for insectivore bats, and a pond can add an interesting structural element to your garden.

In addition, Mies suggests gardening organically, saying that it's beneficial to leave up dead and dying trees. "Climbing vines on the sides of buildings or [a] trellis will provide solitary bats a safe place to roost." It's also important to incorporate some linear features into your garden to open a flyway for hunting bats. This could be as simple as a time-worn trail or as complicated as a made-from-scratch stone wall. Fences, hedgerows, and streams are other examples of linear features that could play a part in your bat-friendly garden.

Lend a Hand

Wojcik encourages all gardeners to support bats, even if pollinating bats live elsewhere. If you do happen to reside in a region in which nectar-feeding bats are common, she suggests helping out as a citizen scientist or supporting local research programs. "Pollinator Partnership works really closely with Bat Conservation International, and they are a group I would encourage people to support," she says.

So, what are you waiting for? Take the initiative this week. Find out what you can do to support bats in your area and how you can promote the value of bats with local gardeners. With millions of bats being inexplicably afflicted by white-nose syndrome—a fatal fungal disease—it's more

Night-Blooming Plants

Confirm your zip code's USDA hardiness zone (www.planthardiness.ars.usda.gov) and then check out these night-blooming possibilities.

- Angel's trumpet: The two closely related species (*Datura innoxia* and *Brugmnasia spp.*) are both known as angel's trumpet and are suitable for zones 9 to 11, although some gardeners in northern climates have success with them as annuals or in containers. Angel's trumpet is extremely poisonous, so take special care when working around it.

Evening primrose

- Evening primrose: Native to North America and a good choice for cooler growing regions, the evening primrose belongs to the *Oenothera* genus and is hardy to zones 3 or 4. Evening primrose provides a nice alternative to so many of the night-blooming plants that require warmer temperatures to thrive.

- Four o'clocks: Colorful and fragrant, these charming little flowers (*Mirabilis jalapa*) are native to Peru and get their name from the fact that they open (theoretically, anyway) at four o'clock in the afternoon and stay open all night. They are easily grown anywhere but can be grown as perennials in zones 7 to 11.

- Moonflowers: The large, white flowers of *Ipomoea alba* can be grown as perennials in zones 8 to 11 and as annuals elsewhere. They are stunningly beautiful as well as fragrant; however, moonflowers (particularly the seeds) are poisonous. Moonflowers can reach substantial heights of 10 feet or higher.

- Night-blooming jasmine: Noted for its perfumed scent at night, *Cestrum nocturnum* is a shrub that boasts tiny green/white flowers as well as berries. Night-blooming jasmine is hardy to zone 8 but does well as a potted plant in cooler climates. This poisonous plant is native to the West Indies.

Night-blooming jasmine

- Night phlox: A nice choice for a patio plant, the South African-native *Zaluzianskya capensis* offers a sweet vanilla/honey fragrance in the evenings and is hardy in zones 9 to 10.

important than ever to work toward promoting the health and safety of bats across North America. Don't let those age-old bat stereotypes prevent you from experiencing all of the wonder and satisfaction that comes from having these nocturnal beings grace your garden.

The Smallest Mammals

In the book *Animal Speak: The Spiritual and Magical Powers of Creatures Great and Small*, Ted Andrews shares insights from traditional cultures on the significance of all kinds of animals. Although modern civilization appears to have no room for what is derogatively termed "vermin," these animals live among us, often because of us. They try to stay unnoticed, tending to their chores of gathering, nesting, cleaning, and making babies that will be the target of every predator in the food web.

Shrews and Moles

Shrews and moles are not rodents, which have flat-tipped teeth that continually grow unless they are gnawing. Shrews actually have tiny spike-like teeth. Shrews possess many interesting traits, yet many gardeners cannot tell a shrew from a gopher. By human terms, shrews live a stressed-out lifestyle. They have the fastest heart rate and metabolism, have the shortest life span, and get the least amount of sleep of any North American mammal. In addition, American short-tailed shrews are the only mammal with a poisonous bite (that can even conquer snakes). Hunting well enough to feed their insatiable appetites requires great skill. Although their eyesight is weak, some species can send out high- or low-frequency signals to echolocate under leaf litter or within snow tunnels.

Like shrews, moles are the size of small mice. They have velvety skin and tiny eyes covered by thin skin. Also like shrews, they are solitary animals, so you aren't likely to find more than three to five moles per acre. They are insectivores that dig tunnels with their broad, paddle-like front feet to get to their favorite foods—beetles, worms, and grubs—and they must eat at least every 12 hours to survive. They have unique adaptations that make life underground possible: no external ears, fur that can point forward or backward, and a fragile, sensitive skull that senses vibrations. They live underground in bi-level burrows, with the upper for feeding, the lower for nesting. Their tunnels may disturb a few plants, but you'll be grateful that moles control root-eating insects.

Voles

Meadow mice, also known as voles, are common backyard rodents that eat grains, seeds, nuts, vegetables, and fruits; they have shorter tails and stouter bodies than other mice. Not to be confused with moles, voles are, on average, about 2 inches longer, social, and herbivores. Voles will burrow in tunnels or use existing mole tunnels, but they also have surface runways. In the wild, voles keep plant crowding down by reducing the abundancy of any one species in a given area, which could help if you have aggressive plants that are taking over. If, on the other hand, the voles are

1. The mole's large front feet enable it to dig underground to find food and build shelter.

2. The shape of the burrow will help you identify the animal that made it.

3. A vole is a type of stout-bodied, short-tailed mouse.

taking over, encourage natural predators to balance the scales. Birds of prey can snatch them up when they are above ground, but the only predator that can follow a vole down its hole is a snake.

Gophers

Gophers are more closely related to ground squirrels than to moles, but they do burrow underground. Gopher-tunnel entrances are more like crescent-shaped mounds, rather than the conical shapes that moles make. You'll likely find only one or two fiercely territorial gophers on your property, but they can create as many as 300 dirt mounds in a year. As a gopher digs, it severs grass roots and sometimes pulls entire plants down into its den. There are thirty-three species of gopher, and the ones known as pocket gophers have fur-lined pouches inside their cheeks to stash food. They can live up to twelve years and have an average of five offspring each year. It may be harder to tolerate gophers, but the gopher's work of aerating and tilling can benefit the integrity of the soil.

Ground Squirrels and Chipmunks

Ground squirrels and chipmunks burrow underneath plants but spend most of their foraging time above ground, eating an omnivorous diet of seeds, berries, slugs, beetles, and even small reptiles, young birds, and other mammals, maybe even baby gophers. Neatly manicured lawns seem to attract ground squirrels because they are natural residents of open meadows.

Chipmunks keep their 2- to 3-inch wide burrow entrances dirt-free by cleverly carrying away any telltale signs of digging and by scattering the soil elsewhere. Their burrows can extend 20 or 30 feet, and they will defend about a 50-foot radius around their burrows. They can have more than one litter of young each year. Rather than hibernating in the winter, they live off stored food and come out on warm days.

Groundhogs, Rabbits, and Tree Squirrels

Many gardeners find it difficult to embrace groundhogs, rabbits, and tree squirrels. Believe it or not, though, they do have some redeeming qualities in addition to their cartoonish cuteness.

Groundhogs

Groundhogs (*Marmota monax*) are marmots, a type of rodent that is closely related to squirrels. Their home range is as extensive as their regional aliases; they are found in all parts of North America and are called woodchucks, rockchucks, whistlepigs, land beavers, and rat bears. They are most well-known for their extensive burrows that can disturb orderly gardens, to put it mildly.

They are herbivores, eating a wide range of fruits, tree leaves, herbaceous plants, and grasses. Adults will eat about a pound to a pound and a half of vegetation each day, invoking the wrath of many farmers and gardeners.

Groundhogs dig burrows between 2 and 6 feet underground, and they can extend for 20 to 30 feet and include separate chambers: one for scat and one for sleeping. Their burrows provide habitat for many other semi-subterranean dwellers as well. Groundhogs are better hibernators than bears, and this adaptation equips them to stay in one location for their entire lives, which could last up to twelve years.

Marlene Condon is an optimistic gardener who has learned to accept groundhogs as part of her garden's ecosystem. In her book, *Nature-Friendly Garden*, she says that groundhogs in her yard prefer plantain, clover, and grasses. When they do nibble on her cultivated plants, they never eat the whole thing, and the results are similar to pruning. Her perennials were actually stronger, bushier, and "more floriferous" because of groundhogs.

When in balance with your garden, a groundhog's burrow will also aerate soil, which can, if done in moderation, help plant roots. They naturally till the soil while depositing pockets of fertilizer.

1. Tiny chipmunks store seeds, berries, and other garden goodies to survive cold winters.

2. Groundhogs are typically destructive to gardens, but their digging can have some benefits.

3. Gophers are prolific diggers in creating their burrows.

Groundhogs lead solitary, individual lifestyles until it's time to find a mate or nurse their young. They like to have 2 or 3 acres to themselves, but they deal with less space in more crowded urban areas. There is a debate as to whether removing a groundhog creates a space for another to move in. A gardener in Lexington, Kentucky, who lives on a small suburban property with a modest-sized backyard, removed an average of eight groundhogs each year for three years. She attributed their persistence to enough habitat in the few adjacent yards to sustain their population. The gentlest approach to dealing with groundhogs is to provide them with enough food in their own special garden that they will leave yours alone (mostly, anyway). Fences can work to protect a garden, but a fence must be buried at the bottom and angled out at the top because groundhogs can dig and climb. The only other humane prevention seems to be a dog that knows how to bark a warning without getting tangled up in a fight.

Rabbits

The eastern cottontail (*Sylvilagus floridanus*) is the most abundant rabbit found in gardens, while fourteen other species fill their niche in various ecosystems, such as jackrabbits in western regions and snowshoe hares in the north. Although rabbits are adorable, people go to great lengths to make their very inviting habitats inaccessible to rabbits.

Rabbits spend a good deal of time in underground burrows, called *warrens*, if the soil conditions are right. They will also use hollowed out trees or logs as a warren. Unlike the solitary groundhog, rabbits are very social and live in communities of eight to fifteen members.

Rabbits are not rodents, but they do have continuously growing incisors, which necessitates their chewing on woody material. They get their nutrition from an all-plant diet, and they recycle unused nutrients by consuming some of their own scat pellets. Plantain, dandelion, and clover—what many lawn-lovers consider "weeds"—are good distractions for rabbits to nibble on, but, like anyone, they prefer variety and quality, so peas, lettuce, and other nutritious spring greens may entice the cottontails more than you'd like. They don't hibernate, so they'll continue to eat whatever they can

find on trees—bark, twigs, buds, pine needles—to survive through the winter. Hungry rabbits (as well as porcupines and other rodents) can chew enough of the phloem and xylem tissue to kill small trees.

Rabbits are known for their prolific reproduction, and this is nature's way of guaranteeing their survival despite a short lifespan of around two years; only about 15 percent of young survive to adulthood. With litters of two to seven young produced up to three times a year, rabbits are hedging their bets that at least a few will grow up. However, young rabbits provide protein for hawks, owls, foxes, snakes, and just about every other garden predator.

The rabbit's best line of defense is to freeze or flee; its camouflage fur hides it well in dry grass, and it can zig-zag at speeds of up to 18 miles per hour. They find cover in shrubs or burrows, often dug by other animals. A rabbit's nest usually consists of a shallow depression in the ground, lined with fur and leaves. Mowing and raking can disturb these nests or even prove fatal for small bunnies, so try to locate them beforehand.

Their abundance in urban settings can be attributed to their mating habits, the reduction of natural predators, and the expansion of habitat. The wild habitat of eastern cottontails is naturally thickets, woodlands, and meadows—spaces that provide resources for both foraging and hiding.

Some gardens provide open invitations for rabbits. If you'd rather not host these furry prey animals, fencing may be your best bet. Rabbit-proof fences don't need to be more than 2 feet high, but they should be buried in the ground a few inches. To protect trees in the winter, encircle the trunk with hardware cloth up to 3 feet high. Space it a few inches away from the trunk so it will not damage the bark. Clearing away dormant herbaceous vegetation around the base of young trees removes protective cover for the rabbits and exposes them to predators.

Tree Squirrels

Tree squirrels' habits are fairly different from those of their cousins, the ground squirrels, because they occupy the canopy rather than the ground and herbaceous layers of the ecosystem.

Tree squirrels also have bushier tails for better warmth, sharper claws for climbing down head-first and performing other harrowing feats, and bigger ears for hearing all kinds of vocalizations and enabling them to communicate. Tree squirrels are omnivorous, eating seeds, nuts, fruit, bark, buds,

1. Rabbits can help rid lawns of weeds, but they also have a taste for fresh vegetables.

2. Squirrels are tenacious in their attempts to get to bird feeders.

3. Tree squirrels can both amaze and frustrate gardeners.

fungi, insects, and the occasional bird egg, baby bird, or small mammal.

Well-treed gardens all over North America are home to at least seven species of tree squirrel: red, western, and eastern gray; Abert's; Douglas's; eastern fox; and flying. Abert's squirrels are found only in the Rocky Mountains, and Douglas's squirrels are limited to the Pacific coastal region. In eastern and urban areas, the gray squirrel has become the most widespread tree squirrel.

Entire books have been written on the love–hate relationship that gardeners have with squirrels. On the one hand, their astounding acrobatics are fun to watch; on the other hand, they have been known to take bites out of perfectly good tomatoes and toss them aside, dig up bulbs, and ransack bird feeders. Although we can do our best to exclude them from certain areas in the garden, we also need to be aware of their natural instincts and the opportunities that gardens provide.

Like rabbits, squirrels don't hibernate. As long as they have stashed enough food, they'll stay in their nests for most of the winter. On warmer days, they make their presence known as they forage. Red squirrels leave distinctive traces of their activities on the snow in the form of discarded bracts and cores of pine cones. Gray squirrels like to break off the ends of deciduous trees branches, eat the buds, and drop the uneaten twigs.

Nut trees attract squirrels, and gray squirrels help the trees by burying nuts, in effect sowing the trees' seeds. They co-evolved this technique in their natural habitats—the eastern deciduous forests—where squirrel competition was fierce and which was similar to many suburban backyards. They are scatter-hoarders, and their survival technique is to spread out their food so that if one stash gets raided, there are back-ups in other locations.

Red squirrels are better at adapting to changes in their environment than are gray squirrels, but gray squirrels make much better companions for hardwood nut trees such as oak, hickory, and black walnut. A single squirrel can bury thousands of caches in one harvest season. Squirrels' excellent sense of smell helps them relocate their caches in winter, but they are bound to miss a few.

Opossums, Porcupines, and Beavers

"Controversial" might be a good word to describe the next trio of mammals. If you can allow them to live out their natural life cycles on your property, you'll be rewarded with glimpses into some of the most misunderstood and well-adapted animals for their environment.

Opossums

"The underdog of the wildlife world" is how Brigette Williams, director of Second Chances Wildlife Center (www.secondchanceswildlife.org) near Louisville, Kentucky begins her description of the

Dispelling the Myths

As a certified wildlife rehabilitator and educator, Brigette Williams houses an educational opossum named Cindy Lou, who was found as an orphaned and injured joey (baby opossum) after her mother was hit by a car. Cindy Lou helps Williams conduct outreach programs to dispel common misperceptions and let people know that they have nothing to fear from opossums. "They are the most gentle, non-confrontational animal that we rescue," she says. Freezing as if dead, or "playing possum," only happens if they are confronted by predators.

Opossums' body temperature runs lower than most mammals, which makes them immune to rabies. They also help prevent the spread of diseases by eating carcasses. Another selling point that Williams likes to share is this: "If you don't want ticks in your yard, thank an opossum." Rather than carrying and spreading ticks as hosts, they eat them.

Virginia opossum (*Didelphis virginianus*). Whether it's the naked tail, the close-set eyes, or the toothy grin, opossums continue to confound gardeners. There's nothing else quite like the opossum that shares our backyard habitat.

They are North America's only marsupials (mammals who carry their young in a pouch on their abdomen), which is why they don't need to make a big deal out of staking a claim and fending off competition. When it's time to move on, they just take the nest with them. As omnivores, opportunity awaits them at every turn. Opossums feed anywhere and everywhere by night, and climb up trees to get out of sight by day.

Opossums spend their days in trees, foraging at night.

With opposable thumbs on their back feet and a prehensile tail perfect for wrapping around branches, they are equally comfortable in the canopy layer or on the ground. Opossums make temporary dens in tree holes, underground burrows, or beneath buildings. Opossums can't survive cold winters, however, because their bodies aren't designed to bulk up on fat, nor can they hibernate. Developed areas unintentionally support them with food year-round, though, and they have little need for territorial disputes.

The Virginia opossum historically lived only in Central America and the southeastern United States prior to the arrival of Europeans. Today, the opossum can be found throughout the central and eastern portions of the continent and along the Pacific Coast. They have become habituated to living in neighborhoods, scavenging from compost piles, garbage, and pet food, and preying on the occasional backyard chicken. "They are really good cleaner-uppers. They eat things like rotten fruit and yellow jackets and can even eat venomous animals and not get sick," Williams continues. They may eat some garden veggies, but because they tend to prefer plant matter that is beginning to rot, compost is a big draw.

Porcupines do not pick fights, but they are more than ready to defend themselves.

Porcupines

Porcupines in North America (*Erethizon dorsatum*) are quiet, reclusive, nocturnal creatures that do very little to provoke fights. They'll climb trees or run away if threatened. However, when they are cornered, they can pack a sharp punch. The only warning a porcupine may give is a musky odor or a clattering of the teeth before displaying up to 30,000 erected quills. Its final move is a quick lash of the tail, aimed at the victim's face. Quills don't shoot out, but they are easily released, and their barbs and scales make it painful or impossible to pull them out.

Porcupines are large rodents, so they have to keep those big incisors busy by gnawing on wood and eating leaves, or their teeth's growth could prove fatal. If wood is scarce, they could upset the ecosystem's balance and kill off too many trees. On the other hand, if there's timber to spare, they contribute valuable ecosystem services. They dislodge twigs and fruit from high in the canopy to fall to the forest floor, where smaller mammals benefit from their nutrients. Porcupines also thin out branches by pruning the canopy, which allows light to penetrate through to the ground below.

Quill Qualms

Interestingly, a porcupine is not likely to hurt itself with its quills. An impaled quill is left to work itself out with no risk of infection. An antibiotic oil coats the quills, likely an adaptation that serves as a safety net for self-inflicted wounds.

Beavers aren't typical garden visitors, but their activity impacts the ecosystem in your area.

Beavers

North American beavers (*Castor canadensis*) are the largest rodents in North America, with a hearty appetite for wood and as many peculiarities as opossums and porcupines. They are semi-aquatic, with webbed hind feet, a nictitating membrane that covers their eyes like goggles, ear and nose flaps to keep water out, and waterproof fur. Their dense fur was in such high demand for hats and coats in the nineteenth century that they nearly went extinct.

Beavers build dams in streams, rivers, and lakes, and the redirected water flow doesn't necessarily work in favor of municipal sewer systems or city planning. Another major source of frustration is that beavers cut down trees. In a robust forest, this helps thin out smaller trees, maintain forest health, and potentially reduce the risk of forest fire due to overcrowding. In urban, suburban, and rural areas, there may not be enough trees to begin with.

If you live near a wetland, you may encounter beavers in your garden; more accurately, your garden may be in their wetland. If that is the case, take the opportunity to watch these masterful natural architects at work. By slowing down water flow—thus reducing silt, cleansing water, and creating a pond—beavers build habitat for waterfowl, muskrats, fish, and other aquatic wildlife.

Carol Buchanan quoted the following anecdote, which presents a nature-friendly point of view, from "Bev in Maryland" in her book *The Wildlife Sanctuary Garden*: "We did have a beaver in our creek a few years back—it built a good-sized dam that was seriously backing up the creek! We were delighted! We were not delighted when we realized that its favorite food was the dogwoods and my neighbor's peach trees! Dogwoods are one of Maryland's most beautiful sights in spring. After a little thought, we decided to let the beaver alone, and my neighbor put wire around his remaining fruit trees. A couple of floods washed away the dam, and we haven't seen any beaver signs for a long time."

In this situation, it worked out that they could protect some trees and allow nature to take care of the rest. Buchanan concludes, "Like beauty being in the eye of the beholder, maybe the pest is in the attitude. You alone can decide what's a pest in your garden."

Skunks and Raccoons

Two more critters that frequently wind up on the least-wanted list are skunks and raccoons. Before calling an animal-control specialist, consider learning more about their natural life cycles and understanding what roles they play in the garden.

Skunks

Four species of skunk live in North America: the descriptively named striped, spotted, hooded, and hog-nosed skunks. The striped skunk (*Mephitis mephitis*) is the most common skunk in North America, but little is known about its behavior in the wild because those powerful scent glands keep everyone at a distance.

A skunk deploys its stink bomb only as a last resort. It gives fair warning by pounding its front paws, waving its tail, and turning around to point its weapon at the target. Skunks have great aim, and the spray can reach 10 feet or farther. Even kits (babies) can spray when they are just about a week old, although their aim improves a few weeks later, when they are able to open their eyes.

Believe it or not, skunks can be more than just a stinky nuisance in the garden.

The spray is oil-based and will sting a predator's eyes, causing temporary blindness.

Typically, you'd only have one skunk on your property because skunks even give each other a wide berth. They eat a wide variety of foods, including grasshoppers, bird eggs, small rodents, frogs, and mushrooms. Because they are nocturnal foragers, you aren't likely to observe them in the garden, but you might find signs that they've visited: cone-shaped holes in the ground where they dug for their favorite food—grubs.

Marlene Condon's *The Wildlife Sanctuary Garden* explains that skunks are helpful in controlling leaf chafers and Japanese beetles and goes on to say, "Without grub control, your plants could die, whereas the physical alterations wrought by [skunks] can be easily remedied. When you find little pits made by a skunk, simply replace the dirt that was dug out and piled right beside them."

Raccoons

Raccoons (*Procyon lotor*) offer us many opportunities to understand how we attract and support wildlife. Brigette Williams of Second Chances Wildlife Center says that raccoons are the number-one nuisance animal about which they receive calls. However, three top reasons for raccoons' becoming a nuisance are directly related to how people attract them: (1) by feeding pets outside, (2) by leaving suet bird feeders out overnight, and (3) by not securing their garbage properly.

Opportunistic omnivores, raccoons in the wild eat a wide variety of plants, fruit, nuts, grains, insects, mollusks, amphibians, crayfish, mice, squirrels, small birds, and eggs. They are highly adaptable creatures. In cities and suburbs, their insatiable curiosity brings them into close proximity with people, and they'll eat all kinds of garbage.

They may live in loose communities of four or five raccoons of the same gender, which could provide some added protection from predators, such as coyotes. A mother raccoon is very protective of her kits; she may have up to six at one time, and she'll stay with them until they are around a year old and can fend for themselves.

Raccoons are able to find enough shelter to stay warm throughout the winter and expand their hunting and scavenging grounds. They have learned to adapt by finding shelter in barns, attics, basements, and doghouses in addition to their natural dens in hollow trees or ground burrows. In urban areas, their paw dexterity serves them well in opening doors, unlatching lids, and otherwise handling human devices. Smart animals indeed, they may be able to remember solutions to challenges for up to three years.

Raccoons are tenacious and difficult to keep out of the garden if they want to get in.

Bird feeders are a main attraction to raccoons in the garden. To keep raccoons out of bird feeders, place the feeders on tall, free-standing poles with baffles large enough to prevent a raccoon from passing. If possible, bring your feeders in at night to prevent all sorts of nocturnal scavengers.

Raccoons may be hard to dissuade from taking up residence, and ethical wildlife professionals generally recommend allowing them to do as they please if they are not causing any harm. If you see more than one raccoon in the spring or summer, you may have a mother with kits, and they will usually move on in a few weeks. There's no need to upset the whole raccoon family by having them trapped and relocated when natural cycles will take care of the problem.

A humane wildlife control company in Florida, 411 Raccoon Solutions (411raccoonsolutions.com), reminds us, "Wildlife trapping is an expensive, temporary 'band-aid;' 99 percent of the time it does not actually resolve your conflict at all!" As long as the food supply and habitat are provided, another raccoon will fill the niche, and there are plenty waiting to move into the open territory.

Deer

Deer get more attention than any other garden wildlife, and you either love 'em or hate 'em. However, as with all wildlife, deer are neither good guys nor bad guys in the garden. They simply live where life is livable. Understanding how our gardens either attract or prevent deer gives us the power to choose whether or not they are welcome and act accordingly.

Two types of deer are native to North America: the mule deer (*Odocoileus hemionus*) and the white-tailed deer (*Odocoileus virginianus*). Mule deer are distinguishable from white-tailed deer because of their longer ears, their larger bodies, and the black tips on their white tails. Mule deer range throughout much of the western United States, while white-tails are found in almost every state. Mule deer often migrate seasonally, whereas white-tails tend to stick together on their territory.

The white-tailed deer's coloration varies from grayish and dark brown in the winter to reddish brown in summer. White fur outlines the nose and underneath the chin and circles the eyes. As the name implies, this deer's most conspicuous white patch is on its backside.

History

Before European settlement, the United States' white-tail population was around 15 million. Because of unrestricted hunting, that number dropped to around 500,000 by 1900. With modern wildlife management practices, the number of deer has rebounded dramatically.

There could be as many as forty deer per square mile in rural areas and up to one hundred per square mile in urban spaces. This large mammal's comeback has unfortunately earned it the distinction of causing more human fatalities (by car accidents) than any other wildlife, and it isn't even a predator.

Habits

Deer browse on tender vegetation during the growing season and graze on woody plants, fruits, and nuts in the fall. They will eat twigs and bark in the winter if their fat reserves are low. Deer will scrape bark with their lower incisors, working on trunks up to 10 feet high and destroying saplings.

Their browsing can stop a generation of young trees from growing and potentially prevent a forest from succeeding naturally. Additionally, the loss of understory, ground-level, and shrub layers limits available nesting habitat for songbirds. The deer's selection of which trees to eat will determine the composition of the forest canopy forty or fifty years in the future. For example, in western New York, white-tails prefer oaks, maples, and ash, while they leave birches and beeches unscathed.

Deer breed in the fall and winter and give birth in the spring. Spotted baby fawns are well-

White-tailed deer can be found browsing in backyards throughout the United States.

camouflaged and may hide in tall grasses and wildflowers, safe places for animals with practically no scent. Mothers will leave fawns alone for long stretches, returning to nurse every few hours, so don't mistake a solo fawn for an orphan. A fawn will be weaned after about a month of nursing and then will venture out to feed on vegetation.

Deer in the Garden

For the gardener who simply wants to grow flowers, fruit, vegetables, and native plants for herself and native wildlife, deer can be tricky. They are too big to ignore. They possess undeniable beauty, yet they consume massive amounts of plants and fear no predators.

Attracting or preventing deer requires understanding of the animals' needs. Food and cover are the most basic habitat needs for deer survival. Most of their water comes from the plants they eat or dew that collects on leaves, but they will drink from water sources if available. Deer are crepuscular, meaning that they are most active around dawn and sunset.

Mow with Caution

Before mowing, take care that fawns are not in the path of machinery. They will instinctively lie still, and many are killed in fields every June. If you can wait until August to mow, the chances are low that you'll encounter a fawn.

Deer eat such a wide range of foods, from lichens and mushrooms to nuts, bark, and forbs, that it is impossible to fill a garden with plants that repel deer. They mainly browse, eating the leaves, stems, and twigs of woody plants. The greater the variety of plants, the more likely it is that deer will select what they need to meet their nutritional needs and leave other plants alone.

If your property is accommodating to deer, and you want to provide habitat for them, keep in mind that, in the wild, with predators present, they may need escape cover (brush or thickets at least 5 feet high) in up to 60 percent of their habitat. If you let your native herbaceous layer grow tall, it could provide excellent fawn habitat.

Deer prevention boils down to good fencing, yet this will not deter them from moving into a neighboring property. Opaque fencing is more effective than chain-link because they won't jump where they can't see. They also dislike leaping across a span, so a double fence also deters them. A cattle guard and a large, barking dog are two other ways to keep deer out.

Smaller fencing can protect selected plants, such as chicken wire over berry bushes or row covers over low-growing vegetables. (Be very cautious about using netting or small fences that other wildlife could get caught in.) Deer don't like to get their feet entangled in cloth, so a fabric cover, such as Remay, can be very effective at protecting young plants. Tree protectors encircle the trunks of young trees and must be removed as the tree grows.

If you'd rather be out pruning hedges than repairing barbed wire or electrical fences, try planting your garden strategically. This may be the most natural, cost-effective, and aesthetically pleasing

As innocent as a young red fox may look, it is still a wild animal and a predator.

solution. Check with your local cooperative extension for a list of deer-repelling plants. Every region has its own selection because tastes vary widely. You may want to weigh the cost of fencing against how much you can afford to experiment with different flowers and vegetables.

Darke and Tallamy present some creative ideas in their book *The Living Landscape*. Deer generally avoid strongly scented herbs, so try a lavender hedge as a border or spicebush interplanted among the deer favorites. Deer leave ferns alone, so experiment with filling edges with ferns.

You may also need to let go of certain delicacies or "deer candy." If you find that nothing will keep them away from your roses, for example, plant something completely different—diversity helps. Variety and change may be necessary to keep deer from adapting their tastes to what is most regularly offered in your garden.

Large Mammals

Top, or apex, predators are those carnivores that are not hunted by other predators and are sometimes considered keystone species: animals whose behavior critically affects all other species in an ecosystem.

North American mammals that are top predators include mountain lions, coyotes, bobcats, grizzly bears, black bears, gray wolves, foxes, badgers, and wolverines. You will have many more encounters in your garden with small mammals, birds, insects, reptiles, and amphibians than with any of these predators.

Most gardens and residential areas are not prepared to welcome wolves and bears. If there are well-managed natural open spaces intermixed with suburbia, and if we learn how to live in harmony with such animals, we can learn to understand and appreciate top predators' place in the ecosystem. If we can accommodate their needs without sacrificing our own safety, we may also benefit from them. The important thing to remember is that wild creatures will never become pets, and they need to retain their wildness as much as we need to keep our guard up while they are around.

The Impact of Top Predators

The populations of most top predators drastically declined after European arrival on the continent. By the 1900s, some states had almost no predators due to habitat destruction for logging or farming as well as indiscriminate hunting and trapping. The human population explosion has continued pushing up against the natural habitats of all kinds of predators, and usually it's only the frightening encounters with predators that make news headlines. However, the vast majority of wild animals that are struggling to survive on the outskirts do not make their presence known to humans.

The effects of removing or introducing top predators have been studied by biologists, hunters, outdoor enthusiasts, and most grade-school children in North America. The big fish eat the little fish, and the big mammals eat the little mammals. But there's more to it, and humans have a big impact on managing the food web.

The reintroduction of wolves to Yellowstone is an ongoing experiment on public land that has provided a wealth of information about the impact of predators. Beginning in 1995, gray wolves were brought from Canada back into Yellowstone National Park and have been closely monitored by biologists and ecologists.

Although there are other predators in Yellowstone (mountain lions, grizzly and black bears, and coyotes) and there are several large prey species (pronghorn antelope, bighorn sheep, elk, white-tailed deer, moose, and bison), the impact wolves have had on reducing the elk population has had a ripple effect on the entire system. Vegetation has less pressure from grazing elk, and trees are growing back in certain areas. Where willow trees are abundant, beavers are flourishing. In turn, they are building dams and creating more habitat for otters, moose, songbirds, insects, and fish. The presence of just one species, the gray wolf, has resulted in a plethora of biodiversity, strengthening and stabilizing the overall system.

Likewise, removing top predators leads to the mesopredator, or mid-sized predator, making a bigger impact in the system. One example is an increase in raccoons where there is a decrease in coyotes. Raccoons often prey on birds' nests, so a reduction in songbirds can be linked to the loss of coyotes in certain situations.

Another nonlinear effect is the fear factor that predators cause in prey species. Deer that are used to eating in peace without the fear of mountain lions lurking nearby will consume more. If predators are a possibility, the deer are more alert and will adopt a different eating pattern, which changes the body chemistry of the deer (increased adrenaline and cortisol) and reduces the amount of vegetation that the deer consumes.

The gray wolf's presence as a predator impacts both animal and plant life.

While wolves may not be in your backyard, and your backyard may not be Yellowstone, learning as much as you can about native and introduced wildlife in your area will help you prepare for the possibility of entertaining a top predator in your garden. Likewise, inviting songbirds, squirrels, or other small wildlife to your garden could naturally lead to attracting larger mammals looking for food.

Meet the Predators
Let's take a closer look at some predators that are gaining ground in suburbs and cities.

Black Bears
Grizzly bears are much less common than black bears. While black bears (*Ursus americanus*) are technically considered top predators, they are much less carnivorous than the canine and feline hunters that stalk the fringes of our gardens. Bears eat a lot, but, in some regions, most of their diet is vegetarian. Fruits, nuts, seeds, and plants make up the foundation of their food pyramid, with some scavenged dead animals thrown into the mix. They will also eat insects, such as wasps, bees, and termites. Bears are strong creatures that are motivated by a powerful hunger, and they will teach their children the habits they need to survive.

American black bears are tempted by gardens that grow sweet corn, apples, berries, and other fruits. Bird feeders can also lure them in. Anecdotes of bears in gardens are plentiful, especially in neighborhoods near wild spaces where bears hibernate during the winter.

Glenwood Springs, Colorado, is a good example of a bear-friendly town with its share of wildlife incidents. Lynn Springer, code enforcement officer for the City of Glenwood Springs, said that in just five months in 2015, she had 500 calls from people concerned about the bears coming into their gardens. While 2014 was a good year and the bears had many cubs, they were then met with

Black bear sightings in neighborhoods are on the rise, causing concern to suburban homeowners.

a harsh drought and not enough water to stay up in the mountains. They came down from the hills and crossed through town to reach the river, sometimes foraging for food in the city. Springer explains that bears are generally afraid of people, and a loud noise will usually send them on their way.

The worst thing you can do is feed a bear on purpose. Habituating them to hand-outs or trash will lead to an aggressive or sick animal, and a very large one at that. One resident cut down all of his fruit trees to prevent problem bears from returning. Perhaps the only fencing that will keep a determined bear out of the garden is electric fencing.

Keep Out!

In bear country, trash must be well secured in metal cans with locking lids. Trash ordinances are serious business in Glenwood Springs. Springer referred to the city's code, which details that garbage and recyclables shall not be kept in a manner that is enticing to wildlife; food, grains, and salt shall not be stored in containers that wildlife can access; and bird feeders left out between April 15 and November 15 must be suspended in a manner to be inaccessible to wildlife other than birds. A first offense is a $50 fine, a second offense is $500, and a third offense will send the offender to court. These rules are in place to protect the animals from the actions of fearful humans as well as to protect humans from bears.

Bobcats

The bobcat (*Lynx rufus*) is not as common as the fox, but bobcats are fairly abundant on the fringes of urban areas. They are watching us much more than we see them.

Masters at the art of hiding in plain sight, bobcats can stalk their prey just a few feet from jogging trails, crouch down in 6-inch-tall grass as people pass by, and then resume their hunt when the coast is clear. Their patience while stalking is legendary. Excellent night vision helps them track subtleties and pounce with perfect timing. In dim light, they can see six times better than humans.

Rabbits and hares are bobcats' main prey, but any small mammal, along with insects and carrion, will do. They can kill mammals up to about 12 pounds and may occasionally kill larger animals and return to feed on the carrion. While it is rare for a bobcat to kill an adult deer, it will prey on fawns.

Bobcats have a much larger home range than foxes, but, in developed areas, they are more likely to stay within 2 to 6 square miles. One of their best strategies for survival is their ability to find a home in almost any terrain. They need den sites and cover for hiding, so they can make use of logs, brush piles, and dense shrubbery in urban areas. Lightly traveled roads will not deter bobcats from their explorations, but heavy traffic and densely populated areas are less appealing.

Bobcats are superior stalkers.

To look for signs of bobcat in your garden, watch for scat and tracks that are about twice the size of a housecat's. The tracks will show no claw marks, distinguishing them from canines.

Bobcats mark their territory by scratching trees, just as a cat would, so look for scratches

A coyote will hunt during the day if there are better opportunities to find prey.

Coyotes in the City

When coyotes make it into the media, most often it's because of conflict. Many suburban and city dwellers don't know what to make of a wild animal like a coyote, and often fear or misinformation clouds objective observation that could be very helpful in understanding the animal's behavior.

at about twice the height that a cat could reach. Bobcats are mostly silent unless mating or competing for a mate, in which cases you might hear startling screams, like those of a child or woman in pain.

A 6-foot fence will not quite discourage these jumpers and climbers from your yard or garden. Protect your animals by keeping all pets indoors and securing any poultry with strong fencing. Bird feeders attract both domestic and wild cats, so bring the feeders in at night.

Coyotes

Excerpted from the article "The Urban Coyote," written by Karen Lanier and originally published on the Urban Farm *website (UrbanFarmonline.com) on December 2, 2015.*

According to differing sources, the word coyote means "barking dog," "song dog," or "trickster." All of these names describe the animals' best-known behaviors and secrets of success. The coyote is a canine, related to wolves and foxes, and resembles a German Shepherd with a narrower muzzle. Mature adults weigh between 25 and 40 pounds; their color varies from tan to buff to dark gray, often tinged with red or frosty-colored tips; and they have black-tipped tails and yellow eyes. They are found in every state except Hawaii.

Coyotes are generally nocturnal, but they will change their habits to match their prey's. They are highly adaptable, elusive, and wily; they are omnivores and opportunists. They'll eat what is easy to get to, such as your trash or compost, if not contained well, but the majority of what urban coyotes eat is small rodents, with fruit, deer, and rabbits constituting the rest of their diet. If you feed birds, take care not to spill excessive seed, which attracts mice and ground squirrels and could thus attract coyotes.

Will coyotes eat your pets? Possibly, but they are more likely to eat your pet's food. Never leave pet food outdoors, and keep cats indoors. Chickens make an easy meal for a coyote, so secure fencing all around and above them is a must. Dogs are more likely to tangle with a coyote if it is protecting its den, especially in the springtime, when its pups are young. Leash your dog if you are in an open space where coyotes could be present.

Will coyotes attack? Rarely. Coyotes are shy, and, despite their frequent forays into suburbia, they are still very wild. They generally avoid people and hide in plain sight. Fragmentation of their natural habitat has forced them to use the green spaces near civilization, such as parks and golf courses. If a dog gets too close for comfort, a mother coyote will protect her den and could become aggressive, but this is a natural instinct and not a random attack.

If you actually see a coyote on your property, it's probably been hanging around for a while. You'd better check your garbage and hope that you haven't been feeding it. Most people hear coyotes' howling and yapping at night rather than see them during the day. They are excellent at hiding in wooded patches or shrubs, and they probably know your routines better than you know theirs.

Understanding coyote behavior is your best approach, and teaching coyotes that they are not welcome on your property is the first step. This is known as *hazing*, and it begins with making loud noises, clapping your hands, waving your hands, acting large, and possibly throwing small things in the coyote's general direction (but not aiming at it).

Most reports of coyotes on residential property are the result of feeding birds, squirrels, or outdoor pets or directly feeding coyotes. If you are providing habitat—food, shelter, water, space—the coyote is more likely to accept your invitation. Simply removing the animal will not fix the problem; taking out one individual will leave a space that another will fill. And if we take out all of the predators, the prey populations will grow to unsustainable levels.

Foxes

Gray and red foxes live in North America, but only the gray originated there. Gray foxes (*Urocyon cinereoargenteus*), also known as forest foxes, are native to eastern forests. An adaptation from their forest evolution, they are able to climb trees to avoid predators—a unique trait for a canine, and something that even the red fox is unable to do. Gray foxes are slightly smaller than red foxes, weighing about the same as a house cat. They have grizzled gray-brown coats with patches of reddish fur. Gray foxes are very territorial, spending most of their lives in a 1-square-mile area.

The gray fox originated in North America and is native to forests in the eastern United States.

Red foxes (*Vulpes vulpes*) were brought to North America by Europeans for sport. They are slightly larger than gray foxes and reddish-colored all over, with the signature white-tipped tails. The same qualities that make red foxes challenging and popular hunting targets are the reasons that they have adapted well to living near humans. They are quick, agile, smart, and resourceful, outwitting predators with their fast maneuvers, ability to disguise their scent, and speeds of up to 45 miles per hour for short sprints.

Foxes eat insects, small mammals, birds, eggs, fruit, nuts, leaves, and carrion. They normally hunt at night, but don't be surprised if you see them out during the day. If they feel safe, they will hunt anytime.

While foxes can be a serious threat to backyard chickens, they shouldn't be a problem if the birds are properly fenced. In the spring, foxes have been known to den under porches or in outbuildings, although they are generally very shy and will avoid people. If you can leave them alone for about nine weeks after kits are born, the kits will begin hunting on their own and set out to find their own territory. You can install a barrier if you don't want them to return to your buildings, but only after you are sure that they are all out.

More Considerations

While most of the animals in this chapter do not fit in into the typical small-backyard ecosystem, more and more encounters with predators are reported as suburban sprawl encroaches on wild space. Meanwhile, our landscaping and excess waste entice and support predators with food, shelter, and water. The national park system, along with other organizations and individual landowners, are doing their best to provide wildlife habitat, but great expanses of neighborhoods, apartment buildings, parking lots, highways, industrial complexes, and other developed areas stand between these pockets of natural systems.

We Are Mammals, Too

Humans are mammals, too. We relate to furry, live-birthing, nursing, warm-blooded creatures more easily than we relate to insects, reptiles, amphibians, or birds. Something about a fuzzy, four-legged creature kindles an instinct to snuggle it, baby it, rescue it, or play with it. No wonder we adopt and domesticate mammals and bring them into our homes as part of our families.

Our compassion toward other life forms is a great asset in our stewardship of the Earth, but it's dangerous to allow these familial tendencies to cloud our judgment regarding wild mammals. When threatened, they will react out of instinct to protect themselves, their territory, and especially their young. They are justified in defending themselves with the tools nature has given them—warning growls, frightening postures, unpleasant odors, sharp claws, and powerful teeth. Know how to respond if you find yourself in a situation with distressed, injured, or sick wildlife.

Be Prepared

Be sure to have the contact information for wildlife professionals in your area programmed into your phone or kept in a convenient place. The National Wildlife Rehabilitators Association (www.

nwrawildlife.org) provides resources for finding a professional in your area. Animal Help Now is a smartphone app and website (ahnow.org) that connects you quickly with the nearest open facility for wildlife rescue. You may want to ask veterinary clinics and your local humane society for recommendations. It is best to find your local wildlife rescue professionals before you need them.

What to Do

If you encounter injured or sick wildlife, maintain a safe distance so the animal does not feel threatened; to the animal, you appear to be a large predator that is ready to take advantage of its vulnerable state. Contact your wildlife rehabilitator and follow his or her instructions for how to keep the animal safe while the rehabilitator coordinates transportation.

The most frequent mistaken wildlife emergency is what appears to be an abandoned or orphaned baby. Brigette Williams of Second Chances Wildlife Center reports that half of all young animals that end up in her rehab center do not need to be there. Mammal mothers come and go, and they do their best to leave their babies in safe places. They will avoid retrieving their young if humans are nearby, so watch from a distance. If the young animal cries for an hour or more without a parent coming to its aid, it may need your help.

Although it may be hard for us to accept, it is a rule of nature, especially in abundant prey species, that not all babies will survive to maturity. Our close proximity to wildlife can make it easy to forget that young mammals regularly become food sources for predators, scavengers, and parasites.

1. An orphaned baby eastern gray squirrel. Rehabilitating wildlife is best left to the experts.

2. A baby animal by itself is not necessarily an orphan.

Disease and Prevention

Bacteria, fungi, parasites, and viruses pass through our systems on a regular basis, cycling to and from other animals and hosts, through our water, and into our soil. Sometimes an imbalance in the ecosystem can lead to an overgrowth and impact our health.

Handling baby animals, injured wildlife, or their scat can expose you to zoonotic diseases—those that are transferred between animals and humans. If you never handle wild animals, you will most likely never have to worry about contracting a serious illness from them. However, other vectors, such as ticks, mosquitoes, and fleas, can transmit pathogens.

Just as we pick up unfamiliar germs at shopping centers and schools, animals share pathogens in more crowded situations. In the wild, home ranges exist for a reason. The space not only reduces competition for habitat, it also isolates diseases to local populations and dissipates an outbreak. After working in your garden, cleaning up around any dens or burrows, and touching any pets, wash your hands thoroughly with soap and water. This one simple step will prevent most exposure to pathogens.

Direct contact with animals is easy to avoid, but working outdoors where pesticides are not used will inevitably expose us to more insects. Ticks, mosquitoes, and fleas can transmit Lyme disease, West Nile virus, and the plague, respectively. These are only a small sample of zoonotic diseases, and they are relatively rare, illustrating why attention to the habitats we provide is important not only for the health and well-being of our wild friends but also for ourselves, our families, and our pets.

In addition to the aforementioned diseases, rabies can be carried and transmitted by almost any mammal, but only through direct contact with body fluids. Ninety percent of rabies cases in the United States involve wildlife, mainly carnivores and bats. Signs of rabies include stumbling, aggression, and foaming at the mouth. A nocturnal animal seen during the daytime does not necessarily have rabies, as urban wildlife often adapt their feeding patterns to human habits, but it is a cause for concern. If in doubt, call your local wildlife authority.

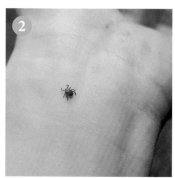

1. Installing fencing around your garden can help to keep certain pests out.

2. The tiny deer tick, *Ixodes scapularis*, transmits debilitating Lyme disease to humans and other animals.

Protect Yourself from Parasites

Be mindful of the times of day when mosquitoes are more active, especially at dusk. Ticks are more likely to be present in tall, thick vegetation and under trees. Fleas can lie in wait in their pupa stage, and they jump to life as adult parasites whenever a warm-blooded host brushes up against them. But don't let these tiny creatures keep you from enjoying your garden. For maximum protection, wear light-colored clothing—long sleeves and pants—and tuck pant legs into socks. The Centers for Disease Control and Prevention(CDC) recommends various insect repellents, but if you want to avoid synthetic chemicals, try oil of lemon eucalyptus on your clothes.

After spending time outdoors, the CDC recommends these simple steps to remove ticks:

- Bathe or shower as soon as possible after coming indoors (preferably within two hours) to wash off and more easily find ticks on your body.
- Conduct a full-body tick check using a handheld or full-length mirror upon returning from tick-infested areas. Parents should check their children for ticks under the arms, in and around the ears, inside the belly button, behind the knees, between the legs, around the waist, and especially in the hair.
- Examine your clothes, gear, and pets. Ticks can hitch a ride home and attach to a person later.
- Tumble clothes in a dryer on high heat for an hour to kill remaining ticks.

Most zoonotic diseases begin with flu-like symptoms: fever, nausea, achiness, and chills. If you experience these symptoms, see a healthcare professional and be sure to tell him or her if you have been in contact with any wild animals, nests, or droppings. It will help them diagnose you properly; additionally, most zoonotic diseases require reporting at either the state or federal level.

Take Responsibility for Your Property

No matter what type of wildlife you hope to entice and support with your garden, understand how it may affect your home. There are plenty of reasons to welcome wildlife, but do so with discernment. We put locks on our doors to keep human intruders out; likewise, if you prefer not to have foxes, raccoons, or bats under your porch or in your attic, install appropriate exclusions over those openings.

As Marlene Condon says in *Nature-Friendly Garden*, "Parents of young children know that they need to child-proof their homes. Gardeners, likewise, need to wildlife-proof their gardens rather than trying to eliminate particular wildlife species from their environment."

Natural Balance

Last, but not least, remember all of the ecosystem services that a good balance of wildlife and habitat will provide. Dragonflies and spiders eat mosquitoes; ducks, wild turkeys, and opossums eat ticks; and beetles, raccoons, and crows scavenge and recycle carcasses. These creatures and many more play an important role in keeping diseases and their vectors to a minimum.

Just as removing any single part of a system upsets the balance, so does an overabundance of a certain element. For example, if you eat too many sweets during the holidays, it takes a while to restabilize your body's internal ecosystem. When you eat a balanced diet, you function better in the long run. Similarly, diversity and soil health are your building blocks for healthy life in your garden. When all the parts are functioning well, natural processes reduce the need to battle any single disease or type of wildlife.

Final Thoughts

We gravitate toward natural areas because they provide us with what we need—beauty, recreation, a spiritual connection, and inner peace—yet the wild world is not a perfect picture of flowers and rainbows; it is a very real place with disease, trauma, and hardship.

Hardships in nature affect all of us; humans are not separate from nature. A drought does not simply mean that we don't get to water our lawns anymore. A drought means that bears will come closer to food sources and that fewer dragonflies will be able to lay eggs when aquatic plants wilt. Times of abundance also mean that insects will thrive, and some of those insects may carry disease or just be plain nuisances.

We may even compete with wildlife for the fruits of our gardens. As John Muir noted on one of his early naturalist explorations in 1867, "What a pity that nature should have made so many small mouths palated like our own!"

Acting as good stewards of the land while we inhabit it is a tall order, but we are up to the challenge. We not only have the tools and the intelligence, we also have compassion. *Biophilia* bonds us inexplicably to nature. By approaching it, interacting with it, and dwelling in it, we become more natural beings. Whether consciously or instinctively, we yearn for nature. Gardening is deeply healing on many levels: through the movement and stimulation of our senses; the absorption of sunshine and fresh air; the invigorating smell of moist earth; the songs of birds; the rewards of flowers, fruits, vegetables, nuts, and legumes; and all of the possibility held within a single seed.

Following permaculture principles in our gardens and lifestyles brings us closer to our wild selves and reawakens our knowledge of how to coexist harmoniously with all life on Earth. If you learn nothing else about the philosophy of bringing permanence into our culture, remember to observe. This one strand of the sustainability web connects and informs all of our actions. Whether you

are considering putting in a pond, fencing a flower bed, or cutting down a dead tree, the first step of observation is the most important.

Marlene Condon provides good reasons to become a keen observer: "When you make your own detailed observations of the natural world, you will have a better idea of which information you can trust as being accurate. We are living in an age when information can be obtained almost effortlessly, but, unfortunately, not all information is good information. If you follow poor advice, you may harm not only wildlife but also the natural workings of your garden."

Here are some reminders and suggestions about how to observe closely. Keep this list on hand and refer to it when you feel uninspired or need to step out of your comfort zone to connect with nature.

- **Keep a field notebook.** Your entries can be as simple as the weather or as complex as daily check-ins on anthills. It takes only a few months of notes to begin seeing patterns and looking forward to the next observation.

- **Use a camera.** Whether it is a phone, a digital SLR, or a simple point-and-shoot, keep a camera nearby. Let your camera show you what you aren't seeing. Take it away from your face, and snap shots down at ankle height. Hold it up high, as far as your arms will reach. Set the timer and put it inside a tree hollow or under a shrub. You don't need motion sensors or long zoom lenses to change your perspective.

- **Use a lens.** Binoculars, hand lenses, and magnifying glasses are easy to keep with you. Turn leaves over and investigate the chew marks, insect eggs, and signs of decay. Look closely at twigs, buds, and leaf scars. Notice the differences between different plants and how they change from month to month.

- **Sense it.** Take yourself on a nature walk through your garden five times. Each time, focus on a different sense. When you look, try to have your eyes follow a path, such as up one tree and down the next. When you listen, close your eyes and notice the depth, pitch, and dimensions of sounds, man-made and natural. When you smell, crush leaves and turn over soil to release hidden aromas. When you taste, be careful about what you put in your mouth, but try unusual things like stones and pine needles. When you touch, remember that your entire body is a sensory organ, so touching happens with every part, including your feet and hair. Take a sixth walk and become aware of any extra sensations (emotions, memories) beyond the physical body.

- **Map it.** Draw your property, even if you aren't in the design process. Map all of the dimensions of your space. Draw a sound map: what do you hear at different times of day? Draw a water flow map: use tennis balls to recreate the flow and notice where they stop. Is this where water pools? Draw a culture map: where do people influence the space? Draw a nest map: winter is a great time to locate birds' nests in trees, and you can watch for activity in other seasons. Make any other kind of map you can think of.

- **Limit yourself.** Take a hula hoop or a 10-foot section of rope or garden hose and encircle a small space. Spend ten minutes looking closely at only the life inside that boundary. Notice the soil texture, count the diversity of plants, identify insects, and look for any signs of life (chew marks, scat, tracks). Think of your tiny space as a miniature nature park. What animals, scenery, or features would be the main attractions? Take the next ten minutes to look around from within the boundary. Without leaving the circle, what are the sights, sounds, smells, tastes, and sensations that interest you?

- **Embrace the dark side.** Go outside at night and make the same observations that you would during the day. Listen carefully. Inhale deeply. Your senses will detect different things at night, and different plants and animals are communicating all around you. Use a flashlight sparingly; try to let your eyes adjust to the dark. Better yet, set up a hammock, sleeping bag, or tent and spend the night in your natural habitat.

- **Find the spectrum.** Colors are everywhere in nature, all year long. Create a natural color wheel by collecting objects from every color in the spectrum. Sketch, photograph, digitally scan, or

make rubbings from the natural objects. Make a new color wheel each season and see which colors are the easiest and hardest to find. Seek out as many different colors from one type of leaf and create a fan, bouquet, or wreath. Get crafty and come up with your own imaginative designs that play with nature's palette.

- **Become the background.** Regular appearances will help you become less threatening to wildlife in your garden. Walking the same path at the same rate, wearing the same jacket or hat, and sitting on the same bench at the same time every day are ways to blend in. Wildlife send out alarm signals when they notice something out of the ordinary, and it takes energy away from their survival activities. As you become more accepted as a "regular" in the scenery, the closer you may be able to approach and make observations without disturbing the animals.

- **Get your kids outside**. Nobody can clue you in to garden life better than a four-year-old. If you don't have children, invite young relatives or neighbors to spend time exploring with you. All of the ideas listed here are even better when a child is involved. Children can be your naturalist partners and help compile observations to share with future generations.

- **Keep your human neighbors happy, or at least tolerant.** In your adventures in wildlife gardening, staying on good terms with your neighbors could increase the likelihood that they will join you in creating wildlife corridors throughout suburbia. It helps if you are already on good terms with your neighbors, treating your community as a garden full of relationships that require tending.

- **Use fencing with aesthetics in mind.** For example, an archway can add a welcoming presence and act as support for hummingbird-attracting flowering vines. Put your most recognizable and impressive flowering species, such as marigolds, sunflowers, dogwoods, and redbuds near the front of your garden and save the wilder looking plants for the back.

- **Identify your yard as wildlife-friendly with a sign.** You can get an official designation from the National Wildlife Federation or Monarch Watch, or you can hand-paint your own sign (cuteness counts here) that says "Pollinator Habitat/No Spray," or something to that effect. Offer a tour through your neighborhood association or garden club. Use the opportunity to educate your neighbors about all of the life that your garden is hosting in the hopes of encouraging them to do the same.

How we approach the land reflects our values and how we want to spend our time. A dear friend shared a realization he had after he had worked all weekend planting trees in a neighborhood park and tending to a friend's garden. With dirt-crusted hands grasping a huge bag of turnip greens, he said, "You know, a garden is really a relationship. You get out of it what you put into it." Reflecting a bit more, he shared, "I've been asking myself, 'What do I want in my garden?'"

Hopefully, you, too, have a sense of your garden as a relationship with nature as a whole. Your garden is the perfect space to ponder deeper meanings. It's so much more than a place to grow flowers and vegetables; it can be a place to keep your world in balance. So, what do you want in your garden?

Resources

Andrews, Ted. *Animal Speak: The Spiritual and Magical Powers of Creatures Great and Small.* Woodbury, MN: Llewellyn Publications, 1993.

Barilla, James. *My Backyard Jungle: The Adventures of an Urban Wildlife Lover Who Turned His Yard into Habitat and Learned to Live with It.* New Haven, CT: Yale University Press, 2013.

Barnes, Thomas G., editor. *Private Lands Wildlife Management: A Technical Guidance Manual.* Lexington, KY: The Kentucky Cooperative Extension Service, University of Kentucky, 1992.

Buchanan, Carol. *The Wildlife Sanctuary Garden.* Berkeley, CA: Ten Speed Press, 1999.

Condon, Marlene A. *Nature-Friendly Garden: Creating a Backyard Haven for Plants, Wildlife, and People.* Mechanicsburg, PA: Stackpole Books, 2006.

Cunningham, Sally Jean. *Great Garden Companions.* Emmaus, PA: Rodale Press, 1998.

Cranshaw, Whitney. *Garden Insects of North America: The Ultimate Guide to Backyard Bugs.* Princeton, NJ: Princeton University Press. 2004.

Darke, Rick and Tallamy, Doug. *The Living Landscape: Designing for Beauty and Biodiversity in the Home Garden.* Portland, OR: Timber Press, 2014.

Flint, Mary Louise. *Pests of the Garden and Small Farm: A Grower's Guide to Using Less Pesticide,* 2nd ed. University of California, 1998.

Heinrich, Bernd. *Winter World: The Ingenuity of Animal Survival.* New York: Harper-Collins, 2003.

Haupt, Lyanda Lynn. Crow *Planet: Essential Wisdom from the Urban Wilderness.* Boston, MA: Back Bay Books, 2009.

Kentucky Department of Fish and Wildlife Resources. Backyard Wildlife Habitat Kit.

Mader, Eric et al. *Attracting Native Pollinators: The Xerces Society Guide to Protecting North America's Bees and Butterflies.* North Adams, MA: Storey Publishing, 2011.

Mills, Dick. *A Popular Guide to Garden Ponds.* Tetra Press, 1992.

Mitchell, John Hanson. *A Field Guide to Your Own Back Yard.* Woodstock, VT: The Countryman Press, 2014.

Mizejewski, David. *Attracting Birds, Butterflies and Other Backyard Wildlife.* Merrifield, VA: National Wildlife Federation, 2004.

Moisset, Beatriz and Buchmann, Stephen. *Bee Basics: An Introduction to Our Native Bees.* USDA Forest Service and Pollinator Partnership, 2011.

Muir, John. *A Thousand Mile Walk to the Gulf.* London, England: Penguin Books, 1992.

Newfield, Nancy L. and Barbara Nielsen. *Hummingbird Gardens: Attracting Nature's Jewel's to Your Backyard.* Toronto, Canada: Chapters Publishing, 1996.

Olkowski, William, Sheila Daar and Helga Olkowski. *The Gardener's Guide to Common-Sense Pest Control.* Newtown, CT: Taunton Press, 2013.

Rutledge, Cooper. *Backyard Battle Plan: The Ultimate Guide to Controlling Wildlife Damage in Your Garden.* London, England: Penguin Books, 1998.

Sayre, April Pulley. *Touch a Butterfly: Wildlife Gardening With Kids.* Boulder, CO: Roost Books, 2013.

Starcher, Allison Mia. *Good Bugs For Your Garden.* Chapel Hill, NC: Algonquin Books, 1995.

Tallamy, Douglas W. *Bringing Nature Home: How Native Plants Sustain Wildlife in Our Gardens.* Portland, OR: Timber Press, 2007.

—. "Conserving Nature by Conserving Food Webs." Presentation at Fayette County Cooperative Extension, Lexington, Kentucky, September 30, 2015.

—. "The Vital Role of Urban/Suburban Landscape." Presentation at Wild Ones National Headquarters, January 25, 2014.

Thomas, Elizabeth Marshall. *The Hidden Life of Deer: Lessons From the Natural World.* New York: Harper Collins, 2009.

Walliser, Jessica. *Good Bug, Bad Bug: Who's Who, What They Do, and How To Manage Them Organically (All You Need To Know About The Insects In Your Garden).* Pittsburgh, PA: St. Lynn's Press, 2008.

Index

Photos

Acknowledgments

I want to express my gratitude to the following individuals for sharing their stories, knowledge, encouragement, feedback, critiques, and inspiration for my first book:

Ann Bowe, Rachael Brugger, Betty Hall, Cory Hershberger, Beverly James, Judy Johnson, Susan Jonas, Janet Lanier, David Lanier, Karen Leet, Beate Popkin, Linda Porter, Lynne Springer, Dr. Iga Stasiak, Russ Turpin, Donna Van Buecken, Shayne Wigglesworth, Brigette Williams, and Bruce, Milo, and Nelly.

About the Editor

Karen Lanier considers herself a naturalist, documentarian, teacher, artist, and gardener who explores the intersections of nature and culture. She has worked as a seasonal park ranger in national and state parks from California to Maine. Wildlife has always been a close ally in Karen's work of connecting people with their environments. As she rehabilitated birds of prey and led educational programs at a wildlife center, she sensed the power that humans have to create change in the world, for better or worse. A common thread throughout Karen's adventures has been finding ways to communicate the preciousness of the natural world and share meaningful experiences. By making a documentary in Brazil about a reforestation project, her mission was to highlight good deeds and promote land stewardship.

Karen holds degrees in photography, foreign language, conservation studies, and documentary studies as well as a professional environmental educator certificate. She is actively involved with the Lexington, Kentucky, chapter of Wild Ones: Native Plants, Natural Landscapes, and she works closely with the Kentucky Association for Environmental Education. Her AmeriCorps volunteer experience with Seedleaf, a community gardening nonprofit, helped shift her migratory perspective on life toward putting down roots. Now, along with the bees and butterflies that return to the flowers each summer, Karen cultivates hope in her urban forest.